Publisher's Summary

A small-town musician from North Carolina tries his luck on the biggest stage of all: New York City. And he hits the jackpot. Mere months into his NYC gambit, guitarist Jeffrey Lee Campbell is catapulted from selling candy in Broadway theaters to touring the world with rock legend Sting. Go behind the scenes with the provincial, wide-eyed rookie as he fakes his way around the globe, shoulder-to-shoulder with his longtime musical hero.

Do Stand So Close is a layered, coming-of-age memoir, recounting Jeffrey Lee Campbell's glamorous (and grueling) twenty-five country, six-continent trial by fire on Sting's "Nothing Like The Sun" World Tour. Filled with humorous anecdotes and poignant revelations, *Do Stand So Close* follows Jeffrey's amazing odyssey—from relocating to NYC and miraculously landing the high-profile gig, to life on the road with one of the planet's biggest rock stars, to his humbling crash-and-burn after the tour. Buckle up!

Do Stand So Close

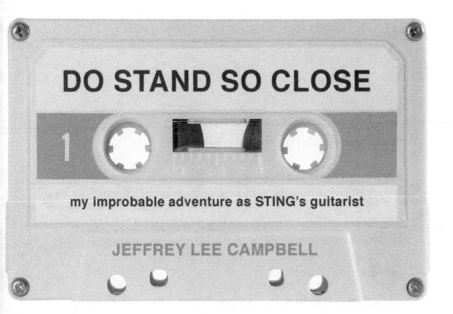

DO STAND SO CLOSE

1

my improbable adventure as STING's guitarist

JEFFREY LEE CAMPBELL

Deeds Publishing | Atlanta

Published by Deeds Publishing in Athens, GA
www.deedspublishing.com

Printed in The United States of America

Cover design and text layout by Mark Babcock

Back cover photo by Ned Matura, NYC

ISBN 978-1-947309-33-3

Books are available in quantity for promotional or premium use. For information, email info@deedspublishing.com

First Edition, 2018

10 9 8 7 6 5 4 3 2 1

To my wife, Patty. The page would be blank without you.

Contents

"No one should come to New York to live unless he is willing to be lucky."

— E. B. White

Wednesday, February 3, 1988

Tomorrow marks my one-year anniversary in New York City, and to say it's been a wild twelve months would be a serious understatement. Last February 4, feeling restless and unfulfilled, I braved the Mason-Dixon Line and basically started over. Swapping the known for the unknown, I dared myself, "Give NYC one year of your life and see what happens." I figured even if things didn't pan out, I'd head back to North Carolina a little more worldly and armed with some damn good stories. But things have panned out—to say the least. I followed through on my word, clocking a whole year in the big bad city, and THAT definitely calls for a celebration. But the party will have to wait; I've got to go to work…

…if it's considered "work" to be playing Madison Square Garden with Sting.

Since childhood, my goal was simple and clear: I wanted to be a professional musician. Rejecting any contingency plans, I was "all in" from the very start. Music is the only life I've ever known. I played my first paying gig at age thirteen—and my most recent one just last night. But out of forty-plus years of strumming, my rookie season in New York City remains the most extraordinary...by far.

In October of 1987, a mere eight months into my New York City gambit, Sting took a chance on a complete unknown and hired me to play guitar on his "Nothing Like the Sun" World Tour. In a blinding flash, I went from the small time to the big time. I was thrust into the spotlight, traveling the globe shoulder-to-shoulder with one of the planet's biggest rock stars—and one of my all-time musical heroes. By the end of my incredible journey, I'd performed for over two million fans in twenty-five countries on six different continents...and learned at least TWO lifetimes of lessons along the way.

How did a newcomer score such a high-level gig? Luck certainly played its part. But as the saying goes, "Luck is when opportunity meets preparation." I worked hard to put myself in a position to succeed—and then an entire galaxy of stars aligned perfectly. The result was a dream-come-true year; one filled with amazing highlights and, not surprisingly, plenty of regrettable lowlights.

Quick, Painless Backstory

I was born in the leafy college town of Chapel Hill, North Carolina, but raised across the tracks in neighboring blue-collar Carrboro. The middle of three boys in a working-class family, I plucked my first guitar (or as my grandfather called it, "the starvation box") around age eight. My older brother, Mike, won a crappy acoustic guitar in a department store raffle. He ignored it, I adored it. Captivated by the instrument, I never looked back. I played in bands from elementary school through high school, honing my skills at dances, frat parties, and bars. Thanks to the continuing emotional—and financial—support from my parents, I went on to study music in college. I was accepted into the prestigious jazz program at the University of Miami, where I quickly learned how little I knew about music...and life. Carrboro's big fish became Miami's minnow. Most of my classmates played circles around me, and the multicultural urban sizzle was more than I'd bargained for. But it planted a seed.

I made it through three years of college before conceding jazz was not my true calling. Miles, Bird, and Trane may have ruled in the classroom, but Earth, Wind & Fire ruled in my dorm room. After growing up on a steady diet of rock and soul music, I realized jazz would never be more than a second language to me. Miami could teach me how to *speak* jazz, but I knew I'd always *dream* in pop. I did some extensive soul-searching and decided to quit school—surprisingly with my parents' blessings.

Officially a college dropout, I moved back to North Carolina, teamed up with a few hometown pals, and put together a damn good band called Steps. (Jazzbo trivia: We were the guys responsible for *encouraging* Michael Brecker to change the name of his all-star NYC jazz ensemble from "Steps" to "Steps Ahead." Sorry, we owned the trademark and they wouldn't meet our asking price.) Convinced we'd conquer the world, Steps chased fame and glory up and down I-85, spreading our soul-flavored rock to nightclubs, roadhouses, and campuses all over the Southeast. We learned a lot, laughed a lot, drank a *few* beers, and managed to eke out a bit of a living. At the height of our popularity, we signed with a local indie label and released a four-song EP of original music. Yet despite our dedication, Steps was never able to break through to the next level. Five years of wear and tear finally took its toll, and the group fell apart. Now what?

Unable to crack the code as an original artist, I wondered if I might have better luck as a hired gun. Between my years of gigging and three-quarters of an undergrad education, I was confident I had the right stuff. I just needed to find some established coattails and hitch a ride.

In search of a spark, I reached out to an old college pal—and fellow guitarist—Doug Travis. Unlike me, Doug had managed to complete the mission in Miami. Degree in hand, Doug had headed north to join the scrum of musicians seeking their fortunes in New York City. I had an open invitation to crash on Doug's couch, so I decided to take advantage of his offer. I saved a few bucks and booked what turned out to be a life-changing flight.

Deplaning in Newark, I climbed aboard a bus bound for Manhattan—and moreover my destiny. I gazed in anticipation at the clump of skyscrapers on the horizon as the driver zoomed up the New Jersey Turnpike. Nearing the city, the thick, aggressive traffic eventually choked on itself and slowed to a crawl. I stared across the Hudson River as we inched down the helix toward the mouth of the Lincoln Tunnel, transfixed by Manhattan's glistening skyline. I was ultimately dumped off at the seedy Port Authority Bus Terminal, where I quickly navigated my way through the assortment of colorful characters to a much-welcomed exit. The moment I stepped onto 42nd Street, the artist in me knew he was *home*.

I spent two exhilarating days being seduced by New York City's charms before heading back to North Carolina—forever a changed man. I was exhausted from my trip but also invigorated. Born again, I no longer cared about my struggles with the North Carolina music scene (or the lack thereof). I'd glimpsed my future and it looked amazing. I immediately began mapping out a strategy to return to the "Center of the Universe" on a permanent basis.

With my sights set on NYC, I committed to a disciplined program of preparation—physically, musically, and emotionally. I knew I'd need to raise every aspect of my game if I wanted to compete on the demanding New York stage. My daily regimen consisted of a five-mile run in the morning, followed by marathon sessions of practicing. I even placed a guitar at my bedside so I could literally begin and end each day with a strum. Regarding emotional preparation, I made a vow to steer clear of serious relationships. A savvy friend had pointed out how a hot and heavy romance could easily derail my aspirations, so I made sure to keep my social life casual. This was a good call. Bachelorhood made it much easier to follow through on my daunting move.

To increase my versatility and, I hoped, improve my odds of finding employment in New York, I bought my first tuxedo and joined The Bill Bolen Orchestra, Chapel Hill's premiere society band. I'd spent most of my life focusing on contemporary music, but the time had come to cast a wider net. As a member of Bill's band, I learned my way around the essential jazz standards, bossa novas, show tunes, and perennial (read: clichéd) crowd-pleasers. This also turned out to be a good call. Playing oldies for the gilded country-club set helped prepare me, as much as possible, for New York's ruthless "club-date" (aka wedding-band) scene.

Despite being armed with a focused, can-do attitude, I was still faced with that all-too-familiar obstacle: money. I knew my plan would be doomed without a sufficient war chest, so I started a rigorous—but painfully slow—savings program. As I struggled to squirrel away the necessary funds, my parents stepped up to help subsidize my musical dreams yet again. Mom and Dad took one for the team and offered to let me move back in with them. I'm a very lucky son. Living rent-free was the exact financial catalyst I needed to follow through on my Manhattan project.

After settling back into my childhood bedroom, I taped a giant, colorful street map of New York City to the wall for motivation…and education. I stared a hole through that map as I ran through my daily picking exercises, dreaming of the possibilities while also schooling myself on the lay of the land. *Avenues go north and south, streets go east and west.*

Hello New York City

It took a couple of years, but I finally reached the point where I felt ready to make my move. Needing one last piece of the relocation puzzle, I jetted back up to New York, crashed on Doug's couch (again), and commenced the cruel hunt for affordable housing. I scoured the rental ads in *The Village Voice* until I found a one-bedroom share that fit my modest budget. After nailing down an official New York address, I flew back to North Carolina, loaded all my junk into my car, tearily kissed my parents goodbye, and made the nine-hour drive "home."

Under my new living arrangements, my landlord/roommate, Sara, occupied the bedroom, and I was relegated to a pullout couch in the tiny living room/kitchenette area. Despite sleeping with my head mere inches from the refrigerator, I felt like a Master of the Universe. I was living in midtown Manhattan, with a view of the Empire State Building from my "bedroom" window...as long as I craned my neck just right.

Now the hard part: finding work. The good news? The city had a ton of musical opportunities. The bad news? The city had *two* tons of musicians—and it certainly wasn't lacking in guitarists. As someone once pointed out, "In New York, even if you're one in a million, that still means there are seven others just like you."

Adapting to my new reality, I learned the meter is always running in NYC. Manhattan was damned expensive compared to the America I was used to. Between my initial outlay and my day-to-day living costs, I'd put a nice dent in my savings account before I knew what hit me. With my nest egg dwindling faster than anticipated, I needed to find some immediate income—musical or not—to help offset the relentless outgo. Kimberley to the rescue.

Doug's girlfriend, Kimberley Spencer, worked for a Broadway theater concession company, and pitched me to her bosses in an act of mercy. I was offered a job on the spot; I accepted the job on the spot. The next day, I embarked on a new career of gouging theatergoers with overpriced cocktails and munchies. The job paid a whopping fifteen dollars per shift (plus dependably shitty tips), but at least I'd have a little bit of money coming in.

I actually kind of enjoyed the concessions gig at first. Even though I was just a lowly candy salesman, it was still pretty cool to be punching the clock inside of various historic Broadway theaters. Maybe I wasn't living the dream, but at least I was living in the same zip code as the dream. Needless to say, the novelty quickly wore off and my job became incredibly boring…usually.

One rainy afternoon at the Gershwin Theater—at the time, home to Andrew Lloyd Webber's inexplicably popular rock 'n' roller skating musical, *Starlight Express*—I drew the short straw and wound up with the dreaded coat-check duty. Working coat-check sucked. Unlike regular concession shifts, which ended after intermission, coat-check duty required you to stick around until the show was completely over. Those coats weren't going to redistribute themselves. But that day, the short straw turned out to be my friend.

After the pre-show rush subsided, I was staring off into space from my lonely cloakroom when one of my biggest musical heroes waltzed through the door. My mouth hung open as I watched Prince (with bejeweled walking cane and burly bodyguard) strut across the deserted Gershwin lobby. I was beyond starstruck, but at the same time, frustrated. I couldn't help thinking, "Damn, I should be playing guitar with a big-time artist like that, not standing here collecting stupid raincoats and umbrellas." Trying to put a positive spin on things, I reminded myself at least I was now living in a city where people like Prince roam free. Stay the course; patience is an action.

* * *

New York City is overrun with people voted "most likely to succeed." But even the shiniest newcomers rarely shoot straight to the top. More often than not, a menial job is a rite of passage for future celebrities. Today's faceless waitress, bartender—or candy salesman—can be tomorrow's huge star. I saw it firsthand.

I schlepped ice buckets with a fledgling writer named Aaron Sorkin, who of course went on to become one of Hollywood's hottest properties, with films including *An American President*, *The Social Network*, and television's *The West Wing*. Legend has it that Aaron actually wrote parts of his breakout play, *A Few Good Men*, during lulls in concession shifts, scribbling down ideas on cocktail napkins whenever inspiration struck. ("You can't handle the truth!") Another one of my candy colleagues, Camryn Manheim, ultimately ditched the Raisinet racket for an Emmy-award-winning acting career, starring in TV hits such as *The Practice, Ghost Whisperer,* and *Harry's Law.* My concession co-workers were all so excited when I landed the Sting gig: one of the inmates had escaped! I may have been the first of our gang to go over the wall, but Aaron and Camryn's time was right around the corner.

I had not moved to Manhattan to sell candy, so I got busy spreading the word: guitarist for hire. I reached out to the small circle of musicians I knew, but tempered my expectations. Most of my pals were struggling to find work as well. The bulk of my contacts were University of Miami refugees, but one non-college connection was pianist—and fellow Tar Heel—Bill Covington. Bill and I had worked on the teaching staff at B&B Music, Chapel Hill's local music store, and I remember being impressed (and jealous) when Bill made *his* move to New York. Our Carolina bond put Bill near the top of my short list of allies, so he was one of my first calls after I got settled.

I was relieved to finally hear some positivity as I chatted with Bill. Unlike the gloom and doom I'd encountered elsewhere, Bill was upbeat and reassuring. But he had reason to be: he was the proud owner of a steady gig. Bill played keyboards with Faze 4, one of the area's busiest club-date/wedding bands, and as a result, his calendar—and wallet—stayed comfortably full. Wedding receptions are big business in the Northeast, and despite reliable abuse from crazy clients (and even crazier bandleaders), the gigs are a good source of income. Unfortunately, Faze 4 wasn't in the market for a guitarist, but Bill did volunteer to put out some feelers on my behalf. Bill contacted a few of his music pals and unearthed a connection that placed me only *two* degrees of separation from Sting. I am forever indebted to Bill Covington for introducing me to the guy who lit the fuse: Delmar Brown.

Delmar Brown, originally from the Chicago area, was a prominent keyboard player on the New York scene. Among his varied projects, Delmar led a jazz/funk fusion group called Bushrock, and played in The Gil Evans Orchestra—a hip, "downtown" big band. Gil Evans was one of the most admired arrangers in jazz, due in large part to his groundbreaking work with trumpeter Miles Davis. Evans had legions of fans worldwide, including one Mr. Gordon Sumner—aka Sting.

While I was busy honing my concession-stand skills, Sting was on the Caribbean island of Montserrat recording his second solo album, *Nothing Like the Sun*. Sting's new record followed in the jazzy footsteps of his first post-Police effort, *The Dream of the Blue Turtles*, offering up an ambitious mix of musical styles and flavors. Somewhat surprisingly, *Nothing Like the Sun* included a cover version of Jimi Hendrix's "Little Wing." And here's where things start to get interesting. Sting's take on the rock ballad was arranged by Gil Evans (and also featured Gil's amazing orchestra). So if you're keeping score at home: my Carolina buddy Bill knew Delmar, Delmar knew Gil, Gil knew Sting. The cosmos was officially in motion.

As I continued to chase employment leads, I kept hearing talk of Europe's summer jazz festivals. These annual events functioned almost like a paid vacation for New York musicians, giving them a chance to get out of town, earn a few bucks, and bask in the glow of the generally more-appreciative European audiences. The Gil Evans Orchestra was a popular fixture on the jazz festival circuit and already had a string of summer dates booked throughout Europe. The resourceful Delmar Brown had decided to take advantage of his itinerary with Gil, and hatched a plan to bring *his* band, Bushrock, along for the ride. Lucky for me, Bushrock was looking for a guitarist.

One of Bill Covington's feelers had gone out to his pal Delmar—and Delmar took the bait. On a mutually agreed-upon night, Bill and I drove up to Delmar's place in Washington Heights for a meet-and-greet. Delmar's wife invited us in when we arrived, but told us Delmar wasn't home yet. We waited around for a half-hour or so, and then…it hit! The apartment door flew open, and in burst one of the most animated characters I'd ever seen in my life. Delmar was a high-energy, dreadlocked ball of fire, a hyper combination of decibels and smiles. I was new to the city, so I just assumed Delmar's intensity was typical of all New York musicians. Wrong. I've lived in NYC for over thirty years; I've still never met anyone like Delmar Brown.

We ended up at a bar in Soho, drinking and chatting until the wee hours. After determining we were musically simpatico, Delmar asked if I wanted to audition for his band. I'd answered yes before he could finish the sentence. Delmar smiled, reached into his shoulder bag and handed me a cassette tape of his latest album. I was psyched. I'd landed my first legit New York prospect. I couldn't wait to get up the next morning—take three aspirin—and dig into the music of Delmar Brown's Bushrock.

I studied Bushrock by day and hawked bad champagne in plastic cups by night. Meanwhile, my fate was unfolding halfway around the world. Gil Evans signed off on a gig that would play a pivotal role in my life: The Gil Evans Orchestra, live at the Umbria Jazz Festival…with special guest Sting.

My shot with Bushrock finally arrived. I showed up at some ratty rehearsal studio and played loud, intense music with loud, intense musicians. New York's ferocity was living up to my expectations—and then some. I felt pretty good about my audition, but Delmar was looking at other guitarists as well. Now for the fun part: the waiting.

I got a phone call from Delmar a few days later. He said I'd sounded great, but he'd decided to go with a more established guy. I was bummed but philosophical; rejection is a cornerstone of showbiz. As my pal Doug loves to say, "Ah the music business, one disappointment after another."

Living in midtown put me only a short distance from the Mecca of musical instrument retail, West 48th Street. The block between Sixth and Seventh Avenues sizzled with music stores, including Rudy's Music Stop, Sam Ash, We Buy Guitars, and the legendary Manny's Music. Owning the leisurely schedule of an unemployed musician, I spent a lot of my free time hanging out on 48th Street.

My favorite spot was Manny's. I'd wander around the bustling store, drooling over the high-end guitars and gawking at the extraordinary collection of autographed photos. Manny's walls were covered with SIGNED 8-by-10-inch glossies from practically every noteworthy musician of the twentieth century. (No telling how many hours I wasted trying to decipher the chicken-scratched inscriptions from The Beatles, The Rolling Stones, Jimi Hendrix, Frank Sinatra, etc.) And since we're talking New York City, those headshots sometimes came to life. One day at Manny's, I was waiting to pay for a pack of guitar strings when I looked up to see rock pioneer Bo Diddley standing right beside me. Jaw meet floor.

I dropped by Manny's one afternoon to do a little loitering—and harass my pal Jack Morer. (Jack, another Miami alum, and yet another guitarist, worked as a salesman at Manny's.) Jack knew I'd been on Delmar's "short list" and was eager to share some insider info with me. Turns out, one of Jack's friends had landed the Bushrock gig, but he was having second thoughts. Jack's buddy had concerns over the tour's murky finances and was seriously thinking about backing out. Jack gave me a "Who knows?" shrug, and suggested I might want to stay near the phone. Jack was right.

I got a call from Delmar a couple of days later. Already in Europe, Delmar told me there'd been a change of plans, and he now wanted me in his band. Delmar laid out the basics: the tour would last a month or so, and it paid $1,000 a week. For a part-time candy salesman like myself, the decision was a no-brainer. Then Delmar casually asked if I could be in Paris by *next week*.

I frantically prepared for my last-minute trip. First things first: the provincial rookie needed a U.S. passport. (A veteran New York musician had advised me to get a passport when I first got to town, predicting "You're gonna need one." I remember thinking at the time, "Yeah, right." I obviously wasn't dreaming big enough.) I also had to make a quick trip down to the concrete canyons of Wall Street to meet with Delmar's lawyer. I signed my contract and was handed a $1,000 check as an advance on my first week's salary. Compared to my measly concession pay, I was already way ahead of the game. The check cleared … and I was off to Europe for the first time in my life.

Europe (France/Italy)

with Delmar Brown's Bushrock

June 23—July 20, 1987

How Ya Gonna Keep 'em Down on the Farm (After They've Seen Paree)?

Bushrock set up shop in a graffiti-covered rehearsal studio at the end of a dreary Parisian alley—and I LOVED it. We jammed day and night, exploring untold musical detours and distractions. Then, with just two days of unfocused practice under our belts, Delmar impulsively booked a last-minute gig at one of the city's trendy nightclubs, La Locomotive (located right beside the legendary Moulin Rouge cabaret). Ready or not, it was showtime.

We loaded our gear into a rental van and began navigating the crazy Parisian traffic. (I lost count of our fender benders during our weeklong stay.) Crawling through the urban gridlock, we came upon a police checkpoint. The cops could barely contain their glee when they peered into our van and saw our *must-be-guilty-of-something* crew. The officers singled me out first and gestured for me to follow. I guess they figured the young, innocent-looking white guy would make a perfect mule for the band's drug stash. Scared as shit, I was placed in the back of a police van and thoroughly searched. The cops rifled through my wallet, pointing and laughing at family photos while making what seemed to be smart-ass remarks. But since I spoke next to no French (and comprehended even less), I was at their mercy. They kept repeating their one word inquisition over and over: "*Cocaïne? Cocaïne?*" And I kept replying with my default phrase, "*Je ne parle pas français.*" ("I don't speak French.") After releasing me, the cops took the other band members one by one into the police van for a friendly frisk. Miraculously, we passed inspection and were permitted to proceed—but not before the frustrated authorities gave us a bogus, *très* expensive traffic ticket. (They claimed we made an illegal U-turn. Never happened.) My African-American counterparts reacted to the episode with a weary, business-as-usual shrug. Not me. The blatant profiling and corruption was an eye-opening experience for this naive white boy. Welcome to the real world, Jeff…and life's unavoidable creep toward cynicism.

Finally arriving at the venue, we double-parked beneath the iconic Moulin Rouge windmill and began unloading our gear. Even the mundane act of lugging amplifiers felt a little more romantic in Paris. After an extended soundcheck, we went back to the hotel to freshen up, before heading out for a fashionably late dinner. I was only a couple of days in, but I'd already surmised Parisian nightlife was like New York's: immune to curfews. I sensed a long evening ahead.

We took the stage around one o'clock in the morning, offering up a high-energy set of Delmar's jazzy funk. I thought we sounded pretty damn good, but the French crowd seemed determined to live up to their notoriously blasé reputation. You could cut the *indifférence* with a knife. We played our last note around 2:30am, and then dove into a boozy post-show hang, consuming near-lethal amounts of tequila before leaving the nightclub around 5am. But we weren't done yet. We returned to our hotel, where the drunken party raged until late morning.

As our occupation of Paris drew to a close, I started feeling guilty about my complete lack of cultural pursuits during our stay. I basically had nothing to show for my time in the historic, art-drenched city (aside from a brief drive-by of the Eiffel Tower). In search of absolution, I literally ran to—and through—the Louvre Museum on our last day in town. It was too little, too late; but I felt marginally better about myself as I climbed aboard the band bus for our overnight drive to Italy. At least I'd laid eyes on the Mona Lisa.

I was awakened the next morning by the groans of our bus engine. I rolled out of my bunk and was greeted by an up-close-and-personal view of the Alps. More accustomed to the mellow Appalachians of Carolina, the majestic snow-covered peaks grabbed my full attention. I settled into a window seat and spent the day admiring the French/Italian countryside.

We made a brief stop at a music store in Milan before heading on to the Pistoia Blues Festival. I got my first taste of Italy's charms that night, playing to a huge, adoring crowd in Pistoia's medieval town square. The following morning, we set out for the next stop on our itinerary: the island of Elba. After a glorious ferry ride across the Mediterranean, we stepped onto paradise. (*This is how they punished Napoleon?*) That evening, we performed at a cliffside amphitheater overlooking the sea. The view from the stage was breathtaking. Europe was amazing and I was drinking it all in, in every sense of the word.

Next, we were off to the Italian college town of Perugia for the Umbria Jazz festival…and a little gig that would change the course of history. Well, my history anyway.

* * *

The Umbria Jazz festival is renowned for assembling some of the greatest musical talent in the world. During my two-week stay in Perugia, I witnessed extraordinary performances by artists including Miles Davis, Michael Brecker, Tito Puente, George Benson…and Sting. And while the music was incredible, the hang was even more exciting. I met and hobnobbed with some of the heaviest hitters from New York's jazz scene. But none of my encounters turned out to be more consequential than meeting saxophonist Branford Marsalis. Making Branford's acquaintance would prove to be immensely valuable down the road.

Friday, July 10, 1987

Bushrock performed at a small club in Perugia tonight. The cramped stage barely held our band, and we played WAY too loud for the room. Attendance was light, fifty people tops. But the headline wasn't "How

many," it was "Who." I'd heard a certain VIP might attend our show—
and the rumor came true. I learned after the gig that Sting had indeed
been in the audience. I was shocked that such a huge star would show
up at some two-bit dive to check out Delmar's band of unknowns. I
never saw the rock god, and ignorance definitely equaled bliss. I was
better off not knowing one of my longtime musical idols was watch-
ing ME play.

The following night, I attended the Gil Evans/Sting show at Perugia's soccer stadium. I'd only seen Sting in concert once before
(with The Police on "The Ghost in the Machine" tour), so I was
pumped. Magnifying my excitement, Delmar had secured all-ac-
cess passes for the Bushrock gang. I felt like such a big shot as
I wandered around the backstage area with that laminate slung
around my neck. When the stadium lights went down to signal
showtime, the crowd erupted. As a teenager, I'd gone to every
rock concert possible, and I'd always wondered what that pre-
show roar sounded like from the performer's perspective. Now I
knew: thrilling.

The Gil Evans Orchestra cranked out a blazing set featuring selections from Gil's avant-jazz library and Sting's rock catalog. Highlights included two Jimi Hendrix tunes, "Up from the
Skies" and "Little Wing," as well as Police gems, "Synchronici-
ty I" and "Tea in the Sahara." The band also performed a swinging arrangement of Sting's "Consider Me Gone" that climaxed
with a soaring vocal duel between Sting and MY friend Delmar. One of Delmar's not-so-secret weapons was his inhuman
vocal range...and he let it fly that night. Sting singled Delmar

out by name when the song ended, and added, "He's bad!" Sting capped off the evening with a compelling solo acoustic version of his classic "Message in a Bottle." After the show, I stared in awe from the backstage shadows as a depleted Sting rushed to a waiting Ferrari and zoomed off into the night—never imagining less than a year later I'd be on tour with Sting, cruising around in *my* Ferrari. To be continued ...

Before I left for Europe, my maternalistic roommate, Sara, had insisted I pack a journal. Not really my style, but I'd complied to appease her—and I'm so glad I did. That little book is one of my most treasured keepsakes. Despite my macho aversion to keeping a diary, certain events demanded their due. My hastily scribbled entry for the Gil Evans/Sting show concludes: "I saw history!"

We stuck around Perugia for another week, doing a couple more gigs, hanging out with the cats, and taking in lots of music. The biggest highlight (as a spectator) was seeing Miles Davis perform at the stadium. After the electrifying concert, a few of us Bushrockers bummed a ride back into town on Miles's bus—unfortunately sans Miles. But the brief commute did give me a chance to meet another one of my idols, Miles's bassist, Darryl Jones. I worked up my nerve and approached Darryl to introduce myself. He responded warmly, "Delmar always gets the hot young players." Who me?

Bushrock performed in Perugia's town square the next afternoon. I was doubly psyched because Delmar had invited saxophonist Branford Marsalis to sit in with us. I tried to play it cool, but I was jittery as hell about sharing the stage with New Orleans jazz royalty. Branford joined us for a couple of songs and of course sounded amazing. During the second (and trickier) number, I was stunned when Branford turned to me after his brilliant solo, shrugged and whispered, "I have no idea what to play." His vulnerability was unexpected—and disarming.

Adding to my exhilaration, pianist Kenny Kirkland came up to me after the set and said he'd really enjoyed our music. Wow! My mind was officially blown. In one incredible week, I'd met Darryl Jones, Branford Marsalis, and Kenny Kirkland—three core members of Sting's all-star *Blue Turtles* band. Only a year earlier, I'd sat spellbound in a North Carolina movie theater, idolizing these same guys in Sting's documentary, *Bring on the Night*. I know life can change in a hurry, but I could not believe the company I was keeping.

Meanwhile, as predicted, the Bushrock money did indeed get *funny*. After only a couple of weeks, my paycheck was AWOL. Delmar's manager bobbed and weaved with vague excuses, but it was obvious our tour budget had been prematurely exhausted. I bumped into Branford on the street one afternoon, and sheepishly confided my financial predicament. Branford shook his head and offered the sage advice, "Fuck 'em. Hit the road, leave 'em hanging." Branford said if it were him, he'd head to the airport, buy a plane ticket, and go home. Good plan...IF your last name happens to be Marsalis. But as a mere Campbell, I wasn't going anywhere. I could only dream of the professional and fiscal clout Branford enjoyed.

I was a bit bewildered by Branford's goodwill toward me. The way I saw it, Branford was a huge star and I was a huge nobody. But we did share a Southern upbringing, and Branford had complimented me for being "true to my heritage." Lucky for me, the music industry is one of the few places where being from the South isn't seen as a liability. Society loves to stereotype Southerners as slow and dimwitted, but thanks to significant musical contributions from cities like Memphis, Muscle Shoals, and New Orleans, a drawl isn't considered a red flag in the music biz. In fact, I like to think of my Southern accent as a certificate of authenticity: 100% soul—or your money back.

After twisting in the wind for a couple of weeks, word finally came down the Bushrock tour was ending. But first we had to fulfill one last gig on the books: a concert at the local prison. Tough room—literally. The inmates cheered enthusiastically as Bushrock dished out our jailhouse funk. (Insert "captive audience" joke here.) Post-show, we were pleasantly surprised when the warden treated us to a large dinner spread. His timing was impeccable; free food fit perfectly with my threadbare budget. As the prison guards embraced their inner roadie and loaded out our gear, Bushrock enjoyed a farewell Italian feast. Food, beer and wine…all on the (big) house.

Scheduled to fly out of Rome, we steeled ourselves for the inevitable showdown with airport security. Bushrock sported the typical musician appearance (long hair, dreadlocks, funky clothes, etc.), so hassle-free passage was never in the cards. As expected, we were subjected to intense scrutiny, including repeated passport scans and drug-sniffing dogs. One lucky customer even got an intimate strip search. But despite their best efforts, authorities were unable to pin anything on us. *Arrivederci Roma!*

After nine hours in the air—and a scary-as-hell aborted landing—Bushrock finally touched down at JFK. I was unaccustomed to the rigors of transatlantic travel, so I couldn't wait to escape my economy-class prison. But as we taxied up to the gate, the plane inexplicably stopped short. Arghhh...so close, yet so far. Powered down, we sat on the tarmac for another half-hour, waiting to be towed the final fifty feet of our journey. To distract from my encroaching claustrophobia, I began making small talk with the attractive blonde sitting beside me. (True to introverted form, I hadn't said one word to the girl for the entire flight.) As we chatted, I learned she was on her way to North Carolina—and lived in my hometown of Chapel Hill. Duh.

Back To My Future: Sting

I was so happy to be back in NYC...initially. Yes, Europe had been incredibly exciting, but it was not without its frustrations. Between the lack of gigs and the lack of paychecks, team spirit had waned. And while it was great to meet so many high-profile musicians, it was hard not to be envious of their success. I wanted what they had. As I dealt with my mixed bag of emotions, New York's harsh reality crept back in. It was late July, the city was hot and muggy, and I was once again peddling booze and bonbons to theatergoers.

In an effort to recover our unpaid Bushrock wages, drummer Ricky Sebastian and I decided to file a small claims suit against Delmar's manager. We scraped together our severely limited resources, went down to the courthouse, paid the nominal filing fee, and filled out the paperwork—only to be told it would be a couple of months before our complaint would even be heard. Broke and unemployed (musically), my memories of hanging around Italy with—uh, make that "near"—Miles Davis and Sting were becoming increasingly bittersweet.

I kept my head down and things gradually started to pick up a bit. Augmenting my concessions career (which seemed even less glamorous post-Europe), I was able to book a few gigs here and there. I continued to work the phones and before I knew it, I'd filled a string of Saturday nights with club-dates. Reinvigorated, I felt like I was finally gaining some traction. Then I received the phone call that changed my life…FOREVER.

* * *

My answering machine blinked innocently as I dragged in from yet another soul-sucking shift at the candy stand. I hit the play-back button without a second thought, and liberated the long-lost voice of Delmar Brown. Delmar dropped a nuclear bomb. "Yo Jeff, Sting is looking for a guitarist for his band…and he asked me about you. Give his manager, Kim Turner, a call." Delmar read off Kim's phone number before reiterating, quite unnecessarily, "Call him!"

I stood there frozen. I know it sounds cliché, but I felt like I was in a dream. After regaining consciousness, I replayed the message and scribbled down Kim's number. I dialed the magic digits, and got an immediate "Hello." When I asked to speak with Mr. Turner, the voice on the other end grunted, "Wrong number" and hung up. In my hysteria, I'd obviously misdialed. I composed myself, and re-dialed—carefully. This time the other end answered, "KRT."

KRT management was founded by Kim Robin Turner, an integral member of The Police family from the start. In the band's infancy, Kim filled whatever role was needed: roadie, driver, soundman, road manager, etc. Kim was there every step of the way as The Police built their massive empire, and ultimately rose through the ranks to a top management position. Miles Copeland was the big cheese, but Kim handled many of the day-to-day managerial duties for Sting Inc.—including things like dealing with freaked-out guitarists.

I spoke with Kim briefly and we scheduled a meeting at his office, conveniently located at 1776 Broadway. I knew the *patriotic* address well. A mere two blocks from my apartment, the building's shiny, brass "1776" plaque always caught my eye as I trotted up to Central Park for my daily jog. (Central Park had provided great comfort as I weaned myself from the flora and fauna of North Carolina to a steady diet of urban concrete.)

I made the short hike over to Broadway and 57th the following afternoon—attempting to stay calm in the face of such a huge opportunity. I gave myself one last pep talk as I stepped onto the elevator and pressed 17. Reaching destiny's floor, I exhaled and walked into KRT Management. Kim offered a quick handshake and cut to the chase:

Kim: "Are you interested in the gig?"
Me: "Yes."
Kim: "Are you married?"
Me: "No."
Kim: "Good, the tour will be long."
Me: "OK."
Kim: "If you're hired, the gig pays $2500 a week—firm."
Me (trying not to smile): "Uh, OK."

Kim's no-nonsense approach caught me a little off guard, but I eventually learned the motivation behind his blunt bedside manner: control. The backup band on Sting's previous tour (*The Dream of the Blue Turtles*) was stocked exclusively with all-stars; a boon for Sting's fans, but apparently not so much for his management. Sting's killer sidemen (Branford Marsalis, Kenny Kirkland, Darryl Jones, Omar Hakim) were all seasoned, A-list veterans with numerous major credits...and a mutually shared manager. Word was, between their professional leverage and managerial solidarity, the *Blue Turtles* bloc had caused a few headaches for Sting's brass along the way. Well, God bless those beautiful headaches; they likely created an opening for an unknown rookie like myself to sneak into the big tent. After wrestling with a band full of self-assured *somebodies*, Sting & Co. probably welcomed the idea of dealing with a submissive *nobody*.

Wrapping up the world's shortest business meeting, Kim sent me downstairs to the affiliated offices of FBI (Frontier Booking International) to grab an advance copy of Sting's new album. The booking/talent agency was founded by Ian Copeland (brother of Police drummer, Stewart and manager, Miles). But unlike its crime-fighting namesake, *this* FBI featured a tropical aquarium, a pinball machine, and lots of pretty girls.

I walked through the glass doors of FBI and was directed to the corner office of Theresa Greene. I introduced myself to the striking Ms. Greene and made a stab at some relaxed small talk. (I felt anything but relaxed.) After the chitchat ran its course, Theresa reached into her desk and handed me a generically labeled cassette tape of Sting's upcoming album. Cue angelic choir. Just being in possession of the exclusive, unreleased recording made me feel more important than I ever had in my life. My head was swimming…but I needed to focus. My audition was only a week away. I had a LOT of studying to do.

To prepare for the opportunity of a lifetime, I began working the only way I knew how: obsessively. Both a blessing and a curse, I'm totally driven when tackling any task (big or small). The concept of moderation eludes me—in work and, unfortunately, *play*. I've finally accepted I have two speeds: ON and OFF. Matter of fact, when I walked away from college, my GPA was a robust 3.98. I was one lone B short of academic perfection. Yep, I'm a dropout with essentially a straight A average. Paging Dr. Freud.

I immersed myself in Sting during the one-week window before my audition. And I'm not just talking about the new album. I learned, or at least familiarized myself with, every single Sting/Police song I could get my hands on. I devoured all five Police albums, Sting's solo *Blue Turtles* record, and even *Bring on the Night*—the somewhat obscure live album from Sting's previous tour (which, at the time, was only available as a European import).

I spent practically every waking minute cramming for my rock 'n' roll exam, but, as much as I wanted to, I couldn't afford to play hooky from work. Each afternoon around 5pm, I'd resentfully put down my guitar and rush off to the Gershwin Theater. (The same place where I saw Prince stroll in. Was it an omen?) Luckily, the mindless drudgery of concession "preset" was perfect for multitasking. Thanks to my Sony Walkman cassette player (the iPod's granddaddy), I was able to continue my Sting studies on the sly as I ran around the theater replacing soda tanks, stocking candy, and filling ice buckets.

I'd decided against telling my co-workers about the upcoming audition, fearing it might somehow jinx things. I'd actually toyed with keeping the news a secret from everyone, but had quickly ruled that out. Being a prohibitive long shot, I recognized the buildup to my audition would probably be the most exciting part of the experience. Family and close friends deserved to be along for the fun part of the ride. Plus, I desperately needed their prayers.

Sunday, September 27, 1987

Audition day. I can't believe I'm going to play music with Sting this afternoon. Hell, I can't believe I'm even getting a chance to meet the guy. Earlier in the week, a well-meaning friend had tried to steady my nerves with, "Just remember Jeff, if things don't work out, there'll always be other gigs." I appreciated his attempt at preemptive consolation, but we both knew life doesn't offer an endless supply of opportunities of this caliber. Today feels like MY Super Bowl or Oscar Night. I worked damn hard to get here. Who knows when—or IF—I'll ever get another shot like this?

Ready for battle, I hailed a cab for my short but fateful journey down to SIR (Studio Instrument Rentals) Studios on West 25th Street. My goal was to arrive fashionably early—aiming for that imaginary nanosecond that effortlessly bisects "over-eager" and "lackadaisical." The dude behind the front desk looked up from his heavy-metal magazine long enough to point me toward Stage Two. I nodded, took a deep breath, and pushed through the door to my future.

I scanned the room, and saw my patron saint Delmar holding court in the corner. I headed straight in his direction. Delmar greeted me with an affectionate bro hug before introducing me to bassist Tracy Wormworth, drummer Marvin "Smitty" Smith, and percussionist Steve Thornton. (There was no sign of heavy hitters Branford Marsalis or Kenny Kirkland—and it would stay that way.) We exchanged hellos, and then did what musicians do best: make noise. We noodled around, weaving in and out of a few funky grooves as we awaited the main event.

A little later, the studio door swung open and in bounced the man of the hour. I willed myself to stay calm, but my cool demeanor was a complete sham. Simply standing in the same room with Sting was blowing my Carrboro mind. After being officially introduced to *Elvis*, we got down to business. To my surprise, the scene was relaxed and unstructured. Instead of the usual two or three songs, followed by a perfunctory "don't call us, we'll call you," we ended up hanging for a couple of hours. Amazingly, the audition was not your typical cattle call. Matter of fact, no other musicians showed up at all.

Sting threw out random titles from his catalog as we searched for songs to play. And thanks to my painstaking preparation, I was ready for anything—and everything. Meanwhile, judging from some of the shrugs around the room, it was clear my colleagues didn't share my freakish compulsion to learn every Sting song under the sun. Nobody likes a know-it-all, so I considered pulling my punches. But the stakes were too high to cede an inch.

Instead, I leaned in, answering the bell, song after song—even at the risk of alienating my peers. Each time Sting asked if we knew a certain tune, I'd chirp, "Sure!" Sting eventually looked over at me. "OK, Jeff, stop showing off." For better or worse, I'd made an impression.

I was still soaring the next day, but resolved not to wallow in any fantasy "what ifs." Conceding my flirtation with rock stardom had probably reached its conclusion, I tried to embrace the ever-popular (but ever-hollow) "it's an honor just to be nominated." Then the phone rang. I picked up to hear, "Hi, Jeff, this is Patty LaMagna at KRT. Sting wants to know if you can come back down to SIR tomorrow." I responded with an artificially restrained, "Yes" before hanging up in a daze. I was numb; I'd gotten a callback. Sitting down so I wouldn't fall down, I trashed my earlier resolution. Unleash the hounds of fantasy. What if?

Tomorrow couldn't come fast enough. But since I was unsure of how the day would unfold, I decided to play it safe and cancel my evening concession shift. God forbid the jam session ran long and I'd have to excuse myself to go sell M&M's.

I returned to SIR on Tuesday afternoon and discovered a hallway full of dudes with guitar cases. Dammit! Word had obviously leaked about the Sting auditions. I didn't want, or need, the additional competition—but I did have to admire my fellow musicians' chutzpah. That said, you can't just show up at high-level tryouts like these. Or can you? I was stunned when Sting threw open the door and welcomed the party crashers into the studio. Hats off to Sting for being such a nice guy, but I wasn't in a position to be quite as magnanimous. I hated that players were simply walking in off the street and gaining an audience with *my* Sting.

But I clearly had no say in the matter, so I just focused on remaining confident and upbeat...externally. Internally, I was working feverishly to shore up my fragile ego. I kept reminding myself I'd not only been invited, but I'd also been invited *back*. Sting let the intruders showcase their wares before thanking them and sending them packing. We then proceeded to dive into another afternoon of the most fulfilling music of my life. As my second day of fantasy camp came to a close, Sting walked over and asked if I could come back again tomorrow. Gulp.

The Cinderella story continued. I'd survived the cut on Sunday and Tuesday—and now I was heading back for round three on Wednesday. But Wednesday is matinee day on Broadway, which meant I was on the hook for a noon concession shift. Forced to wriggle out of my day job yet again, I received a stern ultimatum from my less-than-happy boss: if I missed ANY more work, I would be fired. Despite my precarious financial status, the threat barely registered. Was I willing to jeopardize my candy-jockey career to pursue the gig of a lifetime? I wish all decisions were that easy.

I strutted into the increasingly comfy confines of SIR on Wednesday morning, walking a bit taller than just a few days earlier. After a couple hours of jamming, we broke for lunch. Delmar, Tracy, and I shot over to the Chelsea Commons restaurant to grab a bite to eat...and commiserate over our murky fates. We'd been called back for three days now. Did that mean we had the gig? Sting had been warm and welcoming, but also sphinx-like. He'd dropped no hints as to where his game of musical chairs was leading. Not knowing where we stood was nerve-racking, but we all agreed to just relax (as much as possible) and enjoy the ride.

Meanwhile, staying calm was proving to be equally difficult back home in North Carolina. The stress was starting to take its toll as my parents anxiously awaited any news from the front. Thanks to the nail-biting suspense, my father had developed a painful case of shingles.

After lunch, we strapped in for another round of rock 'n' roll. Kicking things up a notch (or two), Branford Marsalis made his first appearance of the week...and I couldn't have scripted it any better. Branford broke into a big smile when he breezed through the studio door and saw me standing across the way. Branford hollered, "Jeff, my man!" and rushed to embrace me like a long lost friend. Luckily, Sting was standing nearby—and paying very close attention to the public display of affection. I'll never know for sure, but the Marsalis *hug of validation* may have permanently tipped the scales in my favor. Branford unpacked his horn, and we took off on a journey that made the previous sessions pale in comparison. Sting pulled me aside at the end of the day and whispered cryptically, "Come back tomorrow."

Thursday, October 1, 1987

Day Four of the SIR hostage crisis. After another laid back—but electrifying—day of jamming, Sting dismissed the troops and retreated to a couch in the corner. As the room emptied, I wandered over to say goodbye to my reclining host. Sting wished me a good evening, and then said matter-of-factly, "Um, by the way Jeff, you can have the gig...if you want it." IF?!? Am I dreaming? Completely floored, I quickly accepted Sting's casual—life-altering—offer. I felt like I'd hit the lottery. I couldn't fucking believe what was happening. Little Jeffrey Lee Campbell from Carrboro, North Carolina had just landed the Sting gig. Putting a bow on it, Sting smiled and added, "I'm going to make you famous."

Like a rock 'n' roll King Arthur, I'd pulled the sword from the stone—and with a surprising amount of ease. For reasons unknown, I didn't have to run a gauntlet of the world's finest guitarists. Sting apparently took a look at one other guy (Jon Gordon of Suzanne Vega's band) before bringing me back into the fold. I still can't believe Sting only auditioned two guitarists for such a coveted gig. I've heard horror stories about big-name artists auditioning (and re-auditioning) dozens of players on both coasts…and still being undecided. I guess Sting knew what he wanted: me.

I packed up my gear in a fog. Crewmembers Danny Quatrochi and Tom Herrmann extended their congratulations, before offhandedly inviting me to Sting's birthday party—happening that very night. Danny and "Tom-o" were both longtime, valued employees of the Sting machine. Danny's association with Sting stretched back to the early days of The Police, after he accepted a chance offer to handle drum tech for "a new band from England." Over the years, Danny became Sting's right-hand man; in charge of guitar tech, keyboard tech, moral support, photography, cup of tea…you name it. Look up "indispensable" in the dictionary; you'll see a picture of Danny Quatrochi. Most impressive of all, Danny is still at Sting's side today.

Tom Herrmann's area of expertise was audio. A veteran of numerous Police/Sting tours, Tom-o had the impossible task of keeping musicians happy with their onstage monitor mix. ("Yo Tom-o, turn ME up.") Tom eventually escaped the rigors of the road to raise a family, but he didn't stray from the pressure cooker of showbiz. Swapping one superstar boss for another, Tom went to work for the mercurial David Letterman, handling mix duties at *The Late Show* for over twenty years until Letterman surrendered to retirement. But Dave's departure didn't mark the end of Tom-o's tenure at The Ed Sullivan Theater. Tom-o survived *Late Show* regime change and continues to work his sonic magic for keeper of the flame, Stephen Colbert.

* * *

I'd been a member of Sting's band for all of five minutes and I was already being treated like family. I was invited to HIS house for HIS birthday party. Count me in. But I needed to take care of one small piece of business first: find the nearest rooftop and scream, "I GOT THE DAMN GIG!" I rushed back to my apartment, called my family and gave them the incredible news. Next, I phoned my presumptive girlfriend, Denise, and told her to put on her party shoes because we'd been invited to a birthday bash for my new BOSS. I felt like I'd been shot out of a cannon.

At the time, Sting was subletting a luxurious loft in Soho. I'd been instructed to press the buzzer marked "Ben Franklin" when I arrived at the swanky address. (Being privy to a celebrity pseudonym made me feel like such the insider.) Denise and I took the elevator up to "Ben's" floor where the doors opened directly into a spacious duplex filled with fashionable strangers. I had to pinch myself as we entered the exclusive gathering. Was I really partying at Sting's house? Still working on my social graces, it never crossed my mind to bring a birthday present—until I saw Branford show up with a gift bag. Arriving empty-handed was definitely a faux pas on my part, but I'll cut myself a little slack since my head was in the clouds. I watched Sting unwrap Branford's offering to reveal a collection of books. Sting smiled. "Thanks man, you can never go wrong with books." I didn't grasp the wisdom of his words at the time, but I came to see the light over the next year. Nothing makes you appreciate a good book like a sixteen-hour flight.

Denise and I had an incredible evening, mingling with the beautiful people while discreetly exchanging glances of "Can you believe this shit?" As the party wound down, we said our goodnights and floated back uptown.

I awoke Friday morning to my new life as Sting's guitarist. Tackling the first item on my delicious to-do list, I called AJR Concessions Inc. and resigned from my candy stand job. (Adios Twizzlers!) My supervisors were thrilled about my *slight* promotion and wished me nothing but the best. Next on the agenda: cancel my upcoming wedding band gigs. (The exact same gigs I was SO happy to have on the books a mere two weeks earlier.) I dialed my club-date office, eager to share my big news, but this call didn't go quite as smoothly. Rocco, my hard-nosed boss, reacted with a bare minimum of enthusiasm before accepting my resignation—conditionally. Rocco claimed it would be impossible to find a replacement on such short notice, and insisted it was too late to bail on tomorrow night's job. He expected me in Yonkers as scheduled. I was stunned, but responded with a timid "OK." When I mentioned the strong-arm tactics to my pal Doug, he let out a snort and suggested I blow off the gig. I was tempted, but, owing to my across-the-board fear of authority figures (real or perceived), I thought it best to honor my Saturday night engagement with The Frank Terris Orchestra.

Friday afternoon at REHEARSAL (no longer an audition), I asked Sting for permission to leave early on Saturday. I trotted out the perfectly vague "previous commitments" excuse and he said, "Sure, no problem." Thankfully he didn't ask any questions.

The following day will forever live in infamy. After playing a few hours of world-class music with Sting and company, I excused myself and rushed to my car. Using my backseat as a dressing room, I changed into my working-class tuxedo and drove the twenty—or twenty million—miles north to Yonkers. I then kicked off part two of my mind-bending Saturday, strumming my way through a schmaltzy wedding reception at the local Elks lodge. It was an unforgettable dose of culture shock. In one 24-hour period, I played some of the best—and worst—music of my life.

* * *

Seeing the same faces at rehearsal each day, I assumed Sting had settled on his lineup…until renowned jazz-fusion drummer

Dennis Chambers walked through the door. Dennis jumped behind the drums and laid down some serious grooves. It was an impressive display, but I was surprised Chambers was even in the mix. In light of Sting's spotty track record with premium sidemen, I figured Dennis's sparkly résumé might actually be viewed as a liability.

But when we finished jamming—major credits notwithstanding—Sting began quizzing Dennis about his schedule. Dennis listened and nodded, before calmly replying he wasn't currently available due to commitments with saxophonist David Sanborn. I stood there in silence, amazed by Dennis's detached response. Until that moment, I'd assumed if Sting showed interest in you ... *you* started clearing your calendar. I wasn't used to being around musicians who could pick and choose between high-profile gigs. And Sting probably wasn't used to hearing, "Thanks, but no thanks." The drum slot ended up going to Marvin "Smitty" Smith. Sting's new band was officially in place:

Delmar Brown—keyboards/vocals (Pat Martino, Gil Evans)
Mino Cinelu—percussion/vocals (Miles Davis, Weather Report)
Kenny Kirkland—piano (Dizzy Gillespie, Wynton Marsalis, Sting)
Branford Marsalis—saxophone (Herbie Hancock, Art Blakey, Sting)
Marvin "Smitty" Smith—drums (Sonny Rollins, Art Farmer)
Tracy Wormworth—bass/vocals (The Waitresses, Phyllis Hyman)

...and the new guy, Jeffrey Lee Campbell—guitar/vocals (M&M's, Raisinets)

New York City | Palladium | October 16

Our first gig was at the Palladium nightclub on East 14th street. The show was a private event sponsored by New England Digital, the company responsible for creating Sting's favorite new plaything: the Synclavier. The Synclavier was a state-of-the art keyboard/digital recorder—and had the price tag to prove it, costing somewhere in the neighborhood of two-hundred-and-fifty thousand dollars! Sting used the cutting-edge Synclavier to supplement our live sound with digitally recorded fragments ("samples") of background vocals, rhythmic loops, and various sounds from the *Nothing Like the Sun* album.

Today, the use of computers to enhance—or completely generate (ugh)—a band's sound is commonplace. And thanks to exponential advances in technology, a laptop computer can accomplish most, if not all, of the tasks that were once the sole domain of the mighty Synclavier. Best of all, going with a humble laptop will allow you to keep the bulk of your quarter million dollars tucked safely in your pocket. But back in the dawning days of digital, the pricey Synclavier ruled the roost—and it merited an exclusive, invitation-only concert by Sting.

We took the stage at the Palladium, and let the record show: Jeffrey Lee Campbell was officially performing with Sting. I was in heaven. The crowd hung on our every note as we ran through a dream setlist of Sting's music. Knowing his audience, and not above a little pandering, Sting stopped the band cold at one point to gush over his beloved Synclavier. Unfortunately, Sting's spontaneous testimonial came at MY expense. I'd just launched into the exposed, reggae-flavored guitar intro for Sting's new tune,

"History Will Teach Us Nothing," when I suddenly heard Sting shouting for me to stop. I looked up—and, as requested, stopped. Sting leaned into his microphone. "Sorry Jeff, but my Synclavier plays that guitar lick MUCH better than you." The partisan crowd howled on cue. A smirking Sting counted the tune off again, but I kept my arms folded this go-round and let the vaunted machine lead the way. Despite my demotion from guitarist to bystander, you heard no complaints from me. I was happy to play the patsy; I was onstage with Sting.

I felt overwhelmed as we wrapped our set. I couldn't believe I'd actually played a gig with my musical hero. Adding to my elation, I had a profound realization as I exited the stage: for the first time in my life, I wouldn't have to help pack up the band's equipment. After spending years in the rock 'n' roll trenches—serving as both musician AND crew—the concept of simply walking away after the final note was completely alien to me. My deeply ingrained habits told me to change into a dry T-shirt and start rolling up beer-soaked cables. Somehow I resisted the urge and despite my guilt over skipping out on the dirty work, my roadie impulses quickly disappeared. If memory serves, by the very next show.

There was no time to bask in any post-Palladium glory. We had a slightly less-private gig the following evening: the season premier of *Saturday Night Live*. Leading up to the SNL broadcast, the original plan had been to perform "We'll Be Together" and "Be Still my Beating Heart"—the first two singles from *Nothing Like the Sun*. Accordingly, those tunes had received top priority at our daily rehearsals. But we'd also kept our eye on the bigger picture: assembling the full-blown set for our upcoming world tour. Thanks to arranger Gil Evans, our unabridged song list included one of my all-time faves, "Little Wing" by Jimi Hendrix. I was probably only nine or ten years old when I first heard "Little Wing," but I was immediately drawn in. To my young ears, Jimi's psychedelic soul ballad sounded like Curtis Mayfield and The Impressions…on acid.

A few days before our SNL appearance, we innocently waded into "Little Wing" at an afternoon rehearsal. We explored the tune, taking our sweet time as we stretched out into previously uncharted territory. Ten-or-so inspired minutes later, when the last squeals of feedback died out, we stood staring at each other. Our powerful creation had taken us all by surprise. Sting broke the silence. "Do you think we can get that down to four minutes?" (SNL enforced a four-minute time limit for musical performances.) The band let out a good laugh, but the boss wasn't kidding. In a proverbial "New York minute," Sting made an executive decision and unilaterally replaced *his* "Be Still My Beating Heart" with *Jimi's* "Little Wing." My outrageous fortune continued as Sting's impulsive switcheroo transformed my SNL role from anonymous sideman to featured performer. Thank you Jimi, Gil, and most of all, Sting. (One interesting piece of trivia: Sting originally composed "Be Still My Beating Heart" for Whitney Houston, but she took a pass on the song. Take note: even guys like Sting deal with rejection.)

The band swung by Rockefeller Center for a dry run on the Thursday before the broadcast. Just walking into Studio 8H gave me goose bumps. Those sacred walls had soaked up over fifty years of music, ranging from the sublime (Arturo Toscanini's NBC Symphony Orchestra) to the ridiculous (Bill Murray's lounge lizard "Star Wars"). Now it was my turn to add to that legacy.

Sting called in the heavy artillery for the telecast, recruiting über-engineer Bob Clearmountain (Rolling Stones, Bowie, Chic) to handle the mix duties. *Great, just what I needed, more pressure.* Mr. Clearmountain asked for multiple passes of "Little Wing" as he fine-tuned our blend at soundcheck. After a couple of repetitions, I spied SNL bandleader G.E. Smith—another six-string idol of mine—quietly observing from the shadows. *Great, just what I needed, more pressure.* (Is there an echo in here?) I attempted to top myself with each new take of "Wing," and promptly proved the law of diminishing returns. Adding to my butterflies, comedic superheroes like Steve Martin, Dana Carvey, and Phil Hartman kept wandering in to check out the band.

That same afternoon, I was introduced to our road manager, Billy Francis. Billy was a tall, lanky Brit with an unmistakable "Do not fuck with me" air about him. I was having trouble keeping up with the crush of names and faces, but I quickly learned that Billy was indeed a VERY important "name and face." Being new to the touring game, I didn't understand the vital role of the road manager. The demanding gig is equal parts sheriff, den mother, cat herder, and if need be, executioner. To that end, Billy's nearly impossible mission for the next year was to keep eight crazy-ass musicians in line. But Billy's tough, no-nonsense demeanor made him the perfect man for the job. (Billy's impressive resumé included stints with Led Zeppelin, Yes, Rod Stewart, and The Police.) Despite his gruff exterior, Billy actually had a semi-lovable side once you got to know him. We ended up becoming good pals over the course of the tour, and fierce competitors on the tennis courts of the world.

New York City | Saturday Night Live | October 17

October 17, 1987, marked the 13th season premiere of *Saturday Night Live*—and my network television debut. I was psyched that my friends and family around the country would get a chance to see me perform with my new pal Sting..."Live from New York!"

I was picked up at my apartment by an NBC limo and delivered to Rockefeller Center for our 5pm soundcheck. My heart skipped a beat as I exited the elevator and strutted down the same hallway I'd seen featured on numerous SNL production numbers over the years. I pushed through those familiar double doors and stepped onto the hallowed set. I checked in with Team Sting, tossed my guitar up on stage, and dug into the first of many "hurry up and wait" portions of the day.

Left to my own devices, I set out on a self-guided tour of the SNL campus. I wandered up and down the halls, marveling at the vast collection of framed memorabilia. Adrift in my reverie, I rounded a corner and literally bumped into Sting. He took pity on the little lost lamb and invited me to tag along. Next thing I knew, I was standing in Steve Martin's dressing room. Sting doled out the introductions. "Steve, Jeff; Jeff, Steve." I squeaked out a nervous hello and flopped on the couch in the corner. I grabbed a random magazine and pretended to read while the two heavyweights ran lines for their James Bond skit. (For all I know, I was holding the magazine upside down.) Watching Steve "007" Martin and "Gold-Sting" hone their comedic timing was incredible, but MY portrayal of "nonchalant companion" was far and away the most Emmy-worthy performance in the room.

Despite the glut of downtime, musical guests were not permitted to leave the building. NYC is a wonderland of temptation and distractions, and Lorne Michaels was not going to risk having one of his performers turn up MIA come showtime. Like it or not, we were under benevolent house arrest for the next eight hours. Or that was the plan until smoke started wafting into the studio. Jailbreak!

30 Rock was on fire—courtesy of a frying utility cable underneath the sixty-five-story building. Self-preservation kicked in the moment I heard the alarm and saw wisps of smoke. I had no interest in waiting around for a group consensus on strategy. Instead, I located the nearest fire exit and scurried down the stairs—all the while wondering if I was escaping danger, or heading toward it. A metal security gate clanged shut behind me when I reached the bottom of the deserted stairwell. Reversing course was no longer an option. Shit! Where was I? Was I trapped in a basement? Was this the end? So close to my TV glory? Mommy! I pressed the emergency bar on the door in front of me and prayed it wasn't locked. The door clicked open and freed me onto the sidewalk. I looked up and saw flames dancing from a window above the iconic NBC/Rainbow Room marquee. This was definitely not a drill.

The good news: I was safe. The bad news: it looked like my national TV showcase had literally gone up in smoke. I dodged the incoming fire trucks and crossed to the sane(r) side of the street. I saw a couple of Sting's crew guys milling about on the sidewalk, so I flagged them down. Unsure of our next move, we teamed up and set out in search of a place that was not on fire. We dropped anchor at a nearby sushi joint and, with nothing better to do, sat ... and ate ... and drank. (Saké all around!)

Following a couple of hours of uncertainty, official word came down: the show would go on. We rushed back upstairs, but by that point it was too late to do the customary dress rehearsal. (Standard operating procedure at SNL involves an 8pm run-through in front of a live studio audience. Afterward, they clear the house, prune the show, and refill the studio with a new, drunker crowd for the actual broadcast. Our show is reportedly the only episode in *Saturday Night Live* history to hit the airwaves without a dress rehearsal.) Meanwhile, I'd been operating on a full tank of adrenaline *before* the fire drama, so now I was really jacked up. The prospect of performing with Sting on live TV was scary enough; no life-threatening emergencies required. The day had already been extremely memorable—and I'd yet to play a note.

We hunkered down in our dressing room/holding cell after being allowed back in the building. It was too early to start pacing the floor, so I decided to distract myself with some mindless instrument maintenance. I was hunched over, restringing my guitar, when I heard Delmar exclaim, "Yo Hiram!" I glanced up to see the tall, imposing figure of Mr. Hiram Bullock standing in the doorway. Best known for his work with Paul Shaffer on *Late Night with David Letterman,* Hiram Bullock was one of my favorite guitarists. In fact, Letterman's house band ("The World's Most Dangerous Band") was one of my favorite bands.

Shaffer's quartet—and the Letterman show in general—had played a significant role in my obsession with NYC. I was a rabid fan of *Late Night,* watching the show religiously, long before my move north. I'd sit in front of the TV transfixed as Paul's Hammond organ cued the opening sequence. The gritty montage of neon lights, crawling cop cars, and the mysterious steam rising from the streets made New York City seem like the hippest place on earth.

I was thrilled, yet thoroughly intimidated, that Hiram had turned up for our performance. And while I didn't think it possible, the evening's stakes had just gotten higher. In addition to the Letterman show, Hiram was also the guitarist in The Gil Evan's Orchestra—which meant he'd played guitar on Sting's studio version of "Little Wing." One could make the argument that I'd snaked Hiram's gig. Our tiny dressing room suddenly felt a little more crowded...and a lot more awkward. First a fire, and now Hiram Bullock. God had my undivided attention.

That familiar medley of excitement and fear churned in my gut as showtime approached. *Fortunately*, a visionary stagehand had clued me in on a private refrigerator tucked beneath the mezzanine. The secret icebox was stocked full of beer, and I'll confess I snuck off to visit the hidden mother lode a couple of times before our performance. But at the risk of rationalizing, I'm sure I wasn't the first—or last—self-medicated musician to take the SNL stage.

Zero hour. We kicked things off with Sting's funky new single, "We'll Be Together." Our eight-piece band swelled to nine on the first tune as Sting's assistant, Danny Quatrochi, was elevated to honorary band-member status. We were still in the process of sorting out various technical logistics, so Danny had been temporarily charged with triggering the Synclavier samples (horns/background vocals) used in the song. Due to severe space limitations in the 8H wings, the bulky keyboard had nowhere to go but onstage. Accordingly, Danny (aka The Synclavier Whisperer) followed suit.

A few days earlier, when it was determined he'd be appearing on-camera, Danny was required to hastily join the Musicians Union. But Danny wasn't the only one in our camp with labor issues. When I naively asked management if I also needed to be in the union, Kim Turner answered with his typical, dry British wit. "Only if you want to get paid." Sufficiently motivated by Kim's response, I rushed down to the Local 802 offices and signed on the dotted line. I'm proud to say I've been a member in good standing ever since.

After a few more comedy sketches, it was time for "Little Wing." Retaking the stage during a commercial break, I noticed my *buddy* Hiram Bullock planted firmly on the front row. There he sat, arms folded, eyebrow raised, shooting me a chilly "this better be good" glare.

As "Little Wing" took flight, I quickly realized my amp wasn't going to be loud enough to weather the coming storm. I stopped playing momentarily and reached down to boost my volume. The maneuver felt clumsy and amateurish, but I did what I had to do. And boy I'm glad I did. Lack of muscle would've totally undermined what turned out to be my shining hour.

Another interesting piece of body language occurred during the tune, but *this* move came courtesy of our frontman. As I stepped into the spotlight for my solo, Sting retreated to a chair tucked beside the drum set and unceremoniously took a seat. He turned his back to me, placed his chin in his hand and struck a pose of complete indifference. I'll never know if Sting's stagecraft was spontaneous or premeditated, but the tweak (and the mystery chair) was definitely there. In all fairness, Sting spun around after only a few seconds and gave me his full attention.

As my guitar solo reached its climax, Branford joined in on the final screaming note, creating a seamless segue into his sax solo. Branford's lyric soprano calmed the waters and gently guided us back to the last verse. Then we went in for the kill. Sting stoked the coda, tossing Beatles quotes onto the smoldering fire. The intensity continued to grow until the song eventually blasted off into the stratosphere. With the stage volume boiling over, I saw Branford shake his head and grin, as if to imply "now THIS is rock 'n' roll." When the last power chord came crashing down, the audience went nuts. Sting wheeled around and shot me a look of "Hell yeah!" I exhaled. His smile made me feel like TWO million bucks.

We exchanged hugs and high-fives as we triumphantly strutted back to the dressing room. An excited Kenny Kirkland pulled me aside and gushed he'd been temporarily transformed into a spellbound fan during "Little Wing." Kenny confided he'd gotten totally caught up in the moment when he suddenly remembered, "Hey wait a minute ... I'm IN this band!" I was blown away.

Holding down the other end of the accolade spectrum: Miles Copeland. Sting's notoriously brusque manager lived *up* to his reputation by not saying one friggin' word to me as the band huddled in the hallway backstage. In fact, despite standing only two feet away, Miles wouldn't even acknowledge my presence. I felt invisible. I was confident I'd delivered the goods on "Little Wing," and foolishly waited for my "nice job, kid." It never came. A little slow on the uptake, I'd soon learn Miles's true feelings about me.

We joined Steve Martin and the cast onstage at the end of the show for the traditional group sign-off, before heading out to the legendary SNL after-party. Delmar and I climbed into another one of NBC's bottomless supply of limos for the *grueling* three-block journey to the China Grill. The paparazzi sprung into action when our stretch pulled up to the curb. The shutterbugs leaned in as the limo driver opened our door, but much to the their chagrin, out popped two complete nobodies. Clueless to our identities, the posse lowered their cameras without exhausting a single flash.

Once inside, I headed straight to the bar for a celebratory cocktail. Forget my earlier saké-soaked fire drill and clandestine raids on the SNL beer stash—it was now officially party time. I worked the packed room, collecting congratulatory backslaps from friends and strangers alike. During my second or third victory lap, I saw Sting motioning for me to join him at the big boy's table. I zipped over and settled into the hot seat for the umpteenth time of the day. Sting did the honors, introducing me to his pals, *Rolling Stone* publisher Jann Wenner and rock journalist Vic Garbarini, editor of *Musician* magazine. (Like I said: big boys.) The four of us were chatting away when Vic blurted out, "Jeff, you do know Hiram Bullock wants your job?" Vic's news flash came as no surprise, but hearing the words float through the air struck fear in my heart. As I nervously tried to think of a witty comeback, Sting rode to my rescue. "Well, that's too bad. Hiram can't have Jeff's job." I internalized a huge sigh of relief, extremely grateful for the boss's vote of confidence. Turns out, it wouldn't be the last time Sting stuck up for me in the face of a job threat.

The SNL party raged well into the night, but I guess that's to be expected when the festivities don't get underway until 2am. I finally surrendered at some ungodly hour and poured myself into a cab. Despite being doubly intoxicated from the day's crazy events and my massive intake of booze, I had a sober sense of accomplishment as my head hit the pillow. Nailed it.

Sting had personal commitments in England after our SNL performance, so the band *enjoyed* a two-week break from rehearsals. Time off from work is normally considered a good thing, but I hated it. After years of toiling in obscurity, I couldn't get enough of my newfound elite status. I'd become addicted to spending my days at the exclusive SIR Studios, rocking out with world-class musicians, while seeing celebrities like Cher or Paul Shaffer wandering the halls on break from their respective rehearsals. The last thing I wanted was a day off.

Although my career was *en fuego*, my domestic situation left a lot to be desired. I'd grown tired of the sofa-bed life, and my eccentric, clingy roommate was proving to be a handful. (Did I mention she was an amateur witch?) Between her tarot card readings, spell-casting magic candles, and unsolicited neck rubs, things were getting just a little too wacky. I needed some space, physically and mentally. Meanwhile, my pal Doug's cavernous apartment sat dark most nights. Both Doug and his roommate, Richie Douglas, had essentially moved in with their girlfriends—so their deserted bachelor pad seemed like the perfect solution to my housing dilemma. I'd had my eye on their place since first coming to the city, but despite repeated overtures, Doug and Richie were reluctant to take on a third roommate. Then Sting happened. With my impending world tour added to the equation, the idea simply made too much sense. I was going to be out-of-town for most of the next year. Why not split the rent with another absentee tenant?

My buddies finally relented and agreed to let me move into their spacious Upper West Side digs. The view overlooking Riverside Park was incredible, but the apartment's most outstanding feature by far was its ridiculously low rent. Thanks to a long-standing, rent-stabilized lease, my pals were only paying $430 a month for their two-bedroom palace. In today's market, that apartment would easily go for TEN times that much. I've always heard when planning your household budget, one week's pay should cover one month's rent. However, that rule-of-thumb is often adjusted upward in pricey Manhattan. But in my case, the adjustment was downward—way downward. I'd agreed to foot half of Doug and Richie's rent, so my monthly burden was a *mighty* $215. (Considerably less than what I was shelling out for my sofa bed at Sara's place.) Do the beautiful math: one single WEEK of my Sting salary would pay an entire YEAR of my rent. I'll never see that kind of income-to-rent ratio again in my life. I even felt a little guilty about my embarrassment of riches. But what was I supposed to do? I was on a roll.

When Sting returned Stateside, we cranked back up with an eye toward our South American debut, which was only a little over two weeks away. The band dynamic began to take shape as rehearsals progressed, with the veteran members setting the tone. Branford was the affable mayor; Kenny was the enigmatic guru; and percussionist Mino Cinelu was definitely the life of the party. Oozing French-Caribbean charm, Mino was our resident authority on the finer things in life—and thus ran unopposed for the position of band connoisseur. Mino was always in charge of selecting the wine at dinner…or lunch…or breakfast. (Just kidding, everybody knows breakfast means Bloody Marys.)

We were enjoying a vino-infused lunch one afternoon when Mino looked over at me. "*Ooski,* once we're out on the road, I'm going to teach you how to drink." (Mino called everyone "Ooski." I have no idea why. He literally had a language of his own.) I appreciated Mino's offer of mentorship, but I had to chuckle at the thought of anybody teaching ME how to drink. Thanks to my formative years of gigging in bars and frat houses, I'd had PLEN-TY of on-the-job training. But Mino was right. I ended up learning a great deal from him about fine wines and unconventional spirits of the world. Under Mino's expert tutelage, I grew to be a much more sophisticated and discriminating drunk.

With the tour breathing down my neck, I got busy refining my road rig. My cherished Mesa Boogie Mark III amp was at the heart of my setup. (The amp was an incredibly generous going-away gift from Carolina friends and family in honor of my move to New York.) As far as sound processing was concerned, individual effects pedals ("stomp boxes") had fallen out of favor in the late 80's, so I had my eye on a sleek, rack-mounted Roland GP-8. The multi-effects unit seemed like the perfect solution for achieving the requisite Police/Sting sounds and textures. But due to its immense popularity, I couldn't find a GP-8 anywhere. No matter where I looked, the reply was "sold out." I tried crying on Tom-o's shoulder, but he dismissed me with a distracted, half-sympathetic shrug. Or so I thought.

I walked into SIR the next day and found an overnight package waiting for me. I opened the box and discovered MY brand-new GP-8. I slowly began to grasp the attendant clout of rock stardom. "Unavailable" items suddenly became "available" when you worked for an artist of Sting's caliber.

My go-to guitar was a red "Strat" made by Zion, a small boutique company in North Carolina. But I needed a backup for the road, so I placed an order for a second axe; same model, but with an icy white finish. When my new guitar arrived, I couldn't wait to take it for a spin at rehearsal. Meanwhile, for whatever reason, the boss was not having a good day. Sting turned to me after only one or two tunes and bellowed out of nowhere, "I HATE that guitar!" My poor, innocent Zion had become the scapegoat for Sting's sour mood. I took the not-so-subtle hint and decided to tuck my new baby away until the storm clouds cleared. Eventually, my shiny white guitar was able to worm its way back into Sting's good graces (and even land in a music video).

Another fringe benefit of the Sting gig was custom-made stage clothes, courtesy of designer Colleen Atwood. Ms. Atwood had costumed Sting's previous tour, and she'd been summoned to work her makeover magic once again. Colleen dropped by rehearsal one afternoon to meet the gang and literally size up her task. After a brief introduction, next thing I knew, I was standing in my skivvies while some dude measured my inseam. But modesty be damned. I would've stripped naked for the indulgence of bespoke threads. A personal tailor was a whole new level of extravagance for an off-the-rack guy like me.

The finished Atwood designs had a unique flair—perhaps to a fault. Despite the made-to-order luxury, I never really warmed to my outfit. And I wasn't alone. Maybe Colleen's vision was simply too fashion forward, but our custom clothing gradually drifted out of sight. Little by little, band members replaced Colleen's handiwork with their own stylistic choices. But hey, you win some, you lose some—and Colleen has certainly done her share of winning. She's gone on to great success in Hollywood, winning four Oscars for costume design (including 2003's "Best Picture," the smash hit *Chicago*).

Affirming the slow wheels of justice, I received a letter around this time from the New York City Small Claims Court. "Campbell v Bushrock" had finally bubbled to the top of the docket. But thanks to the beautiful upheaval in my life, my complaint against Delmar's manager had completely slipped my mind. My case was airtight, but I had no interest in pursuing legal action. In light of recent events—e.g. landing the gig of a lifetime—I let the court date slide. Based on my calculations, the Gods had repaid that debt a million times over.

Our six-week residency at SIR started drawing to a close. We spent our remaining days putting the final touches on our twenty-five-song setlist (give or take), as well as grooming a temporary replacement for Branford. Turns out our in-demand saxophonist would not be joining us for the first leg of the tour, due to previous commitments…in Hollywood. Thanks to a show-stealing performance in Sting's *Blue Turtles* documentary, Branford was busy parlaying his natural, on-screen charisma into additional movie roles. Sting signed off on Branford's leave of absence, permitting him to go to his bullpen. Branford tapped pal Steve Coleman to cover woodwind duties in the interim.

Branford had recently finished shooting Spike Lee's latest movie, *School Daze*, so I wasn't surprised when the Brooklyn filmmaker turned up at one of our rehearsals. Spike chatted with the band for a bit, and then stuck around to check out a few tunes. A couple of days later, I was walking up Eighth Avenue when I saw Spike Lee heading in my direction. I was certain he wouldn't remember me, so I kept my eyes forward as we passed. (I had no intention of humiliating myself with a one-sided hello.) Imagine my shock when Spike stopped in his tracks, turned and shouted, "Hey I know you—Sting's guitarist!" For that brief moment, I was THE man. Later that same week, I was waiting in line at a coffee shop when some guy said, "Dude, you look just like Sting's guitarist." I replied, "Guilty." He laughed and warned I better get used to the attention. Life was beautiful. I was right in the sweet spot—still savoring the honeymoon phase of the gig while standing on the edge of a worldwide adventure. I'd never been happier.

New York City | The Ritz | November 15, 16

We played two nights at The Ritz in New York City prior to setting out for South America. The shows served as our final tune-up before graduating to the gigantic soccer stadiums of Brazil and Argentina. The Ritz (originally and now known as Webster Hall) was a hip and happening nightclub in the East Village, with a capacity of about 1500 people. A small crowd for Sting, but a huge crowd for me...at least for the time being.

We were still in the process of working out the kinks, so our shows got a little shaky at times. But the loose vibe only seemed to fuel the voodoo, making the cozy gigs even more memorable for the fans. We were navigating our way through the brand-new "Rock Steady" one night when Sting got hopelessly lost in his tongue-twisting lyrics. Sting accepted defeat and stopped the band mid-song, sheepishly confessing to the crowd he'd forgotten his own words. A quick-thinking fan leapt to the rescue, offering up his handy copy of the *Nothing Like the Sun* CD booklet. The sold-out room watched and waited as Sting playfully perused (and admired) his liner notes, before eventually locating the lyric in question. Sting studied the troublesome passage for a minute or two and, after milking the moment for all it was worth, counted the band back in. The crowd roared with delight as Sting aced his make-up oral exam.

In addition to the adoring fans and industry bigwigs, the Ritz audience held an extra special treat for me. My best buds, and erstwhile roommates, Doug and Richie (along with their girlfriends, Kimberley and Pattie) were on hand for our farewell show. Seeing my friends cheer me on from their ringside balcony seats made for the perfect send-off. Goodbye NYC; Hello World.

South America
November 18 — December 12 (7 shows in 6 cities)

After years of playing dances, bars, and weddings, fantasy became reality: I was on the road with a big-time rock 'n' roll tour—with the emphasis on BIG. All of our South American concerts were booked in giant, outdoor soccer stadiums. (The smallest venue on the itinerary held a *mere* 50,000.) But despite the humongous settings, the shows were still viewed as something of a warm-up—kind of like the NFL's preseason games. Sting was extremely popular in South America, so he could count on his fans to embrace us unconditionally as we jelled into a real band. The strategy of combining a relaxed performance schedule with super-sized, but forgiving, audiences was a great way for us to ease into our mission. It allowed Sting to figure out what did (and didn't) work before the high-stakes madness really kicked in.

First stop: Rio de Janeiro—an ideal jumping-off point for my global fairytale. I'd played songs about Ipanema and Corcovado for years, but I never dreamed I'd get a chance to actually visit these bossa-worthy spots. Experiencing the musically immortalized places firsthand made it easy to understand why composers celebrated Brazil.

Although I was officially on the clock, it felt more like I was on Spring Break. The *caipirinhas* (Brazil's national cocktail) and the thongs (Brazil's national bikini) were both essentially bottomless, so the party raged full tilt. Lady Rio was quite the skilled seductress and I made for easy prey. Being a newbie, I hadn't grasped that the same debauched storyline would be repeated at practically every turn over the upcoming year. We might not have always received the "key to the city," but we ALWAYS ended up with the "key to the bar." Overindulgence became my default standard of living. The thought of pacing myself never crossed my mind.

Rio de Janeiro, Brazil | Marcanã Stadium | November 20

We were scheduled to kick things off at Rio's Maracanã Stadium, but simply getting to the venue proved to be an adventure in itself. We were cruising down the highway when our chartered bus lost power and sputtered to a stop. The driver made several attempts to restart the engine, but had no luck. Our bus was dead—and the lack of air conditioning quickly drove us out of the vehicle. We loitered on the shoulder of the freeway as cars whizzed by. I could see the massive stadium on the horizon, but it did not qualify as walking distance. We were stranded.

Fortunately, we'd been followed. A few carloads of Sting chasers had fallen in behind us as we departed the hotel, and they'd had the *cojones* (and/or common decency) to pull over when they saw our bus limp to the curb. Realizing our loss could be their gain, the benign stalkers offered to ferry the band the rest of the way. Billy weighed the spontaneous proposal and, with no better solutions on the table, instructed us to split up and pile into the cars of complete strangers. Win-win, I guess. We were rescued—and some Sting fans got the thrill of a lifetime. Funny, in all my rock-star fantasies, I never envisioned being chauffeured to my big-stage debut in the cramped backseat of a Toyota.

After reaching the stadium, courtesy of our makeshift motorcade, we settled into our dressing rooms. My guitar was in need of fresh strings, so, like I'd done my whole life, I sprawled out on the floor and began the humdrum task of restringing my axe. Sting wandered in a few minutes later, paused, and gave me a bit of a funny look before moving on. I didn't think much of it at the time, but it later dawned on me that instrument maintenance probably wasn't considered a part of my job description up in the big leagues. Sure enough, I was assigned my own personal guitar tech the very next day. (OK, if you guys insist.) Mike Strout, a proud Jersey dude, was put in charge of keeping me happy, and he did one helluva job. Mike took great care of me and—damn him—succeeded in spoiling me for life. My pampered showtime routine entailed:

1. Walk on stage as Mike hands me my polished, freshly strung guitar
2. Play awesome music in front of gigantic, adoring crowds
3. Toss my abused, sweat-drenched guitar to Mike as I walk off stage
4. Accept a towel, a cold beer, and a pat on the back from Mike

All musicians should be lucky enough to have a "Mike." I've missed him on every single gig since.

Ironically, our first concert ended up being the largest of the entire tour. With a flair for the dramatic, Sting unveiled his new band to a mob of over two hundred thousand fans. It was an incredible evening. Hearing the roar of a quarter million people is something I'll never forget.

* * *

With three days off in Rio after our inaugural show, I embraced the role of hedonistic rocker to the hilt. I dedicated the bulk of my waking hours to drinks, chicks, and relentless beachcombing. But despite the nonstop fun, I couldn't wait to go back to work. At that early juncture, I found a "day on" to be much more enjoyable than a "day off." Being a rock star was a lot cooler than being a civilian.

Belo Horizonte, Brazil | 7 de Setembro Stadium | November 24

What a difference a year makes. I'd spent last Thanksgiving in Carrboro with Mom and Dad. This Thanksgiving? Rio de Janeiro with Sting. I kicked off my expat Turkey Day with a round of doubles tennis (celebrity edition): Billy and me versus the formidable team of Sting and "the missus," Trudie Styler. I absentmindedly wished my three British playmates a "Happy Thanksgiving" as we convened on the court. Duh. The culturally flawed sentiment hung in the air until Sting sneered sarcastically, "Thanksgiving? Stupid American holiday." OK, I deserved that.

We swatted and sweated as Christ the Redeemer peered down from atop Corcovado Mountain. I was patrolling the net midway through the match when a fat, juicy lob came my way. I licked my lips and reared back for my dependably erratic overhead smash. Whack! I crushed the ball—but I crushed it right into Trudie's forehead. (Shit.) Before I could attempt to beg her forgiveness, Sting's better half calmly turned to him and pointed at me. "FIRE HIM!" Sting looked over at me. "Jeff, you're fired." More British wit…I hope?

Brasilia, Brazil | Mané Garrincha Stadium | November 28

I was rocking along in my usual state of bliss when I noticed a commotion out of the corner of my eye. A woman from the audience had made her way up on stage—and she was rushing straight toward Sting. Like any good soldier, my first instinct was to protect the King. I abandoned strum mid-tune and tried to intercept the charging fan, but she was not going to be denied. She pushed past me and latched on to our leader like an amorous octopus. The crowd cheered with delight as the woman devoured her quarry with hugs and kisses. A couple of crewmembers eventually wandered out from the wings and peeled the sexy assailant off of Sting. As I watched the grinning roadies escort the woman away, I got the feeling I may have overreacted. Sting's guitar tech, Danny, pulled me aside after the show. "If that ever happens again, just keep playing. We'll take care of it." Chalk up yet another rookie misstep. But at least my heart was in the right place.

* * *

With another three-day break on tap, Sting—one of the world's leading Rain Forest advocates—made a quick visit to the Amazon. Joined by Trudie, Mino, and Belgian filmmaker Jean-Pierre Dutilleux, Sting ventured into the jungle to meet with Chief Raoni and members of the Kayapo tribe to discuss the ongoing plight of deforestation.

When Sting and company returned to civilization, they entertained us city slickers with harrowing stories from the bush. The fearless foursome had lived side by side with the tribesmen, *enjoying* activities like skinny dipping in the Amazon, dodging tarantulas, and staring down poisonous snakes. Apparently, simply making it back in one piece was a feat in itself. Word was, the "white man" didn't always live to tell his jungle tale.

I admired the intrepid spirit of my band mates, but I wasn't the least bit envious. Thank God they hadn't invited me to tag along. Peer pressure would've forced me to say yes, and I would have been scared to death the entire time. As a friend of mine used to say, "Sure, I LOVE camping…at the Waldorf Astoria."

Porto Alegre, Brazil | Olympic Stadium | December 2

We were psyched to tackle another stadium full of fans, but Mother Nature had other ideas. A downpour of biblical proportions pelted our bus as we pulled up to the venue. I dropped my belongings in the dressing room and wandered outside to assess the *fluid* situation. I shielded myself under an archway and watched as the storm unleashed its fury on thousands of unprotected humans. Rain poured, thunder clapped, lightning popped—but the hardcore faithful stood their ground. They wanted some Sting.

Whispers of a possible cancellation swirled backstage, but our opening act, Capital Inicial, elected to suck it up and brave the near-apocalyptic conditions. The group's tenacity was admirable, but it came at a price as the overhead canopy ultimately proved no match for the heavy weather. After their set, I watched (and winced) in sympathy as the keyboardist lifted his synthesizer from its stand, triggering a cascade of rainwater from inside the now-ruined instrument.

Sting's brain trust huddled with concert promoters backstage as conditions continued to deteriorate. The powers that be discussed options that hovered somewhere between bad and worse. Should we pull the plug on our show? And if we did, which *lucky* person would get to tell 60,000 death-defying fans that Sting would not be performing? Needless to say, the waterlogged masses would not be pleased with such a development.

Brainstorming different ways to proceed, Sting offered to go out on stage, break the bad news, play one song by himself and say goodnight. That idea was shot down immediately. Our promoters recognized the potential wrath of the huge crowd and insisted—in the event of a cancellation—the band would have to be LONG gone before any official announcement was made. That seemed like a smart plan (in my unsolicited opinion). I had no desire to be trapped in the middle of a Brazilian riot, especially one that could be blamed on me. As the debate roiled, the storm mercifully blinked. The winds calmed and the rains subsided, allowing us to finally take the stage—two soggy hours behind schedule. But Sting came prepared. Good Boy Scout that he was, Sting had a note of apology (written in Portuguese) tucked in his pocket, just in case we needed to run for cover mid-song. In the end, we were able to deliver our entire set to the patient, wrinkly throng—although our last note wasn't sounded until after 1am.

São Paulo, Brazil | Anhembi Exhibition | December 5, 6

Our next stop was the imposing metropolis of São Paulo, the largest city in the Southern Hemisphere. I checked into my upper-floor hotel room and stared out the window in disbelief. With no perceptible horizon, the city appeared to be infinite. The vast urban sprawl created the sensation of being surrounded by ten Manhattan skylines—at least. The view was breathtaking, but almost in a scary, "Make it stop" kind of way.

Feeling hungry, I located my room service menu and ordered lunch. I'd only been on tour for three weeks, but I already had the traveling businessman routine down pat: inhale a club sandwich while sitting on your bed in antisocial seclusion. Sufficiently carb loaded, I decided to head for the hotel gym. I was determined to work off at least two or three of those french fries.

I walked into the pool area, and was immediately confronted by my repressed American upbringing...and a roomful of naked men. The hotel's health club was clearly "Male Only," because the use of swimwear was graphically optional. No Shoes, No Pants, No Problem. Suddenly the thought of an itty-bitty Speedo seemed downright modest. But my provincial sensibilities took an even bigger hit when I noticed the abundance of female employees milling around. I settled into a deckchair and watched in amazement as the women nonchalantly catered to the club's nude clientele. The uniformed matrons went about their duties (serving beverages, distributing towels, etc.), completely unfazed by the free-swinging anatomy. For the record, I chose to remain covered.

Sting strolled in a little later (with pants on) and pulled up a chair. Within moments, an eagle-eyed club manager was all over us. He excitedly welcomed Sting and launched into a spiel extolling the facility's features. Of the various amenities, "high-pressure water therapy" piqued our interest the most. The manager persisted until Sting and I agreed to a demonstration. We were escorted to a tiled space where we found ourselves face-to-face with a shiny, slightly menacing, machine. The contraption featured numerous gauges, switches, and a large hose; it was essentially a pressure washer for humans. Trying to show off for my boss, I volunteered to go first. A burly club employee took her place behind the industrial Super Soaker and told me to face the wall. (I felt like I should've been offered a blindfold and a cigarette.) I obeyed the command and assumed the position. Ready,

Aim, Splash! Torrents of pressurized water exploded from the machine, pummeling my back, arms, and legs with an invigorating massage. After my backside had been taught a lesson, the dominatrix ordered me to turn around. But before unleashing her frontal assault, she instructed me to cup my hands over my sensitive *parts*. This ended up being a damn good suggestion. I survived round two of my aqua beatdown and moved aside to let Sting step into the line of fire. Ready…Aim…

* * *

I was having the time of my life, but the pressure to excel was intense. To that end, certain songs required a little (or a lot of) tweaking as we found our way. Sting had expressed frustration with the "feel" in one of our reggae numbers, and—despite being the runt of the litter—I was confident I'd identified the problem. I talked with Sting one-on-one before a show, giving my theories on why the groove wasn't grooving. Sting endured my *expert* analysis and countered, "Great! Now go tell the band what you just told me." Maybe Sting was testing my mettle, but away I went on a suicide mission to enlighten my veteran co-workers.

The band sat quietly as I shared my views on how to fix our reggae problem. I spouted some overly academic bullshit about "underlying duple versus triple feel" and *blah, blah, blah*. When I wrapped up my lecture, Kenny responded with polite but deadly aim. "Yeah man, I can definitely tell you went to music school." Kenny's left-handed compliment found its mark. I heard him loud and clear: don't say it, play it. (Like Thelonious Monk said, "Talking about music is like dancing about architecture.") Our drummer, Smitty, was more than happy to give Kenny's dagger a twist. "Thanks, Jeff. Now sit down and shut the fuck up."

(For the record, everything is cool between Smitty and me. Long after the tour, we bumped into each other one afternoon at Manny's Music in NYC. Smitty had since moved to LA and was holding down the drum chair for Jay Leno's *Tonight Show* band. Smitty greeted me with a big smile and a warm hug, before making a point to apologize for any unfriendly behavior "all those years ago.")

Unfortunately, Smitty wasn't the only one who seemed less than thrilled with Sting's choice of guitarists. Branford's sub, Steve Coleman, appeared to be ambivalent (at best) about my presence on the bandstand. This wasn't surprising; Steve and I were definitely cut from a different cloth. Steve is a cerebral, hardcore jazzer—not to mention, a 2014 recipient of the prestigious MacArthur Fellowship "Genius Grant." Me? I'm just a simple pop/rock guy with a half-baked college education. One had to look no further than Sting's souvenir program to discover the glaring *religious* differences between Steve and myself. In Steve's bio, he was asked to name his "guilty musical pleasure." He answered "Prince." Huh?!? In my world, Prince rates as a stone-cold genius. No disrespect to John, Paul, George and Ringo, but Prince was MY Beatles. And while I have plenty of "guilty" songs in my music library, Prince isn't responsible for any of 'em. (Lawrence Welk, yes; Prince, no.) But forget about Prince, I sometimes wondered if Steve even liked Sting's music. Thanks to Steve's permanent cold shoulder, I had no idea what made that guy tick.

Meanwhile, Steve's scowl appeared to be contagious. He and Smitty were close friends, and they spent a lot of time together on the road. As we made our way around Brazil, I picked up on a subtle shift in our drummer's demeanor. Smitty had been cheerful and gung ho at the start of the tour, but as the miles mounted, he'd gradually adopted Steve's sullen attitude.

After a lackluster opening night in São Paulo, Sting called a midnight meeting at the hotel. (Never a good sign.) We assembled in a penthouse boardroom and sat quietly as an enraged Sting tore us a new orifice. Nervously glancing around the room, I was stunned to see Smitty leafing through a magazine, while completely ignoring the tongue-lashing. I couldn't believe my eyes; Smitty was fiddling while Sting burned. Apparently I wasn't the only one who noticed the passive-aggressive "dis." A couple of days after Smitty's flagrant insubordination, I began hearing whispers about a mystery drummer en route to South America to shadow the band ... "just in case."

São Paulo wrapped up our commitments in Brazil. ¡Hola Argentina! We continued our brutally relaxed pace of three days off in between every show, and I was quickly discovering just how boring the road could be. I was always on the prowl for diversion, so I jumped at an invitation to join Sting and Trudie for lunch. We dined at an exclusive Buenos Aires racquet club, but before breaking bread, I added yet another virgin experience to my ever-expanding repertoire: a game of squash. My rock-star coach gave me a crash course in the sport, and then we dove into a friendly, but competitive, match. Luckily, we were only playing singles that day, so I didn't run the risk of clobbering Trudie again... and getting fired again. Squash with Sting? In Argentina?

My life kept getting more and more surreal. But I understood my mission: keep smiling and fake it.

Buenos Aires, Argentina | River Plate Stadium | December 11

During our Buenos Aires performance, we were joined onstage by *The Mothers of the Disappeared*—the inspiration behind Sting's new song, "They Dance Alone." The organization had been founded by women who'd lost children under Argentina's former military dictatorship. (The ruthless regime was known to "disappear" citizens who dared challenge governmental authority.) As a form of non-violent protest, the courageous women would dance in public while holding pictures of missing loved ones. Sting's somber, yet ultimately joyous, song was always an emotional highlight of the evening, but the sight of Sting dancing with the actual *Mothers* was especially powerful.

On a much lighter note, "They Dance Alone"—or at least a snippet of it—proved irresistible to the mercenaries of Madison Avenue. (I guess advertisers figured if something's good enough to denounce evil dictators, it's good enough to sell stuff.) I was vegging on my couch one afternoon when a TV commercial jolted me from my stupor. I thought it was my imagination at first, but, upon closer scrutiny, my ears were not playing tricks on me: the Sheba Cat Food jingle was blatantly ripping off "They Dance Alone." Some shameless ad agency had pilfered Sting's opening 4-note theme, and even had the audacity to use the same synth sound for the stolen motif. I made a mental note and jokingly alerted Sting to the overt plagiarism at our next show. He looked at me like I was crazy—and like I watched way too much TV. But a week or so later at soundcheck, Sting says out-of-the-blue, "OK guys, let's play the 'cat food' song." It took me a minute to figure out what the hell he was talking about.

* * *

Buenos Aires was our final stop in South America before drastically changing gears and heading UP to Jolly Olde England. Christmas was less than two weeks away, so I couldn't wait to swap the Southern hemisphere's summer for the more holiday-appropriate chill of England. But escaping the clutches of South America was easier said than done. Our flight to London was booked out of Rio—and Brazil was in the middle of an airline strike. Fortunately, the work stoppage was supposed be over before our departure to the UK, so we crossed our fingers and flew on to Rio. If necessary, we'd just have to wait things out. And wait is exactly what we did.

We made it to Rio without a hitch, and then the *fun* started. We sat and sat—mainly in an airport bar, of course—as Brazil's airline industry slowly flickered back to life. We waited around so long we even got tired of drinking. (You know things are bad when rockers tire of drinking.) After repeated delays, the heavenly sound of a boarding call boosted morale. We let out a drunken cheer and staggered onto the jet, but our optimism was unfortunately short-lived. Subjected to another interminable wait, we realized we'd accomplished next to nothing: we'd simply exchanged bar stools for airplane seats. The cabin door remained wide open with no signs of intelligent life. We were going nowhere fast.

Eager to begin the twelve-hour journey, our rowdy group began chanting, "Close the door! Close the door!" Our shouts were in vain, but we were buoyed by the sight of a flight crew eventually straggling onto the scene. Half an hour later, amid sarcastic applause from the weary passengers, a flight attendant finally closed the plane's door. But our celebration was premature yet again. We just sat there—and now we had the added bonus of being sealed in an airtight metal tube. With things going from bad to worse, a new chant was born: "Open the door! Open the door!" Our cries went unheeded; we were hostages of Varig Airlines. We endured another mind-numbing chunk of downtime before our foxhole prayers were finally answered. The plane pushed back from the gate and, at long last, Team Sting was on its way to London. HO! HO! HO!

Dateline: London

Prim and proper London was a welcome change of pace after spending the past month in wild and loose South America. It was my first visit to England, but compared to Brazil and Argentina, I felt right at home. (Except for that driving on the wrong side of the road business.) I could finally exhale...or so I thought. Unfortunately, my peace of mind was fleeting as I detected a heightened sense of urgency from the boss.

Despite being on Sting's home turf, it was clear the ante had been upped. The unconditional love of South America was in our rearview mirror, and Sting was faced with debuting his latest venture to a more discriminating—and jaded—audience. Hedging his bets for our London stand, Sting added background vocalists Dolette McDonald and Tessa Niles. Dolette had been a member of Sting's *Blue Turtles* band, so she was family. Tessa was one of London's top-call singers, with credits including Eric Clapton, Tina Turner, Duran Duran, and The Police. (For the record, Dolette ended up staying onboard for the rest of the tour.)

In other personnel news, the drama surrounding our drum chair continued to simmer in secret. But Smitty wasn't the only employee on the endangered species list. Unbeknownst to me, there was also a campaign afoot to replace…the GUITARIST! (Cue *Psycho* violins.)

Sadly, with such a high-profile, high-pressure gig, I spent a large part of the Sting tour worrying about job security. In my recurring nightmare, I was exposed as a fraud and summarily sent back to where I belonged: the candy stand. And it certainly hadn't helped matters when my guitar tech Mike had confided during a late-night bender in Brazil, "Hey man, we're all pulling for you." Pulling for me? Obviously my paranoia was not unfounded.

As I later discovered, management had quietly set aside an afternoon in London for Sting to look at potential replacements for yours truly. Apparently, Miles Copeland—my old pal who'd ignored me backstage at SNL—had been urging Sting to make a change. Among my alleged crimes and misdemeanors, Miles thought I was "too short" for the gig. WTF? I'm at least as tall as Police guitarist Andy Summers, and that situation seemed to work out pretty well. Nevertheless, as I was frolicking around London in ignorant holiday bliss, my future with Sting hung by a thread. As best as I could later piece together through band gossip, Sting looked at a couple of British guitarists, but ultimately decided to stand pat. Whew! Christmas came early for me—and I didn't even know it. My angels were clearly still on the j-o-b.

So it was official: I was an underdog. But at least I was Sting's underdog. According to music journalist Vic Garbarini, I reminded Sting a bit of his younger self; when *he* was the new guy playing with the older, wiser musicians. During Sting's formative years, his musical elders had affectionately dubbed him "The Kid." Luckily, I guess Sting saw some of "The Kid" in me. In fact, in the tour program, Sting poked fun at my youthful appearance:

"Jeff looks like he is twelve years old... but actually he is fourteen and a half. I discovered him in the Port Authority Bus Terminal."

* * *

My stay of execution underscores the most important lesson I've learned over the years: Be nice! Musical skills are just one piece of the puzzle. Trust me, EVERYBODY at the audition knows how to play, or they wouldn't be there in the first place. Consequently, people skills can often mean the difference between landing and losing a gig. I once heard a big-time road manager spell it out in a candid interview: "I don't care how good you play. If you're an asshole, I don't want you on my bus." Amen to that; camaraderie counts. If Sting hadn't liked me, I'm sure he wouldn't have hesitated to ax me. There are plenty of excellent guitarists out there. Any one of them would've gladly taken my place.

Years after the Sting tour, I auditioned for the guitar slot in *Saturday Night Live's* house band. The show was replacing Lukasz "Dr. Luke" Gottwald, who was moving on to seriously greener pastures as one of the world's top record producers (Britney, Pink, Avril, etc.). My audition turned out to be a laid-back, one-on-one hang with SNL's musical director/saxophonist Lenny Pickett. We chilled for a couple of hours in Lenny's office, casually playing through a few charts while philosophizing about the biz. In Lenny's opinion, there are three simple keys to a successful career in music:

1. Be on time
2. Be prepared
3. Have a good attitude

I agree with Lenny wholeheartedly. But you'd be surprised how many technically qualified musicians struggle to deliver those three *simple* things. (For the record, the SNL gig went to the talented Jared Scharff.)

* * *

Christmastime in London was magical. Stoking the holiday spirit, Sting threw a party for the band at his 17th century English townhouse. In a span of three months, I'd been a guest at Sting's birthday party in NYC, and his Christmas party in London. (A beach party at his house in Malibu was still to come.) A lavish spread of food and drink, along with a crackling fire in the over-sized hearth, made for an evening worthy of Currier and Ives. But despite the wonderful memories, I'm somewhat embarrassed when I see photos from the party. My bargain-basement wardrobe screams "amateur with little money—and even less fashion sense." Thankfully, none of the big boys ever made fun of my questionable clothing choices, at least not to my face. Constantly surrounded by cosmopolitan types with a flair for style, I eventually realized I needed to dig a little deeper into my wallet and try to at least *look* like I belonged.

But, then again, sometimes you just can't win. Our road manager arrived at Sting's Christmas party sporting an expensive suit with a bold pinstripe. As Billy mingled across the way, Sting leaned over to me and mused about the double-edged sword of fashion. "Like they say, Jeff, sometimes the man wears the clothes; other times, the clothes wear the man." When I nodded in agreement, Sting pounced, "For example, take a look at that suit wearing Billy." Ba dum ching. Don Rickles would've been proud.

London, England | Wembley Arena | December 15, 16, 18, 19, 20

We were set to tackle Wembley arena, but our drummer issue was still unsettled. And secretly knowing Smitty's potential replacement was circling like a vulture made the situation even more uncomfortable. Adding to the melodrama, Smitty's wife had decided to jet over to London for a little pre-Christmas revelry with the gang. This could get ugly.

Our performance schedule called for two shows, a night off, and then three more shows before heading home for the holidays. The critics weighed in after the first two concerts, heaping praise on Sting's latest endeavor. I heaved a sigh of relief, and held out hope the glowing reviews might soothe Sting's drummer frustrations...at least temporarily. I did not want to see ANYBODY getting fired right before Christmas, especially with their spouse occupying a ringside seat. Bah Humbug indeed.

But I obviously underestimated Sting's anger. Sure enough, Sting pulled the trigger on our day off and canned Smitty. With only three shows left before our break, Smitty was out—and Jean Paul Ceccarelli was in. I hated to see things go down that way. I liked Smitty and, whether he deserved it or not, the timing of his dismissal seemed unnecessarily cruel. Sting's actions epitomized the cold-blooded reality of our industry. As Jay Mohr's character says in the film *Jerry Maguire*, "It's not show FRIENDS, it's show BUSINESS!"

Jean Paul had obviously been paying close attention from the shadows. He jumped right in and nailed the three remaining shows. Nevertheless, I was still somewhat guarded about JP's chances for full assimilation into the band. A native of France, our new drummer barely spoke a word of English.

Our final night at Wembley felt like the last day of school. Accordingly, we blew the roof off the dump. Jack Bruce (bassist from the legendary rock trio, Cream) was in the house, and came backstage after the show. The holiday spirits flowed freely as Mr. "Sunshine of Your Love" held court in our green room. The chummy rock star was clearly feeling no pain, and kept insisting we all come out to his estate sometime. Then his whiskey chimed in. "But ONLY when I'm home…because I don't trust you horny musicians around my sexy wife." And yes, she was sitting right there.

Unfortunately there was more band drama yet to unfold— with me smack dab in the middle of it. Throughout history, musicians have been known to attract a certain *overly friendly* element of female admirers. The scene in London was no different. We'd made our fair share of acquaintances during the weeklong stay, and some of the local ladies had been unable to resist the charms of our brooding sax man. One girl in particular was a bit of a fixture around our hotel, so I wasn't surprised when Steve invited her to be his guest at the final show.

All was calm, all was bright during the concert. But as the post-gig festivities marinated backstage, Steve seemed much more interested in chatting with fellow musos than keeping his date entertained. Bored and restless, the attention-starved kitten started shooting frisky glances in my direction. My instincts told me this chick probably wasn't going to be the future "Mrs. Steve Coleman," so I happily played along with her *harmless* game of peek-a-boo.

When the after-party finally fell to earth, we piled into our vans and made our way back to the hotel. I said my goodnights as we dispersed in the lobby and retired to my room. A little while later, I heard a faint knock at my door. I threw on my thirsty five-star bathrobe and answered to find Steve's companion standing in the hallway. Apparently she was fed up with her escort's continuing neglect, and had decided to pay me a visit. We sat on the edge of my bed making small talk when, out of nowhere, she leaned over and kissed me. She looked deep into my eyes after the glorified peck, then jumped up and bolted out of the room. I shrugged off the amusing interlude and went back to my post-gig decompression.

Meanwhile, Little Miss Kiss and Tell obviously made a bee-line back to Steve's room to confess her sins. Shortly after her hasty exit, my telephone rang. I picked up and was greeted by a highly agitated saxophonist shouting obscenities while ordering me to leave HIS woman alone. At that point, I did what I rarely have the nerve to do. Mid-expletive, I hung up. Silence was golden—but only temporarily. Less than a minute later, there was a violent pounding on my door. (Hmmm, I wonder who that could be?) Steve had stormed down to my room and was screaming for me to show my face. But I'm a lover, not a fighter. I ignored the ruckus and Steve eventually left.

The New York contingent headed out to Heathrow the following morning for our flight back to the States. Steve and I did an excellent job of avoiding each other at the airport, but, in a flash of maturity, I decided to take a shot at diffusing the situation. The whole thing seemed a bit overblown—especially considering the larger context. Steve didn't realize it, but I'd actually helped him out of a jam with the girl in question only a couple of days earlier. I'd bumped into the young lady outside our hotel, and she'd started quizzing me on Steve's whereabouts. I played dumb, but, truth was, I'd seen him minutes earlier—in the company of another woman. Observing the unwritten law of male *omertà*, I did Steve a solid and covered for him. Oh well, "No good deed goes unpunished."

Oddly enough, my desire to make amends with Steve didn't stem from a meaningless smooch from some groupie. Instead, I felt bad about my uncivilized telephone etiquette. In my book, hanging up on someone is the height of rudeness. I approached Steve as we waited on the check-in line and apologized for my boorish behavior. Steve accepted my olive branch, albeit half-heartedly, and I assumed we'd turned the page. Wrong.

We boarded our flight and, thanks to fate's devilish sense of humor, Steve and I ended up seated beside each other. The now-tiresome topic reignited as the plane sat on the tarmac, but I was done with the *mea culpas*. Words became heated and the situation escalated quickly. Steve exploded, "Stand up, I'm gonna fuck you up!" I replied, "Oh yeah? YOU stand up, I'm gonna fuck YOU up!" But before I could pretend to make good on my empty threat, Steve (who was trained in the martial arts) jumped from his seat and punched me in the mouth...HARD. Stars started spinning around my head, just like in the cartoons. A couple of flight attendants leapt into the fray and separated the two macho idiots before somebody (read: me) got hurt. I couldn't believe what was happening. I hadn't been punched in the face since third grade. Airline personnel insisted I change seats, even offering to bump me up to first class, but I refused. I'd survived five weeks of Steve Coleman; I could handle six more hours.

Although my relationship with Steve had been far from buddy-buddy, I never expected to end up a victim of friendly fire. But between Steve's baseline antipathy toward me AND his anger over Smitty's dismissal, I was dead man walking. That trivial kiss was probably just a convenient excuse to kick my ass. Softening the blow (figuratively, anyway), at least my bandmates took my side in the dust-up. They were longtime friends with Steve, but they unanimously condemned his violent behavior. Adding to my transatlantic enjoyment, I only had three thousand miles to figure out how I was going to explain my swollen lip to my girlfriend, Denise. (I told her the *varnished* truth.)

Of course the "Thrilla on the Tarmac" made perfect fodder for the rest of the tour. In the next itinerary, Billy, our editor-in-snark, roasted each band member with an embarrassing nickname. On the "Tour Personnel" page, I was listed as:

Jeff "Rocky" Campbell — womanizer

* * *

Years later, I was surfing the web when I saw a news item about a fistfight on a plane departing Heathrow airport. Sound familiar? Imagine my reaction when I noticed the report was courtesy of "TSA spokesman STEVE COLEMAN." (Nope, different guy.) I couldn't resist emailing the link to Branford. He replied instantly, "Un-fucking-believable!" I could almost hear Branford's peals of laughter echoing through cyberspace.

Christmas: It's a Wonderful Break

After navigating the craziest three months of my life, I spent a blissful Christmas unwinding in North Carolina. Being off the hot seat for a couple of weeks was one of the best gifts Santa ever brought me. The living was easy; eating, drinking, and chilling with friends and family. My younger brother, Will (a saxophonist of the non-violent persuasion) was also home for the holidays, so we made sure to squeeze in a bit of music between all of the over-indulgence. We were jamming away one afternoon when Will stopped to compliment my maturing "time feel." I thanked him and boasted I'd been practicing a lot. Will nodded in agreement before astutely adding, "And playing in a band with Kenny Kirkland." He had that right. Running with the big dogs was making me a stronger player.

I rang in the New Year down south and then raced back to

NYC, eager to return to the grind of being a rock star—or at least hanging out with one. We were scheduled to begin a three-month tour of North America in mid-January, but we had a couple of side projects on tap first: a video shoot and a recording session.

There isn't a single note of guitar on "Englishman in New York," but, proving once again he was a stand-up guy, Sting included me—and my *hated* white guitar—in the music video anyway. (Warning: Do not blink or you will miss me.) In fact, when we played the song live, I ditched my guitar altogether and picked up a percussion mallet. My sole responsibility was nailing the huge gong crash that heralded the song's out-of-nowhere, hip-hop breakbeat. For the record, I was also in charge of gong duties whenever we performed Sting's Prokofiev-inspired, anti-war anthem, "Russians." Not exactly a toe-tapper, that number usually stayed in the trunk.

Shortly after I landed the gig, Sting asked if I found anything on his new album "surprising." Without hesitation, I cited the abrupt drum break in the middle of "Englishman in New York." The non-sequitur from swinging pizzicato strings to noisy funk seemed extreme—if not downright wacky. Sting smiled and explained he was trying to evoke the juxtaposition between British gentility and NYC's grittiness. Sting defending his creative choices to me? Priceless.

In typical showbiz fashion, the date for our video shoot was changed at the last minute. Management scrambled to notify everyone, but the free-spirited Delmar was off the grid and missed out entirely. With Delmar on the lam, and our new drummer, JP, still in France for the holidays, we ended up using a three-quarter, skeletal band for the clip. (Our percussionist Mino assumed the drum throne.)

The band gathered on a snowy morning at a vacant, heat-challenged building in Greenwich Village to shoot "Englishman in New York." Director David Fincher elected to go with an artsy single-camera setup, which translated into a long day involving multiple takes. (Lights, Camera, Inaction!) After a few passes with the entire band (sans Sting), we moved on to the individual close-ups. The band's hierarchy was clearly defined, so it was pretty much a foregone conclusion the guitar-playing rookie would go last. It wasn't rocket science; Branford was the one with the personal barber in tow, not me. I did a whole lot of standing around that afternoon, but I didn't care. I was ecstatic to be a part of a professional music video, destined for my beloved MTV.

Sting wasn't an on-camera participant that day, but he showed up later to offer moral support. After twiddling my frost-bit thumbs for hours, it was finally my turn to make love to the camera. But just as the director yelled "Action," Sting up and walked out of the room. Maybe he wanted to give me some artistic space...or maybe he simply couldn't bear to watch. Trying to tamp down my jitters, I channeled my inner Brando and summoned as much swagger as possible. Sting reappeared after I'd finished filming my bit and asked, "How'd it go? Were you great?" I had no clue. But I stayed in cocky character, replying, "Absolutely."

Sting invited the stragglers over to his loft in Soho after the final shot of the day. His place was only a couple of blocks from the video location so, like all respectable New Yorkers, we set out on foot. Prior to living in NYC, I'd assumed celebrities were *re-*

quired to use limousines; I had no idea they were allowed to walk freely amongst the little people. Heads turned and eyes widened as me and my rock-star pal strolled down the icy sidewalks of Manhattan. Could life get ANY cooler? And where the hell is that pesky paparazzi when you need them?

I hadn't seen Sting since our final show in London, so he was eager to hear the gory details regarding the Heathrow fisticuff (singular, not plural). Sting shook his head in disbelief as I recounted the absurd story. After noting it was a felony to disrupt an international flight, Sting pointed out I could press assault charges if I were so inclined. I appreciated Sting's paternal instincts but I'm not the litigious type. No thanks, case closed.

Arriving at *Casa de Sting*, we grabbed some beverages and kicked back to compare notes on our Christmas vacations. The conversation eventually turned to music, prompting Sting to break out a couple of guitars. Next thing I knew, I was sitting on the couch, jamming one-on-one with the King of Pain. I did a decent job of keeping cool—until we segued into "Message in a Bottle," At that point, I briefly left my body. Halfway through the tune, Sting stopped to show me the harmony guitar part. Private instruction from the actual composer? Turns out life *could* get cooler.

As we continued to strum, I confessed to Sting that Police guitarist Andy Summers had been a major influence on my playing. Sting looked up and sniffed, "Those guitar parts were mine. I taught them to Andy." Meow. I'd obviously touched a nerve. But I had no reason to doubt Sting's claim. He may have achieved worldwide fame as a bassist, but he also plays a mean guitar.

We had one other assignment before hitting the road: record

a new version of the Police tune, "One World (Not Three)." The reboot was earmarked for a documentary focusing on the world's underdeveloped nations. I was psyched about the opportunity to play on a studio recording with Sting, and, as a bonus, we were booked at Manhattan's legendary Record Plant. The midtown studio had a rich history including Bruce Springsteen, The Eagles, Aerosmith, and John Lennon. (In fact, Lennon was heading home from the Record Plant the night he was tragically gunned down.)

Hanging out in the lobby before our session, I got the chance to meet another one of my musical heroes: Bernard "Pretty" Purdie (aka "The World's Most Recorded Drummer"). I was thrilled to shake hands with the man responsible for the deep grooves on countless classics by Aretha Franklin, James Brown, B.B. King, Steely Dan…the list goes on and on. I'd had no delusions of grandeur when I moved to New York, I had one *simple* goal: I just wanted to be one of the "cats." And that modest dream was becoming a phenomenal reality. Blues great Buddy Guy said it best, "I came looking for a dime…and found a quarter."

Sting reimagined "One World" as a duet, and invited reggae artist Ziggy Marley to ride shotgun. We performed the tune live in the studio, banging out the track in a single day. The session was loose and low-key, but once again, I was forced to play it cool in the presence of musical royalty. Working side-by-side with Ziggy, the voices in my head kept reminding me I was only one degree of separation from reggae god Bob Marley, Ziggy's late father.

When we were done, I slung my gig bag over my shoulder and wandered out into the wintry night. The Times Square sidewalks bustled with people, all completely oblivious to the magic that had just occurred on the other side of those unassuming concrete walls. I flashed back to a few months earlier, when a couple of friends from North Carolina had visited me in NYC. I'm sure I'd been guilty of over-hyping my new zip code, but my pals seemed somewhat underwhelmed by The Big Apple. From their perspective, Manhattan looked similar to other, less-exalted Southern cities … "just more of it." (You've seen one tall building, you've seen 'em all.) Being a relative newcomer myself, I'd grudgingly conceded their cosmetic point. But I eventually came to realize New York City's prominence doesn't come from its skyline. It's the cutting-edge creativity going on *inside* its skyscrapers that makes New York the greatest city on earth.

USA/Canada

January 16 — April 2 (48 shows in 46 cities)

I received a letter from Sting's management before we set out on the first official leg of our world tour. It read (in part):

"At a great expense to the US tour, we have decided to charter a private plane."

This was awesome news. For the next ten weeks, we'd be flying in glorious rock-star seclusion. But with our travel squad numbering at thirteen (bare minimum), a small corporate jet couldn't accommodate our cubic needs. Therefore, management opted for a larger, albeit slower, airplane—formerly owned by the Prime Minister of Canada. Our airspeeds might not have been lightning fast, but the ride was oh so sweet. Feeling more like a lounge than an airplane, the cabin featured a couch, leather recliners, coffee table, bar, TV/VCR/stereo, and a full-time flight attendant that spoiled us rotten.

Having our own plane also saved us the hassle of checking in and out of hotels at every stop on the itinerary. When geography permitted, we'd plant ourselves at a central location for days (or weeks) at a time, and make quick day-trips to our nearby gigs. Right after the concert, we'd rush back to the local airport and fly "home" for the night.

It didn't take long to get addicted to our new mode of travel. Private planes are like personal roadies; once you've had one, you never want to be without one again. And thanks to the exclusivity of *Air Sting*, my trips to the airport now ended ON the tarmac. Climb out of the car, climb onto the plane. No crowded terminals, no check-in lines, no nosy security searches.

Whenever we flew out of New York, I received door-to-door pampering. A limousine would pick me up at my stoop and deliver me directly to the stairway of our aircraft at New Jersey's Teterboro Airport. (Even *going* to work was fun on the Sting tour.) Enhancing the experience, my chauffeured pomp and circumstance was often played out in front of an audience. The high-rise construction site across from my apartment would grind to a halt each time my stretch pulled into view. Whoops and hollers would rain down from the gawking hardhats as my sexy, blonde female driver held the door for me and my 6-string. The blue-collar peanut gallery made it easy to keep the gratitude in my attitude. I was leading a charmed existence.

Tampa, Florida | Sundome | January 20

Late January, the band happily swapped arctic New York for balmy Florida. I immediately took advantage of the Gulf Coast's notion of winter and hit the beach for a jog. I was walking back up to the hotel after my workout when I saw Sting playing tennis with our tour accountant, Mike "The Goon" McGinley. (I'm not sure about the origin of Mike's nickname, but it fit.) Emboldened by my endorphins, I approached the fence around the courts and started *lightly* taunting Sting about his tennis skills. Sting played along, returning sarcastic fire before telling me to "get lost." Meanwhile, our little joke was sailing right over The Goon's head. New faces were still sinking in as the fully staffed tour got underway, and my rookie mug obviously wasn't registering with Sting's tennis partner. Assuming I was just some annoying fan, The Goon stomped toward me and barked, "Hey you, leave us alone and get the hell out of here." Sting stood by in silence as The Goon attacked, clearly enjoying the spectacle of his accountant berating a stranger... who just happened to be on the payroll.

Miami, Florida | Knight Center | January 21, 22

Following our stateside debut in Tampa, we headed south to Miami for a two-night stand. Unfortunately, with only one concert behind us, Sting's voice was hurting. He pushed through the first show in Miami, but he was nowhere near the top of his game.

Sting flagged me down backstage after the show and introduced me to his friend, Don. I shook Don's hand and offered a polite hello before returning to my post-show schmooze. A little later, I overheard Sting tell Branford, "Don Johnson said he really enjoyed the concert." (At the time, Johnson was king of the airwaves as the star of *Miami Vice.)* I was excited to hear we'd had a celebrity fan in the audience, and expressed regret over not meeting the white-hot actor. Sting looked at me sideways. "But you did!" Yep, generic, backstage Don was, in fact, Don Johnson. I know it's cliché, but I'd expected TV's sexiest man to be much taller. I confessed to Sting I had no idea the "short dude in the floppy hat" was actually *Detective Sonny Crockett.* Sting just rolled his eyes and lamented how quickly I'd become a jaded rock star.

Departing the venue, a few of us thirsty types decided to investigate the newly trendy Miami Beach. The area had undergone a drastic makeover in the ten years since my college days, morphing from a sleepy retirement community into a hipster destination. We ended up at the notorious den of iniquity known as The China Club, where I befriended a tall, slinky woman. Sparks flew and, although I'm not sure I believed her, my towering date insisted she was into shorter men. (Shorter men who just happened to play guitar with Sting?) One thing led to another and I eventually found myself cruising down Collins Avenue in my playmate's Mercedes convertible.

Full disclosure: along with the unlimited drink, other substances were usually available to keep the party going. Pot and cocaine were a reality of "life in the fast lane," so there were one— *or maybe two*—occasions where I was running on more than distilled spirits. What can I say? It was the Big 80's, I was young and dumb, and on tour with a huge rock star. Plus, on that given night, I was carousing around decadent Miami, the nation's leading purveyor of *Vice* (according to *TV Guide* anyway). My statuesque friend and I ultimately wound up back at my hotel where we enjoyed an extended nightcap.

The Key Biscayne sunrise heckled me through the curtains as I crawled into bed. And thanks to my overly ambitious scheduling, I only had time for the briefest of power naps. Lacking any foresight, I'd scheduled a late-morning lunch with my former college guitar teacher: the esteemed (and intimidating) Randall Dollahon. At least I had enough presence of mind to set my trusty alarm clock before I crashed. I figured I could grab a couple hours of sleep, and then rush over to campus. File that under "best laid plans."

It was past noon when I regained consciousness. Shit! I was already over an hour late for my lunch appointment. My "trusty" alarm clock had proven no match for my self-inflicted coma. I frantically tried to call Randall's office to apologize and offer some lame excuse, but I got no answer. If anything, I'm punctual, so I felt like a schmuck—an extremely hungover schmuck. Then MY phone rang. Heaping a scoop of anxiety on top of my self-loathing, Billy was calling to inform me the plug had been pulled on our two-day-old tour.

After seeing a doctor, Sting was placed on full vocal rest—and our second Miami show had to be scrapped. Unfortunately, *that* was the night Randall (if he was still speaking to me) and the head of the UM jazz department, Whit Sidener, were to be my guests at the concert. But Sting's vocal cords were calling the shots, and they'd croaked "no show." I was bummed to lose out on my golden opportunity to make my former teachers proud...and maybe even a little jealous.

The band was told Sting would miss four shows—at least. I felt bad for Sting, but I felt bad for me, too. I didn't want a vacation, I wanted to rock. Adding to the Miami disappointment,

Sting's sick leave was gobbling up two historic venues on our itinerary: Atlanta's Fox Theater and Nashville's Grand Ole Opry. But if Sting ended up needing additional recovery time, then I *really* had a problem. After Atlanta and Nashville, our next scheduled stop was Chapel Hill, North Carolina—my hometown.

Ever since the Chapel Hill concert was announced, "The Jeff and Sting Show" had been a hot topic around my old stomping grounds. Not surprisingly, many of my friends and family had circled January 28 on their calendars. But here we go again. Just like my *Saturday Night Live* adventure, another highly anticipated milestone was suddenly in jeopardy. Based on Sting's projected recovery, the tour was scheduled to relaunch in Chapel Hill—but that was only a guesstimate. If Sting's throat didn't heal in time, the Carolina show would be the next domino to fall. My television debut had miraculously survived a raging fire. Could my homecoming concert survive a sore throat?

With the tour on indefinite hiatus, the band was shipped back to New York. But since Chapel Hill was our targeted return, I decided to take my chances and head to North Carolina instead. My plan was to hang with family—and pray Team Sting would come to me.

While my bandmates simply jumped back on our private plane, I was forced to fend for myself in the real world of commercial aviation. I booked a flight from Miami to North Carolina and was quickly reminded of how much *fun* it was to fly "public." I was waiting in a long line at the X-ray machines, when airport security agents singled me out and pulled me aside. They rummaged through my carry-on bag, checking every nook and cranny—even inspecting the battery compartments on my portable stereo speakers. I was baffled by the intense scrutiny until I caught a glimpse of my reflection in a nearby window. There I saw a rumpled, unshaven guy, sporting a leather jacket, sunglasses, and one serious hangover. Now it all made sense: I looked like one of those oily drug dealers my pal Don Johnson pursued every Friday night on TV. Thank God, I possessed no contraband. (I'd consumed it all the night before.) I passed inspection and was sent on my wobbly way to Raleigh-Durham International.

After a few anxious days of waiting around the family hearth, Billy called with good news: Sting's golden tenor was on the mend. The Chapel Hill show would take place as scheduled. My lucky streak continued.

Chapel Hill, North Carolina | Dean Smith Center | January 28

The big night finally arrived. I'd been strumming around the Chapel Hill area since childhood, so the Sting concert was a culmination and validation beyond my wildest dreams. It's impossible to convey the thrill of performing with one of the world's biggest rock stars in front of my family and friends—some of who went back as far as elementary school. And since the venue was located practically next door to the hospital where I was born, it was a true homecoming.

The lights went down and the arena exploded as we launched into "The Lazarus Heart." Since our very first show of the tour, Sting always made a point to introduce the band during a vamp near the end of our opening number. Typically, I landed somewhere in the middle of the roll call, but our savvy emcee shuffled the deck in Chapel Hill and saved the homeboy for last. When Sting finally yelled, "And on guitar, Jeff Campbell," the place went wild. But he was just getting started. As the band simmered pianissimo, Sting continued, "Gee, I wonder if any of Jeff's friends or relatives are in the house tonight." More cheers. Really milking it, Sting peered out into the audience and gestured, "Oh yeah, there's his cousin, there's his dog" and so on and so on. He had 'em eating out of his hand. Closing with his pièce de résistance, Sting crowed, "And in case anybody doesn't know who I am...I'm Jeff's friend!" The crowd roared its approval, and we pressed forward into two hours of kick-ass rock 'n' roll. Later in the show, after we finished my big feature, "Little Wing," Sting walked over and shook my hand. If I'd died that night, it would've been okay. I'd been to the mountaintop.

I hosted a large party at our hotel's nightclub after the show. I was smothered with support, congratulations, and love; making the evening feel like a birthday/graduation/wedding day—all rolled into one. It was overwhelming to watch my old and new worlds lovingly collide. No matter what gifts my future may hold, performing with Sting in my hometown will always rate as one of the best days of my life.

But when the sun came up, "King for a Day" had run its course. I awoke to find Billy's daily sheet already slipped underneath my door. The day-at-a-glance printout provided pertinent travel and performance information—and, when applicable, a dollop of smart-ass commentary. With only a short trip to Virginia on tap, our departure time seemed unusually early. But our unsparing road manager elaborated at the bottom of the page:

"Please don't ask why we are leaving [Chapel Hill] at this time, the simple answer being that it's BORING. (P.S.— Don't tell Jeff as he may get offended, this place does answer a lot of questions about Jeff's personality)"

The 24-hour ceasefire was officially over. I was once again fair game.

Williamsburg, Virginia, | William and Mary Hall | January 29

Fairfax, Virginia, | Patriot Centre | January 30

After rocking Virginia's College of William and Mary, we performed in the DC suburb of Fairfax. I thought the band was hitting on all cylinders, but Sting had a *slightly* different take on things. Post show, we were dispatched to Sting's dressing room for an epic dressing down. Sting was furious. He accused the band of being boring and lethargic—and threatened to "fire everybody!" Singling me out, Sting fumed, "And Jeff, YOU look like you're over there [on stage] waiting for a fucking bus." Ouch.

I was dazed from Sting's verbal haymaker, but still lucid enough to wonder if I was truly the intended target. Something told me Sting might've wanted to direct his venom elsewhere— possibly at certain, more-tenured band members, and their chronically detached demeanors. But I was low-hanging fruit, the perfect scapegoat for Sting's generalized wrath. I had no interest in arguing and/or being fired, so I absorbed the abuse like a good (and scared) soldier. Message received: Step it up…or else.

Ironically, I agreed with the gist of Sting's rant. The level of showmanship from his sidemen had been pretty minimal up until that point. The band's de facto leaders, Branford and Kenny, were extremely cool customers, both off and ON stage. I'd just assumed I was supposed to follow their lead. Reasoning it would look stupid for me to jump around like a maniac while surrounded by laid-back hipsters, I purposely took an understated approach to my on-stage persona. I aimed for a muted swagger, one consistent with Sting's sophisticated music. So much for THAT theory. Plus, being embarrassingly naive, I actually worried if I were too demonstrative, I might be accused of trying to upstage Sting. Ha! That's a good one. I quickly realized it wouldn't matter if I performed in the raw. All eyes would still stay glued to THE STAR.

Me and my bruised ego made our way downstairs the following morning. We entered the hotel lobby and spied our freshly minted adversary sitting across the room. I took a deep breath, loaded up an apology, and approached The Artist formerly known as Pissed. But before I could say a word, Sting jumped up and beamed, "Jeff, MY MAN!" Huh? Did I miss something? I was confused, but nevertheless relieved to be back in the boss's good graces. Shortly thereafter, I learned the identity of my redeemer: *USA Today*. The McPaper had unwittingly saved my ass with a rave review of the previous night's concert. It read in part:

"Though [Sting's] compositions dominate, it's 'Little Wing,' Jimi Hendrix's psychedelic sonnet, that steals the show. Sting's nostalgic rendering, lush with stirring vocals and

Jeff Campbell's soaring guitar, does justice to a hard-to-top '60's chestnut."

Just like that, I went from being *persona non-grata* to *persona grata*.

* * *

Perfect timing. We had the day off in DC; it was Super Bowl Sunday; and the hometown Redskins were playing in the big game. The NFL fans among us convened in the hotel's sports bar to watch the contest...and maybe even consume a few beers. Always up for a little wager, I'd put my money on the enemy Denver Broncos. First play of the game, Denver quarterback John Elway stepped back and launched a bomb for a touchdown. I jumped to my feet and cheered—for my wallet. Bad idea. Boos rained down from the heavily partisan crowd. Coming to my senses, I sat down and shut the hell up. I had no problem staying quiet; Washington annihilated *my* Broncos by the score of 42-10.

There was plenty of time for socializing during the blowout, and we ended up making friends with one of Washington's lively locals. After the game, Billy, Kim, and I decided to head out for a little grub, and we invited our gal pal to tag along. Kim wanted to swing by his room before hitting the street, so the four of us made a quick detour upstairs. While Kim gathered his belongings, our bubbly companion strolled out on the balcony to take in the view. As she stood with her back to us, Kim tiptoed over and locked the balcony's sliding glass door. He turned to Billy and me and flashed his mischievous grin. "OK guys, let's go eat." (Despite being a top member of the management team, Kim was as crazy as any of us. Unlike the stern Miles Copeland, Kim was a bombastic, larger-than-life sweetheart. The man loved to have his fun.) Our date spun around when she heard the click of the lock and immediately recognized her predicament. I'd grudgingly resigned myself to the road's endless stream of practical jokes, but I was NOT going to leave that poor woman trapped outside on an upper-floor terrace—in January—while we went to dinner. Braving the peer pressure, I walked over and unlocked the door, freeing the momentary captive. Kim insisted he was just kidding, and our party girl seemed to take it all in stride, but I had to draw the line on that prank.

Making our way back downstairs, we walked out of the elegant Four Seasons Georgetown—and into a war zone. The Redskins championship had turned the upscale neighborhood upside down. I'd never been in the middle of a Super Bowl celebration before, but this did not look like a party to me; it looked like a riot. People were running wild in the streets—drinking, screaming, and climbing on top of moving vehicles. I watched in amazement as an out-of-control car careened into a fire hydrant and sent a plume of water shooting high into the air. Right after *Old Faithful* erupted, a deafening explosion rocked the block. The concussion from the blast was staggering, it felt like an actual bomb had gone off. Bedlam reigned, but we were undeterred. Full of liquid courage, our Gang of Four fearlessly, and foolishly, wandered out into the night in search of a nice, *relaxing* dinner.

Bethlehem, Pennsylvania | Stabler Arena | February 1
Philadelphia, Pennsylvania | Spectrum | February 2

New York City | Madison Square Garden | February 3

Following a couple of shows in Pennsylvania, we stormed NYC for a concert at "The World's Most Famous Arena"—Madison Square Garden. For me, it was excitement x 3:

1. I was home
2. I was hanging with my friends
3. It was the eve of my one year anniversary in New York City and…I WAS PERFORMING WITH STING AT MADISON SQUARE GARDEN!

Unfortunately, there was one drop of rain on my Garden parade: an unexpected cameo by my UK sparring partner, Steve Coleman. I was chilling out before the show when I glanced up to see my nemesis stroll through the dressing room door. I felt somewhat betrayed as my bandmates greeted Steve with open arms, but I was even more bummed nobody bothered to give me a courtesy heads-up. (Somebody had to know Steve was on the guest list.) Looking for a silver lining, I hoped the evening might present an opportunity for an overdue truce. I made a few attempts at eye contact in an effort to jumpstart the peace process, but Steve wouldn't even acknowledge my presence. And while I was willing to put the macho bullshit behind us, I wasn't going to bend over backwards; my fists were clean. But détente was clearly not on Steve's agenda and our stalemate continued. Adding to my indignity, I learned *Apollo Creed* would be sitting in with the band that night. Steve and I ultimately went through the entire evening pretending the other didn't exist—backstage AND onstage. It's pathetic that two guys sharing the Garden limelight weren't even on speaking terms. Then again, that probably happens more often than one would think. Rockers can be a childish lot. Hey Steve, I'm sincerely sorry.

Playing Madison Square Garden ranks high on the musician bucket-list. But despite the magnitude of the moment, the venue seemed surprisingly intimate when I stepped out onto the stage. The gig felt huge, the room did not. In fact, when the house lights came up during our encore, I was able to pick out a few familiar faces standing in the back of the arena. Thanks to the gigantic soccer stadiums of South America, my perspective on crowd size had been permanently skewed. (A couple hundred thousand Brazilians can have that effect on you.) Reality check: when an audience of fifteen thousand people feels like a modest gathering, you are riding high.

Boston, Massachusetts | Boston Garden | February 5
Albany, New York | RPI Field House | February 6

My bandmates latched on to my full name as the tour progressed, ditching the utilitarian "Jeff" in favor of the more lyrical "Jeffrey Lee." Sting lit up when he overheard the guys tossing around my new handle and suggested I go with it. When I informed Sting "Jeffrey Lee" was not some contrived term of endearment, but the official name on my birth certificate, he rebranded me on the spot. From that day forward, Sting introduced me at every concert with, "On guitar, Jeffrey Lee Campbell!" Maybe he thought my southern-fried middle name lent an air of rock 'n' roll gravitas. Fine by me, I was more than happy to be lumped in with Jerry Lee Lewis and John Lee Hooker. (Let's leave Kathie Lee Gifford out of it.)

Uniondale, New York | Nassau Coliseum | February 7
Quebec City, Quebec | Colisee de Quebec | February 10
Ottawa, Ontario | Civic Center | February 11
Montreal, Quebec | Forum | February 12

Toronto, Ontario | Maple Leaf Gardens | February 15

Heading north, I chalked up yet another first: Canada. And Canadian February was exactly as advertised—cold and snowy. We played shows in Quebec City, Ottawa, and Montreal, before hitting Toronto for a three-day stay at what was increasingly becoming my standard address: the plush Four Seasons Hotel. After spending many a childhood vacation at spartan public campgrounds, it didn't take me long to get addicted to the life of luxury with Sting.

I was awakened the next morning by a siren—inside my room. The earsplitting wail was accompanied by a prerecorded announcement insisting all guests evacuate immediately. Living in hotels full-time had inured me to the occasional fire alarm, but

I took them seriously nonetheless. Unsure whether I was *enjoying* a crack-of-dawn fire drill, or trapped in The Towering Inferno, I stumbled to the window in search of corroborating smoke or fire trucks. I pulled back the curtain and saw nothing but white; just your typical Canadian blizzard. Deciding to err on the side of caution, I threw on some clothes and made my way to the stairwell. I trudged down the fifteen or so flights and pushed through the emergency exit, but instead of finding myself in the lobby as expected, I was out on the sidewalk...standing in a foot of snow...in my slippers. Not a happy camper, I hurried back around to the front of the building and skated into the hotel. The mysterious emergency was eventually declared under control and we were cleared to return to our pillows.

Unfortunately, the lobby was now swarming with yawning, grumpy guests, all jockeying for an elevator. I had zero interest in climbing fifteen flights of stairs, but I had less-than-zero interest in waiting on line for the pleasure of being crammed into an overcrowded elevator. Choosing my poison, I grudgingly began my assault on Mount Four Seasons, completing my daily cardio requirement long before breakfast.

That afternoon, as we waited around for soundcheck to start, I bitched to Kenny about our sunrise scramble. He shrugged and confessed he'd ignored the alarm altogether, opting to simply roll over and stay beneath his toasty covers. Shocked—and also impressed—by Kenny's death-defying audacity, I asked, "What if it had really been a fire?" He smiled and replied philosophically, "We all have to go sometime."

Ritzy hotels apparently have a universal credo: the higher the floor, the higher the prestige. Reception staff always seemed extremely proud of themselves as they placed me in the strato-sphere. *Welcome Mr. Campbell, we have a beautiful room for you on the 42nd floor.* I guess I was supposed to be thrilled, but I wasn't. As a practicing claustrophobe, I couldn't stand being a slave to the elevator. But this was my cross to bear. Thanks to our relent-less air travel and skyscraper lifestyle, I was forced to face my fears on a daily basis. Sadly, Dr. Sting's desensitization therapy did nothing to remedy my condition. My claustrophobic tenden-cies flourished on tour. Feeling like a wuss, I suffered in silence, combating my anxieties with deep breaths...and deep swigs.

Syracuse, New York | War Memorial | February 16
Cleveland, Ohio | Public Hall | February 17

Detroit, Michigan | Masonic Temple | February 19, 20

We blasted through a couple more frigid cities before heading to Detroit for a pair of shows at the Masonic Temple. Hungry for some non-musical entertainment on our hard-earned night off, a few of us decided to take in a pro basketball game. There was just one problem: Detroit's NBA franchise didn't actually play in De-troit. The Pistons' "home" games were instead played some thirty miles away at the Silverdome in suburban Pontiac. Undaunted, we solved our dilemma the old-fashioned way: we threw money at it until it disappeared. We ponied up a sizable chunk of our per diems and chartered a limousine for the hefty commute.

Kenny, Delmar, percussion tech Nico Wormworth (bassist

Tracy's brother), and I piled into our rent-a-stretch and set out for Pontiac. Voting to stock up on refreshments for the long ride ahead, we asked our driver to stop at the nearest liquor store. When the car pulled over, it was clear we weren't in one of Detroit's finer neighborhoods. A fortified pawnshop and a pack of stray dogs confirmed our location: Funky Town. I heeded my inner wimp and chose to stay in the car while the others went inside for party supplies. I was surveying the menacing landscape from the safety of our limo, when I saw a guy come tearing out of the pawnshop and disappear down the alley. Seconds later, another guy dashed out of the store in hot pursuit. (I assumed the *chasee* had availed himself to the proverbial "five-finger discount.") All was quiet for a minute or two, and then the pursuer re-emerged from the shadows. He was limping and nursing a bloody nose, but maybe worst of all, he was empty handed. Justice denied. Okay guys, shake a leg, let's get the hell out of here.

The Silverdome made for quite a disorienting basketball experience. Designed for professional football games, the 80,000-seat venue effectively swallowed up the intimate five-on-five contest. But we didn't care, we simply wanted diversion, and the NBA delivered. We enjoyed an evening of hotdogs, beer, and off-color conversation, hardly paying any attention to the action on the court. We were much more interested in the final buzzer anyway. Delmar had finagled a post-game invitation to the locker room.

Proving it was indeed a small world, Detroit power forward John Salley was a Delmar Brown fan. But John came by it naturally: his brother was Delmar's manager. In fact, it was my understanding the NBA star bankrolled some, if not all, of Delmar's beleaguered European Bushrock tour. (The one that stopped paying me halfway through.) Rumor was, after Bushrock had burned through its budget prematurely, Delmar's manager went back to his affluent brother for another infusion of cash. A vigilant accountant nixed the request and—poof—Bushrock's payroll evaporated. Remember, it's called Show BUSINESS.

Entering the Detroit "Bad Boys" lair was like stepping into The Land of the Giants. I'd never been that close to a bunch of professional basketball players. Those guys were huge. But, despite the crush of reporters and visitors, it was locker room business-as-usual for the players. There wasn't a hint of modesty on display as we chatted with the sweaty titans, in varying degrees of undress. I tried to remain nonchalant, but I was forced to avert my eyes on several occasions. Like I said...huge.

Oxford, Ohio | Millett Hall (Miami University) | February 21

News outlets were buzzing about a sex scandal involving televangelist Jimmy Swaggart as we invaded Ohio. The well-known preacher had landed on Sting's shit list a few years earlier after condemning the Police song, "Murder by Numbers," and referring to the rock trio as "The Sons of Satan." But now the devil's shoe was on the other foot. The self-righteous Swaggart had been caught cavorting with a New Orleans prostitute, and Sting couldn't wait to exact a little revenge.

Sting gathered the band at soundcheck and announced we'd be adding Swaggart's *favorite* tune to the show—immediately. Tom-o pressed play and "Murder by Numbers" started pumping through the air. We huddled over our monitors, deciphering the bloodthirsty ditty on the fly while Sting stood by twirling his imaginary mustache. I scuffled to pick out Andy Summer's jazzy guitar part amidst the chaos, but we were eventually able to hack our way through the song. Sting proclaimed, "Great! We'll play it tonight. Jeff, you'll be in charge of starting it out."

Everything was sailing along smoothly that evening—until I looked down at my setlist and saw "Murder by Numbers" was up next. The intro was my responsibility and I was drawing a blank. What was the feel? What was the tempo? Shit, I was screwed. Panic attacked as Sting set the scene for the newest addition to our repertoire. Sting went off on a lengthy comedic rant about Swaggart's damnation of The Police, before gleefully pointing out the minister's current fall from grace. After wrapping up *his* sermon, Sting nodded for me to start the tune. Cue flop sweat; I could remember the chord progression, but my addled brain could not access the groove. I had no idea what to play, but I knew I had to play something—fast.

I banged out the opening E7#9 chord and blindly plowed forward...for a few seconds anyway. Sting started waving his arms, yelling, "Whoa, Whoa, Stop, STOP!" Humiliation washed over me as I meekly quit strumming. Our short-lived rendition of "Murder" had sputtered to a stop, and there we stood in front of 10,000 confused people. Sting looked at me incredulously before asking (on microphone, no less), "Jeff, what the hell was that?" Utterly embarrassed, all I could offer was a shrug. Sting shook his head, then turned to our drummer, Jean Paul, and yelled, "JP, YOU start it." Sting counted us back in and Jean Paul fell into the jazzy shuffle that had completely eluded me. The crowd loved the real-life blooper moment. Me? Not so much.

West Lafayette, Indiana | Elliot Hall of Music | February 23
Bloomington, Indiana | Assembly Hall | February 24
St. Louis, Missouri | Fox Theatre | February 26, 27
Chicago, Illinois | Pavilion | February 28
Milwaukee, Wisconsin | Riverside Theatre | March 1
Madison, Wisconsin | Dane County Coliseum | March 2
Minneapolis, Minnesota | Northrop Auditorium | March 4
Omaha, Nebraska | Civic Auditorium | March 5

Onward through the heartland of America. New day, new city; rinse and repeat. After touching down at the airport du jour, we'd climb into our waiting van or limo and promptly ask the driver, "How far to the hotel?" Nine out of ten times, the friendly but noncommittal answer was, "Oh, not too far." The reliable response became a running joke with the band. It didn't matter if the drive was five miles or twenty-five miles, it was always "not too far." Of course, that vague answer rarely pacified the troops. Like fidgety kids on a family trip, we'd turn to "Daddy" (Billy) and whine, "How long 'til we get there?" Billy loved to counter our played-out question with his go-to Zen retort, "Who knows? How long is a piece of string?" Stymied by Billy's existential riddle, we'd surrender and quietly return to our Walkman headphones. That's why Billy made for the perfect tour manager. He could silence a vanload of cranky musicians in one fell swoop.

Upon our arrival in almost every new city, the well-traveled Kenny would ask, "Hey Jeff, have you ever been here before?" I had to keep reminding him I was a certified bumpkin. I'd never been *anywhere* before.

Kansas City, Kansas | Memorial Hall | March 7

I was surprised to see a sizable number of civilians standing in the back of the auditorium as I wandered out on stage for sound-check. (Local radio-station contest winners?) Sting had decided to work on a new tune that afternoon, and he was asking band members to chime in with background vocals as the arrangement fell into place. Unfortunately, pulling a supporting vocal part out of thin air has never been one of my strengths, so I tentatively sang "off mic" as I searched for an acceptable contribution. Sting glanced over and apparently mistook my incompetence for in-difference—and stopped the song cold. Gulp. I got the sinking feeling our guests were about to get a titillating peek behind the showbiz curtain. *Hurry, Hurry, step right up! See the rock star berate a lowly employee before your very eyes.*

With the room's rapt attention, Sting asked why I wasn't sing-ing. I choked under the pressure and offered up the lamest excuse in history. "Because the melody is too high [for my voice]." Sting rolled his eyes and sarcastically replied—on mic of course, "Mel-ody? Haven't you heard Jeff? There is a *new* invention in Western music. It's called 'harmony.' Find one ... AND SING." My band-mates dropped their heads and tittered. I didn't appreciate Sting humiliating me in public, but I took my lumps in silence. He had a point. I was in the major leagues, no excuses allowed.

(Note to younger musicians: Learn to sing. Growing up, I saw peers with natural vocal abilities and mistakenly assumed "either you got it, or you don't." Not true. Your voice is like any other instrument. Practice!)

Somewhere in the muddle of Middle America, Sting brought in a choreographer to punch up our act. Nothing elaborate, just a little something to get us moving and grooving with a tad more flair. (Musicians don't like to admit it, but people *listen* with their eyes, too.) Tracy and I were summoned to our hotel's fitness room one morning to join Sting and our instructor for Dance Party 911. Tracy had a background in dance, so she fell right in line. But in the other corner stood a guitarist with below-average boogie skills—even by white-guy standards. The coach spent a few hours working with the three of us, doling out remedial moves to help energize our show. Being dedicated students, we incorporated the simple steps into our nightly routine. But let's just say we were never any threat to the *Soul Train Gang*.

Fortunately, Sting's audiences tend to value music prowess over spectacle. They don't purchase their tickets with the expectation of fancy footwork. But thanks to my big mouth, our no-frills choreography didn't escape industry ridicule entirely. Six months after the Sting tour, I was in Los Angeles preparing to hit the road with singer-songwriter Sam Phillips. (We rehearsed at producer T Bone Burnett's beachfront apartment in Santa Monica. Best rehearsal view ever.) Being in LA gave me a chance to hang out with one of my closest friends, Tony Bowman. Tony and I first met in the eighth grade and we were instantly joined at the hip. We played in bands together from junior high school through college—and beyond. Tony eventually chased his dreams westward, relocating to Southern California around the same time I'd moved to NYC. A lifelong friend, and a helluva piano player (and singer), Tony is one of the most talented guys I know.

Tony and I were carousing around LA one evening when we bumped into his pal and colleague, Niki Haris. Tony handled the introductions; leading with my Sting credit before mentioning Niki was one of Madonna's primary backup singers and dancers. Despite being a Madonna fan, I couldn't resist taking a gratuitous swipe at Niki's publicity-hound boss. (Demon alcohol strikes again.) Niki, no shrinking violet, smiled a half smile before returning fire. "By the way Jeff, I caught one of your Sting shows—*nice* dancing. Who did the choreography? Jane Fonda?" (At the time, Ms. Fonda had a hugely popular line of aerobic workout videos.) Niki had me dead to rights. Sadly, our rudimentary moves did look more like calisthenics than dance steps.

Austin, Texas | Frank Erwin Center | March 9

Should we stay or should we go? Whenever we had a day off between cities, management made every effort to let us unwind in the more attractive location of the two. And with hip and happening Austin up next on the itinerary, it was a no-brainer to bid farewell to Kansas City and head south for our day of *rest*.

In search of some Texas-sized fun on our night off, all local advice pointed toward Sixth Street. Austin's Sixth Street reminded me of Bleecker Street in New York's Greenwich Village; a neighborhood jam-packed with bars, live music, and rowdy drunks. In other words, the perfect setting for restless musicians to get into trouble. I wandered up and down the strip, sampling numerous honky-tonks while consuming my fair share of whiskey and Texas blues. Considering the combustible atmosphere, you knew someone was going to end up with a classic war story. In Austin, Delmar took the prize—hands down.

Delmar's assault on Austin apparently dissolved into one big blur. Losing all track of time, Delmar glanced down at his watch and saw 7:30 staring back at him. 7:30?!? Red alert! Our concert was scheduled for eight o'clock, so Delmar frantically hailed a cab and zoomed straight to the gig. Arriving at the venue, Delmar ran inside and rushed up onto the stage, shouting, "Don't worry, I'm here!" But nobody was worried. Yes, it was almost eight o'clock, but it was still in the A.M. Delmar wasn't late; he was early…by about twelve hours.

If one wants to be charitable (and I do, because I love Delmar dearly), one could argue dusk and dawn look very similar—especially after a few too many cocktails. As the fog lifted, Delmar realized the stage, along with the entire arena, was empty. In fact, if it weren't for a couple of stage riggers enjoying their morning coffee, Delmar's circadian mistake would've remained his own little secret. But no such luck; word would inevitably spread. Grasping the true time of day, Delmar slinked out of the venue and headed back to the hotel for some much-needed sleep.

Delmar's boozy blunder left him a marked man. Reminiscent of high school—or maybe even elementary school—the road could be a cruel place. Not surprisingly, a couple of roadies couldn't wait to crow about Delmar's gaffe when the band showed up for soundcheck. (Sting's road crew was fueled by a colorful, macho mix of British, Scottish, Irish and New Jersey-ish personalities. "Tough crowd" would be an understatement.) Much like the aftermath of my Heathrow fistfight, Delmar would simply have to ride out the wisecracks. Tag Delmar, you're it.

Roadies are the rock 'n' roll equivalent of older brothers. They are protective, loyal, and above all else...sadistic. They weren't laughing *with* us, they were laughing *at* us. Friendships notwithstanding, I came to accept the dynamic between band and crew is inherently adversarial. Fish got to swim, birds got to fly—and roadies got to break balls. They figure we deserve it. Ask any crewmember, they'll tell you the musicians have it easy. Is that so? Let's examine the facts:

1. The band stays at the Four Seasons; the crew stays at the Holiday Inn.
2. The band lounges by the pool all day while the crew toils in a darkened venue.
3. The band flies private; the crew rides all night on a smelly bus.
4. The band gets all the glory—and most of the pretty girls, too.

Hmmm...I rest *their* case.

* * *

One of the many perks of touring is the opportunity to catch up with friends and family scattered across the land. Texas offered me a chance to reconnect with Stephen Hartsell, the drummer from my high-school rock band. Steve had chosen a nobler path than the rest of us delinquents, trading in his drumsticks for Med school years ago. He'd flourished and gone on to become a successful physician in Salt Lake City. Unfortunately, Sting's itinerary didn't put us anywhere near Steve's neck of the woods, so he hatched a plan to come to me instead.

Temporarily ditching his stethoscope, Steve stepped into the *exciting* world of long-distance vehicle delivery. A friend of Steve's, Tom MacKenzie, was connected with a high-end auto dealership, and a couple of their luxury cars needed to find their way to Texas. Steve and Tom agreed to lend a hand (and foot), and jumped into the sleek rides, destination Austin.

My older brother, Mike, was the car buff in our family, but I still felt a tingle when Steve and Tom rolled up to our hotel; one in a black Porsche, the other in a bright red Ferrari. I greeted my guests and immediately cracked, "Which car is mine?" Tom replied without hesitation, "Take your choice." The Porsche looked mighty sweet, but there was no debate: I wanted to spend some quality time with the Ferrari. It was late afternoon by that point, so my test drive was pushed to the next day. Nevertheless, I was fantasizing about my playdate before the cars could disappear into the Four Seasons garage.

I called Mino the following morning, looking for a partner in crime. I invited him to join me for a spin in *my* Ferrari, and being a red-blooded male with a pulse, Mino was game. We met in front of the hotel and waited breathlessly while the valet retrieved our Italian chariot. I fell in lust all over again as the $200,000 vehicle rolled into view. Our main agenda was to troll the streets of Austin and wave at hot coeds, but first we wanted to take the car out on the highway and see what she could do. Unfortunately, as we were climbing down into the low-slung vehicle, the garage attendant cautioned, "Hey, I noticed a nail stuck in the front left tire. Be careful, that could cause trouble." The tire looked okay, but with no desire to experience a blowout at the speed of sound, we vetoed taking the red rocket out on the open road. We skipped ahead to phase two and kicked off our low-speed, one-car parade around Austin.

My cockiness quickly morphed into angst as the Ferrari proved to be quite the temperamental mistress. Despite being accustomed to driving "stick," I had ongoing problems simply getting the car into gear. I struggled to move forward at almost every stoplight. (It's hard to look cool with beads of sweat dripping from your brow.) After a lifetime of driving clunkers, I clearly lacked the delicate touch the finicky automobile demanded. However, for the short stretches where I was able to maintain momentum, the Ferrari felt sexy and powerful. To quote Mino, "The car looks like it's speeding, even when it's standing still." Nevertheless, between the grinding gears and repeated honks from impatient drivers stuck behind me, my stress easily outpaced my enjoyment. We did manage to turn a few heads as we cruised through campus, but I was relieved when the diva-mobile was parked safely back at the hotel. In the end, she just wasn't my type.

Houston, Texas | The Summit | March 11

Being around so many Brits, soccer was a popular topic on the road. (Personally, I've always had trouble getting excited about a sport where the final score can be 0-0. Zzzzzzz.) On Sting's previous tour, the band and crew had organized a friendly little game of soccer—for fun, and, of course, the highly-coveted bragging rights. Incredibly, the underdog musicians won that contest by the lopsided score of 1-0. A heated rivalry was born, and talk of a rematch had been in the air since the beginning of our rehearsals. After chewing on their loss for over a year, the roadies vowed sweet revenge.

"Put Up or Shut Up" day finally arrived as the city of Houston played host to the much-anticipated *Sting Cup Deux*. The whole gang gathered on our day off for a little fresh air, a lot of trash talk, and hopefully, a non-lethal dose of cardio.

Taking the grudge match maybe a bit too seriously, Billy and Kim ordered top-secret, custom uniforms for Team Band. Come game time, we rushed onto the field as one, screaming like savages as we peeled off our sweats to reveal our menacing "skull and crossbones" jerseys (with cute matching shorts). Unfortunately, our efforts at sartorial gamesmanship didn't intimidate the crew in the slightest. They knew exactly what they were up against: nerd musicians.

The whistle blew—and pandemonium ensued. Our level of athleticism basically resembled a Benny Hill skit (cue "Yakety Sax"), but damned if we didn't have a load of fun. Guilty of numerous whiffs throughout the afternoon, I quickly came to appreciate the difficulty of kicking a ball while running at full speed.

When time mercifully expired, the band had retained its crown, defeating the crew once again by the embarrassing score of 1-0. Good had triumphed over Evil, thanks in large part to the "tenacious D" of tenor goalie Branford Marsalis.

We headed out for a victory dinner after the match. Give us ANY excuse to party and we were there. Selecting the perfect spot for our testosterone-infused celebration, we stormed Houston's local chapter of the Cadillac Bar—a festive Tex Mex chain known for rowdy, drunken behavior. (Naturally, I'd visited the Manhattan outpost on numerous occasions.) Part restaurant, part floorshow, the Cadillac Bar was notorious for its roving tequila waitresses. The sexy servers were armed and dangerous; packing liquor bottles in holsters while shot glasses crisscrossed their chest like bullets in a Mexican *bandolier*. Whenever a thirsty soul volunteered, one of the waitresses would whip out her bottle and pour a shot. The saucy *bandita* would then drum the shot glass loudly against the table, screaming "Arrrriiiba, Arrrriiiba" to rally the crowd. Chants of "Drink! Drink! Drink!" echoed throughout the restaurant as the showboat guzzler basked in his fifteen-seconds of fame. Young knucklehead that I was, I found the frat-like atmosphere totally entertaining. But my more discriminating boss was clearly not amused. Sting leaned over to me during one especially boisterous outburst and whispered in his refined British accent, "I imagine Hell must be just like this." I didn't get it at the time. Today, I couldn't agree with him more.

New Orleans, Louisiana | Lakefront Arena | March 12

Our massive entourage also included a video crew, commissioned to enhance the concert-going experience for the nosebleed seats. A team of gray-clad cameramen discreetly shadowed the band throughout the show, projecting close-up images to the large video screens that flanked each side of our stage. But with boys being boys, the videographers were also known to use their technology for less legitimate purposes on occasion. (Specifically: scouring the audience for sexy ladies.)

Our video director zoomed in on three beauties in New Orleans and dispatched a cameraman to befriend them. After the show, the delta ladies were escorted backstage to meet the boys in the band. And thanks to our keen-eyed surveillance unit, this "boy in the band" made the acquaintance of an extraordinarily attractive *N'awlins* girl that night. I ultimately coerced the women to join me back at the hotel, where I hosted a small after-party in my room for the photogenic trio—plus our crazy accountant, The Goon. Our little gathering quickly devolved into the usual drunken nonsense, with the five of us sprawled out on the floor passing around a giant bottle of scotch. (Hardcore booze even by my standards.) The Goon and his two pals eventually disappeared, and I had an enjoyable evening, or what was left of it, with my sultry friend.

The next morning, gentleman that I am, I escorted my Southern belle downstairs to the hotel's taxi stand. As we strolled through the lobby, I noticed Sting sitting in the corner, sipping a cup of tea while closely observing our "Walk of Shame." When I bumped into my boss later that afternoon, he immediately asked about the "gorgeous" girl he'd seen on my arm. His curiosity made my male ego soar. You're doing something right when an international rock star drools over *your* companion.

* * *

Unfortunately, it didn't take long for the glamorous life to become somewhat routine. I know I sound prematurely jaded for such a low-mileage rookie, but many aspects of the road were incredibly tedious. Ask any touring musician: the hardest part of the gig is filling the twenty-one hours a day you're OFF stage. To battle the boredom, tennis became one of my favorite pastimes— at least of the healthy variety. A couple of sweaty sets were the perfect way to vanquish an idle afternoon, while simultaneously reducing my exposure to bar stools.

The tour boasted a number of tennis bums (including Billy, Kim, The Goon, and Sting) so it was usually easy to rustle up some action. Billy and I developed a friendly tennis rivalry over the course of the year, hitting the courts whenever possible. With our skills pretty evenly matched, we could always count on a nice blend of exercise and conversation.

Things were a bit more complicated when Sting was my opponent. Doubles was cool; singles was another story. Thoroughly intimidated by Sting's awesomeness, I tended to prefer his company in groups. But despite my efforts to stick with the "safety in numbers" approach, there were a few times where Billy was able to dupe me into *mano a mano* combat with the boss. Laying his trap, Billy would call to see if I was interested in a game of tennis. I'd assume he meant with *him*, and answer yes. Billy would drop the hammer. "Great! Meet STING in the lobby in twenty minutes." Curses, foiled again. Our hotels usually had their own tennis courts, but there was one instance where Sting and I were forced to trek to a private racquet club across town. Outsmarted by Billy's bait-and-switch tactics, I found myself alone in the backseat of a taxi with Sting. And despite my daily interactions with the man, the intimate one-on-one setting had me completely flustered. I felt like a nervous teenager on a first date, struggling to make small talk as our cab crawled through traffic. Six months in, and I was still totally starstruck.

San Antonio, Texas | Municipal Auditorium | March 14

Dallas, Texas | Reunion Arena | March 15

A few of us made plans to grab a nightcap after our show in Dallas. Returning to the hotel, I ran up to my room for a quick shower before heading back downstairs to the lobby bar. When I attempted to enter the lounge, the maître d stopped me dead in my tracks. He gave me the once over and sniffed, "No jeans allowed." Despite my budding sense of entitlement, I decided against trotting out the unseemly "Do you know who I am?" routine. (Answer: Nobody.) I didn't have the energy for a showdown, so I retreated to my room and changed into a pair of hotel-approved slacks.

By the time I got back down to the bar, Sting was already holding court in a corner booth. He saw me standing in the doorway—shoulder-to-shoulder with Mr. Dress Code—and waved me over. I joined my pals and immediately noticed Sting's extremely casual attire: a tattered denim jacket and (gasp)...JEANS. I'm no dummy, I understood the double standard, but that didn't mean I had to like it. I glanced back at the fickle fashion cop as I took my seat in Sting's inner circle. The maître d just looked at me and shrugged. He knew he'd been snagged.

* * *

Soundcheck sometimes wound up being the highlight of our day—especially when it turned into a master class from our brilliant pianist, Kenny Kirkland. Kenny would noodle around, exploring his prevailing musical mood as we awaited Sting's arrival. Sometimes it was jazz, sometimes funk, or salsa, or classical...but it was dependably amazing. And if Kenny was really feeling it, we'd get to see an even lesser-known side of the virtuoso. On a couple of occasions, Kenny came out from behind his keyboard rig, grabbed Sting's center stage microphone, and unleashed his killer James Brown impersonation. Out of the multitude of musicians I've had the honor to play with, Kenny Kirkland was absolutely THE man.

We'd get down to business once Sting arrived. Some days there was real work to be done, other days we'd just jam on random tunes. During those moments of spontaneity, I loved it when Sting reached into his untapped Police catalog for sound-check fodder. The instant Sting started vamping on one of his un-used chestnuts, I'd jump right in. Between my cover band experi-ence and my exhaustive audition prep, I stayed locked and loaded for any (and all) Police material. Sting would sometimes seem surprised by my familiarity with his deeper cuts. He'd smile and say, "You know *that* one?" It was almost like he didn't grasp the far-reaching impact of his music. I had to gently remind him The Police were pretty darn popular.

At one loose soundcheck, the band reeled off an impromp-tu version of The Police classic, "Walking on the Moon." Sting seemed caught off-guard by his own composition, remarking, "Wow, that's a pretty good tune." I agreed with him, but I could already see his wheels turning. Sting continued, "Maybe I should write a bridge for it, and we could add it to the set." Unable to hold my tongue, I jumped to defend MY beloved Police song. "Don't you dare touch that tune. If we play it, we should play it as is." I guess Sting heard me because he just grinned and moved on. Thankfully, that was the end of that crazy talk. *If it ain't broke…*

Although I'm a fan of the entire Police catalog, I'm partic-ularly drawn to the band's earlier stuff. The songs are so viscer-al and minimalistic, yet dripping with integrity. I still get excited whenever "So Lonely" or "When the World is Running Down" randomly shuffles up on my iPhone. Maybe it's primal instinct, but I've always responded to music from the bottom up: groove first, followed by harmony/melody, and lastly, lyrics. Accordingly, I tend to gravitate toward rhythmic artists like James Brown, Led Zeppelin, or Prince. Give me a funky beat and I'm a happy boy. In fact, if the groove is deep enough, I'm usually willing to overlook any lame-ass lyrics. But the music of The Police checked all the boxes, satisfying me on every level. Irresistible grooves, cool chord progressions, strong melodies, topped off with intelligent lyrics…well, most of the time anyway. Despite my repeated requests, Sting refused to go anywhere near his nonsensical "De Do Do Do, De Da Da Da." (I love that tune.)

But—and there always seems to be a but—I have to confess that Sting's music has become a bit too sophisticated for my tastes as his career has progressed. I miss the raw, concise power of his early Police work. Even toward the end of the Police era, I felt Sting got a little too cerebral at times. I never could resist poking fun at the heavy-handed imagery of skeletons choking on crusts of bread. But then again, "King of Pain" was one of Sting's biggest hits, so what the hell do I know?

In Sting's defense (not that he needs it, or wants it), I can imagine how difficult it must be for a successful artist to evolve, while still maintaining a) relevance, and b) their fan base. And if a rock star is fortunate enough to be blessed with longevity, they're faced with the hardest trick of all: growing old gracefully. I believe Sting has acquitted himself nicely on this front, staying hip, classy, (and good looking), year after year.

Any recording artist with a multi-decade career has their share of misfires. Remember the old joke about rockers who die young? "Good career move!" Their genius is frozen in time. They didn't stick around long enough to release the inevitable stinker— or two. But Sting is still out there, continually putting his reputation on the line as he tries new and different ideas. I have nothing but respect for performers (like Sting) who are willing to take creative chances, rather than simply repeating their hit formula *ad nauseam*. Despite my personal fantasy of Sting returning to his leaner, meaner style, he's more than earned the right to follow his muse. If Sting wants to spend the rest of his life composing for the lute—or penning Broadway musicals*—more power to him. Sting mastered streamlined, pop/rock years ago. He's got nothing to prove.

Las Cruces, New Mexico | Pan Am Center | March 17
Tempe, Arizona | ASU Activity Center | March 18

Dateline: Los Angeles

Hollywood Swinging, indeed. Although I'd already experienced Paris, Rio, London, etc., I was stoked to add The City of Angels to my "been there, done that" list. We set up camp at the trendy Mondrian Hotel in West Hollywood and, despite being a die-hard East Coast guy, I loved LA.

Even in a city lousy with VIPs, we received the star treatment. The finest restaurants, the hottest clubs, you name it—LA was ours for the taking. One evening, our promoter invited a few of us to join him at the celebrated rock hangout, The Rainbow Bar and Grill. Arriving at the hotspot, we were whisked past the velvet rope and straight to our reserved table, completely bypassing

---

* Box-office struggles notwithstanding, *The Last Ship* was a profound work of art. Sting's thirty-five year arc from reggae punk to Broadway composer is remarkable—and unparalleled.

the long line of *civilians* patiently waiting to get into the club. Let them eat cake.

But always remember, karma is a bitch. I returned to LA the following year and decided to revisit The Rainbow. No longer wielding the lofty title of "Sting's guitarist," I was quickly reminded how the other half lives. Now it was MY turn to wait in line as the big shots and hot babes waltzed past. I felt invisible as the doorman openly ignored my buddy and me while cherry-picking scenesters from the eager mob. Frustrated, and, of course, inebriated, I started griping about the biased admission policy. Not surprisingly, my complaints didn't endear me to the gatekeepers. Thank God, my pal swept me away before the thick-necked bouncers decided to deposit me in the nearby dumpster. Let ME eat cake.

* * *

Continuing to sample the LA nightlife, I made a trip to The Roxy—the legendary rock club on Sunset Strip. Coincidentally, North Carolina transplant Parthenon Huxley was performing that night so I ended up seeing a few semi-familiar faces from back home. Small talk inevitably led to questions about life with Sting. I obliged and tossed out a few tour anecdotes—including the one about Sting's dangerous visit to the Amazon. When I recounted the "white man doesn't always make it out of the jungle alive" aspect of the story, one hipster interjected, "You mean someone had a chance to kill Sting ... and they let him go?"

Even in jest, I didn't appreciate the remark. I'm allowed to talk shit about my boss, but YOU sir, are not. Unamused, and growing bored with the cynical bohemians, I said my goodnights and decamped to my luxury hotel suite—provided by my apparently passé employer.

Los Angeles, California | The Forum | March 20, 21

The band was fully dialed in by the time we hit Los Angeles. We channeled our East Coast pride and gave The Forum a show to remember. Post-concert, the green room was overflowing with Hollywood's top movers and shakers, but I kept reminding myself that WE were the center of attention; the glitterati were out in force to see US. Then I spied Quincy Jones across the way, and my cocky façade crumbled instantly. I'd worshiped "Q" from afar for years, and now we were standing in the same room. The brilliant musician/arranger/producer had shepherded some of my favorite recordings by artists including Ray Charles, Frank Sinatra, Michael Jackson, and the oh-so-funky Brothers Johnson (not to mention, helming a little session known as "We Are the World.") I HAD to meet the master.

Waiting for an organic opportunity to approach the living legend, I sprang into action when I saw Branford and Quincy strike up a conversation. I marched right over—with all the subtlety of a stalker—and demanded Branford introduce me to my hero. Simply saying hello to Mr. Jones made my night…and my week. Looking back over the entire tour, Quincy Jones was the only celebrity I ever ambushed—and I have zero regrets. I may have come off like a giddy groupie, but I couldn't care less. I got to shake hands with King Midas.

Our LA audience was packed with celebs, but the most intriguing attendees (in my opinion) were Sting's former business partners, Messrs. Copeland and Summers. Yep, all three members of the estranged Police were together under one roof—a roof atop a building that happened to contain guitars, drums, and 17,000 Police fans. That's right, POLICE fans. (I knew where I stood with the public. One night, I saw an audience member holding up a large hand-made sign that read, "Sting, PLEASE put The Police back together!")

Before the show, I overheard Kim delicately ask Sting, "Hey, would you maybe want to play a tune with the guys?" Sting's answer was an immediate and firm "No." I assume Sting figured if he played even one song with "the guys," headlines would scream "POLICE REUNITE"—and drown out his solo message in the process. Sting chose pragmatism over sentimentality (if any existed), and stuck to the script.

I got a chance to meet both Police-men before the show, but neither offered more than a chilly "Hello." After the concert, Sting pulled me aside and whispered, "Hey Jeff, Andy says…(I waited for praise from my fellow guitarist)…you're playing a wrong chord in 'Murder by Numbers'." Jeez, everybody's a critic. Sting continued, "Andy said to tell you there's a Bb in the second chord of the song." Oh really? Despite the unimpeachable source, I was skeptical. I tracked down a guitar backstage and gave Andy's *suggested* voicing a strum. Of course, Andy was correct. My ear had missed that sneaky Bb when we'd haphazardly learned

"Murder" for the horny Reverend Swaggart. I should've picked up on that harmonic rub, but, in all the commotion, I was outsmarted by Andy's jazzy Phrygian chord. Maybe I needed that fourth year of college after all.

We finally closed down the Forum and began making our way out across the parking lot to our waiting vans. As we strolled along, I noticed Sting and Trudie peeling away from the group. I was confused at first, but then it hit me: they weren't going back to the hotel with us, they were going home—or to *one* of their homes, anyway; in this case, a beachfront house in Malibu.

Forgoing a chauffeur, Sting and Trudie were bumming a ride with one of their Malibu neighbors, actor Larry Hagman (aka bad boy "JR Ewing" on the hit TV show *Dallas*). Mr. Hagman was known as quite the party animal at the time, and his mode of transportation that evening did nothing to dispel that notion. In typical larger-than-life, Hollywood fashion, Hagman was traveling in a massive, bright-white Chevy Suburban stretch limo, tricked out with blue-neon running lights. Certainly NOT the type of vehicle you'd associate with Sting's cultivated sense of style. I couldn't resist cracking, "Hey, nice ride!" as Sting and Trudie climbed into the garish prom-night battleship. Sting turned and shot me his patented lethal stare.

* * *

Sting invited the band out to his place in Malibu one afternoon for some fun in the sun. But before hitting the beach, we made a stop at one of Nike's corporate showrooms to partake in a little conspicuous consumption. Years earlier, Nike had stumbled upon a newspaper photo of Sting wearing one of their logo'ed T-shirts. The sporting goods company was ecstatic over the unsolicited celebrity endorsement and, in a show of appreciation, rewarded Sting with a lifetime supply of *swooshes*. Nike extended their generosity to include friends of family, and insisted the band swing by for a shopping spree—on the house.

It felt like Christmas morning when we walked into Nike-Town. The entire product line was on display, and we were encouraged to help ourselves to anything (and everything) our greedy hearts desired. Shoes, clothing, hats, etc.—all ours for the asking. Our complimentary duffle bags were bursting at the seams by the time we finished bingeing on the unlimited swag. It is one of life's true enigmas: when you have money, you don't need it as much.

A couple of weeks later, Billy and I were sitting in a hotel lobby when Delmar came bouncing in, dressed head-to-toe in crisp Nike clothing. Never missing a trick, Billy quipped, "You know Jeff, if it weren't for Sting, Delmar would be naked right now."

San Diego, California | Sports Arena | March 22

Oakland, California | Oakland Coliseum | March 24, 25

Although we were performing in Oakland, management opted to house the band in San Francisco. And no disrespect to Oakland, but management made the right call; San Francisco was awesome. My brother, Will, was living in San Fran at the time, so, with two-thirds of their brood in the same zip code, my parents were easily talked into a cross-country trip. Two sons, one Sting, and the Golden Gate Bridge proved to be an irresistible vacation package for the folks.

We had great shows in Oakland, but then again, we AL-WAYS had great shows. Audiences were psyched to see us no matter where we went. Unlike my years on the cover-band circuit (where I sometimes played to apathetic—or hostile—crowds numbering in the single digits), there were never any bad nights at the Sting level. Enthusiastic, sold-out houses were the norm.

But crazy as it sounds, I still felt like I was in a cover band at times—albeit a damn good one. Let's face it; I wasn't performing any of MY music. I didn't write "Every Breath You Take" (dammit), or any of the other tunes in our show. Just like my gigging days back in North Carolina, I was being paid to crank out familiar, crowd-pleasing hits. But at least in this *cover* band, the audiences were huge, the money was great, and I was standing twenty feet from the guy who wrote those crowd-pleasing hits.

Technically speaking, we were a cover band. Sting peppered our setlist with borrowed tunes from time to time, most notably the Squeeze classic, "Tempted" and Frank Zappa's "Idiot Bastard Son." I still have no idea why Sting included that bizarre Zappa number in our show. The audience response was always a unanimous "HUH?" when we finished the *ambitious* head-scratcher. Billy couldn't resist winding Sting up one afternoon, and asked if he'd heard about the injury at our previous performance. An alarmed Sting wanted details. Billy responded with a straight face. "A bored fan fell asleep last night during 'Idiot Bastard Son,' slid out of his chair and hit his head on the floor." Zing! Even the boss couldn't escape our road manager's sarcastic wrath. In fact, Billy doubled down in our next itinerary, editorializing on the tour personnel page:

Sting — God forbid the day he gets his Zappa medley together

Like most working musicians, I'd spent the bulk of my career playing places where the band often served as little more than a glorified jukebox. The kind of gigs where audiences feel like they deserve a say in the song selection, "*Faster! Slower! Louder! Softer! Play something good—NOW!*" But I was breathing rarified air on the Sting tour. People came to hear whatever we wanted to play. (Well, whatever HE wanted to play.) Nevertheless, Sting fans are just like every other audience in the world. They want to hear their favorites. Crowd response was always much more enthusiastic for Police classics than the less-familiar titles from Sting's (or Zappa's) solo catalog. From the roadhouses to the stadiums, you've got to give the people what they want: HITS.

* * *

The backstage scene in Oakland was the typical three-ring circus…with my parents added to the mix. I felt like a plate spinner after the show, trying to be an attentive son while also squeezing in a little face time with the local hotties. We eventually made our way back to the hotel, where I uncharacteristically decided to call it a night. (My usual ritual involved moaning about "last call" in the lobby bar.) I was settling in for the evening when my phone rang. I should've known better, but I answered. It was Mino. So much for calling it a night.

A slice of the Oakland revelry had staggered back across the Bay Bridge to Mino's room, and he was in need of reinforcements. I gave in—with only the tiniest amount of arm-twisting—and agreed to drop by. ("I'll sleep when I'm dead" was a popular refrain on the road.) Walking into Mino's cozy *after* after-party, I recognized a couple of faces from the earlier backstage hang. One of the girls was exceptionally pretty, so I set sail in her direction. With time being of the essence, we dove straight into some serious speed flirting. But unfortunately, the object of my desire turned out to be highly skilled in the art of playing hard-to-get. *Stop, Go, Yes, No.* I didn't have the time, or the patience, for her mixed messages at that late hour, so I elected to punt. Redirecting my energies, I moved in on one of the beauty queen's considerably less-attractive accomplices. Bachelorette #2 was a strapping, hunk of a woman who looked like she could break me in half. But so what? I didn't care if people thought I was crazy. I was.

A darkness had crept into my psyche as the tour unfolded. My prodigious intake of booze was fueling a vicious cycle of reckless behavior and self-loathing. "Bad Jeff" was always lurking nearby, and he was definitely with me in San Francisco. Shifting my self-destruction into high gear, I made a play for the brawny runner-up. And while Lust was firmly in the driver's seat, Spite was right there riding shotgun. Pissing off the coy ringleader absolutely factored into my calculations.

After a bare minimum of chitchat, my husky friend and I slipped away to my room to get better acquainted. Just as things were heating up, my phone rang. I had a hunch who was calling so, despite being *busy*, I crudely answered. (Chivalry died a gruesome death that night my friends.) Greeted by a livid female on the other end of the line, I simply passed the phone to my equally busy companion. The abandoned diva proceeded to rip into her cohort for disappearing with me. Mission accomplished; I'd succeeded in both love AND war. Of course, in hindsight, this is not one of my prouder moments. I'd not only crossed the line of scumbaggery, I'd obliterated it. But there's more ...

Only a few hours later, I joined my brother, his girlfriend (now wife), and my parents for brunch. Nursing yet another brutal hangover, I would've had to get better just to die. I was in desperate need of *medicine*, so, the minute our waiter appeared, I requested my old reliable: vodka and grapefruit juice. We scanned the menu, placed our orders, and then sat back to rehash the previous evening's festivities. Just as my breakfast cocktail was starting to perform its miracles, my mother leaned in. "Who was that ONE girl backstage last night?" Mom lowered her voice and continued. "I hate to say it, but she looked like a MAN." Ouch. I played dumb, but I knew exactly who my mom was talking about. And despite being able to vouch for the debutante's gender, that topic didn't really seem to be family-brunch appropriate. My well-mannered mother didn't mean any disrespect, but her innocent—and unfortunately, accurate—observation didn't help my precarious state of mind, body, or soul. (*Waiter! Another "grapefruit juice" pronto.*) Dark days indeed, but I only had myself to blame. My bleakness was self-inflicted.

* * *

I began to appreciate the value of a good book as we circumnavigated the globe. Between our incessant air travel and endless downtime, reading became a lifesaver. Before the tour, I hardly read anything except easily digestible newspapers and magazines. I thought books were for old, boring people. And my youthful ignorance was on full display in Sting's souvenir tour program. In the personal profile section, I responded to "Current reading?" with this embarrassingly shallow answer:

> *"Magazines mostly, Time, Newsweek and Rolling Stone, because I want to know what people like Bon Jovi are doing, whether I like their music or not."*

Spoken like a true college dropout. I wish I could have another crack at that question. Today, I love to read, and could offer a much more respectable answer:

> *"Well, lately I've been enjoying works by a variety of authors. Updike, Wolfe, Franzen...just to name a few."*

It's also funny—and maybe clairvoyant—that my illiterate response randomly namechecked Bon Jovi. Long after the Sting tour, I had the pleasure of getting to know Jon Bon Jovi personally. Hopefully he'll never see my smug remark from 1987. Color me moron; Bon Jovi rocks.

I was introduced to Jon by Jeff Kazee. Jeff is a phenomenal

musician/singer—and one of my dearest friends. Jeff handled auxiliary keyboard/accordion/vocal duties on Bon Jovi's "Have A Nice Day" World Tour, and was also a longtime member of Jon's solo project. When Jon mentioned he was looking for someone to help him polish his guitar skills, Kazee immediately gave him my number. Jon and I hit it off and ended up working together on a regular basis for a few years. People always ask me why a huge rock star would need a guitar teacher. I'll answer that question with a question: Why do the New York Yankees need a hitting instructor? In the pursuit of excellence, there is no finish line.

Mirroring one of my greatest NYC thrills, I found myself back in the catbird seat: lounging on a rock icon's couch, sipping coffee, and strumming guitars. But this time around, instead of plucking out "Message in a Bottle" at Sting's loft, it was "Wanted Dead or Alive" at JBJ's penthouse. Jon's friendly vibe put me at ease, but tutoring a superstar still proved to be somewhat ticklish. I felt a bit like Geoffrey Rush's tough-love character in the film *The King's Speech*. Except in my case, I'd been hired to exhort (and when needed, admonish) ROCK royalty. Complicating matters further, unlike teaching *civilians*, the "bad cop" routine was completely off the table with Jon. It would've been kind of pointless to threaten Bon Jovi with, "Man, if you don't practice harder, you're never gonna make it in this business." All kidding aside, threats weren't necessary. Jon was dedicated and hardworking, and his efforts paid real dividends. Attending one of Bon Jovi's sold-out shows at Giants Stadium, I felt like a proud papa when Jon stepped into the spotlight and cranked out a blazing guitar solo, temporarily stealing gunslinger Richie Sambora's thunder. Moving to New York was the smartest thing I ever did. Amazing things happen here.

Reno, Nevada | Lawler Events Centre | March 26

Before leaving Reno, Sting got his hands on a less-than-glowing review from our recent Oakland stand. ("First-degree drubbing" would be a more apt description.) We usually received pretty positive write-ups, but that was definitely not the case with *The San Francisco Chronicle.* Staff critic Jesse Hamlin tore into Sting—on a surprisingly personal level. The hatchet job included lines like "Sting would be much easier to stomach if he weren't so taken with himself," and Sting should just "shut up and sing." The spiteful critic went on to describe Sting as "pompous," "pretentious," "tiresome," and "annoying." (How do you really feel, Jesse?)

Hamlin's blood-spattered review included enough abuse, typos, and inaccuracies that Sting couldn't let it slide. Breaking the cardinal PR rule of "staying above the fray," Sting responded via a letter to the editor—which *The Chronicle* promptly printed. After pointing out the numerous errors in the review, Sting's letter concluded:

> *"And finally, let's talk about being 'pompous' and 'pretentious.' Hamlin has a perfect right to evaluate my personality as he sees fit. I have broad shoulders and a thick skin, but it's difficult for me to imagine a more pretentious occupation than that of a professional critic, a task commonly inherited by a failed actor, the failed musician and in Hamlin's case, the failed writer. It's all very well to speak of the arrogance and pomposity of a performer, but it's very rare for anyone to speak of the courage it takes to walk on a stage in front of 20,000 people and attempt to entertain them for 3 hours. It's rare because so few people have ever tried it. Here's a serious offer Jesse, the next time I*

perform in the area, I'm offering you 10 minutes of stage time, you can do whatever you want, dance, sing, read poetry or even one of your articles, but it must be entertaining. To accept my offer will take a degree of courage, skill, and humility possessed by only a few. Love and Good Health to you — Sting"

Bravo. I don't know if Jesse ever took Sting up on his offer. My guess is no.

Seattle, Washington | Coliseum | March 28
Portland, Oregon | Memorial Coliseum | March 29

Sacramento, California | Arco Arena | March 31

Operating out of our comfy home base in LA, we cruised over to Burbank Airport for a day-trip up to Sacramento. I climbed aboard the plane and spotted a new—but familiar—face among our intimate crowd. To my starstruck excitement, Sting had invited Sean Penn to tag along on our adventure. (Hey, wait a minute, nobody told me it was "Bring your Movie Star to Work" day.) I was surprised Hollywood's reigning bad boy wanted to join us in sleepy Sacramento, but maybe Sean's choice was strategic. Between his volatile marriage with Madonna and repeated run-ins with the paparazzi, Mr. Penn was *enjoying* an extremely high profile in the media at the time. Maybe Sacramento sounded like paradise. The perfect place to lay low and avoid trouble—at least for a day, anyway.

I had a chance to spend a little one-on-one time with the intense actor after dinner. Chatting at a picnic table out back of the arena, our conversation turned to performing for large crowds. I puffed out my chest, bragging my first official concert with Sting was in front of over two hundred thousand people in Rio. Sean nodded politely before countering his wife had recently played to over three hundred thousand people in Paris. Impressed, and sufficiently one-upped, I asked Sean if he'd attended the French concert. His reply was concise. "Nope, I was in jail."

Foot meet mouth. How was I to know while Madonna was rocking Paris in her cone bra, Sean had been behind bars for assaulting a photographer? Those two lovebirds were a match made in heaven—divorce lawyer heaven.

Santa Barbara, California | County Bowl | April 1

Las Vegas, Nevada | Aladdin Casino | April 2

I'd never been to Las Vegas, but so what else was new? Scheduled to make a quick, surgical strike in Vegas before beating it back to LA, we zoomed straight to the venue after touching down in the desert. But unlike a lot of our gigs, I didn't have any trouble finding a way to kill time before the show: we were playing at a casino. Being a card-carrying yokel, I typically gravitated toward the most obvious touristy experiences. In Paris, it was the Eiffel Tower; in Vegas, it was the slots. After all, what could be more cliché than losing some of my hard-earned money to a one-armed-bandit in Sin City?

During our extended residency in Los Angeles, I'd introduced Branford to my old Carolina co-conspirator, Tony Bowman. Tony and I had played hundreds of gigs together over the years—and he had crates of incriminating memorabilia to prove it. But with Tony being at least as mischievous as he is sentimental, he couldn't resist slipping Branford a recording of one of my earliest performances. The ancient tape featured my junior high school rock band, Lotus, playing at our eighth-grade Christmas Dance. Among the cassette's many nuggets was my *timeless* rendition of James Brown's "Sex Machine." Branford knew he'd struck gold the minute he heard my virginal 13-year-old voice squeaking out the Godfather's classic intro: *"Hey Man, I feel like doin' it Man, like a Sex Machine, Man. Can I count it off? 1-2-3 …"* The recording is indeed embarrassing, but I couldn't be happier it exists. The lo-fi treasure confirms I've paid my dues.

With the blackmail tape in his possession, Branford schemed to "out" my musical puberty in spectacular fashion. He passed the cassette on to our sound crew and instructed them to unleash the beast at our Vegas soundcheck. The trap was set.

As the band straggled out onto stage for the afternoon walkthrough, *The Ghost of Christmas Dance Past* paid me a visit. Without warning, our massive speaker system began blasting my castrato voice throughout the arena. I was confused—until I saw Branford doubled over with laughter. I immediately knew the score. I'd been punked by the tag team of Bowman and Marsalis. A befuddled Sting looked up from his guitar and moaned, "What the hell is that?" Tom-o mercifully stopped the tape, but not before everybody got an earful of young Jeffrey Lee screaming about "doin' it like a Sex Machine." Just imagine Alvin and the Chipmunks covering James Brown, you'll get the basic picture.

Las Vegas was the final stop on our FIRST trip around North America. (We'd make the rounds again later that summer.) One more show, and then two glorious weeks off. We'd logged two-and-a-half grueling months on the road, so everybody was looking forward to a much-needed breather—especially considering the fact we were staring down the barrel of a three-month stretch in Europe.

The plan was to fly back to LA after the concert, and catch a commercial flight to New York the following morning. But in an effort to wring every single drop out of Spring Break, a few band members decided to book a "red-eye" from Vegas to NYC right after the show. The idea sounded tempting, but the window between our final note and the plane's departure seemed a little tight for my tastes. I'm averse to any nonessential stress, so the thought of rushing through post-gig traffic as the "now boarding" clock ticked down didn't grab me. I stood pat. I was more than happy to kick back and enjoy one more night of our private plane—and my Hollywood address—before confronting the spartan realities of my New York life. No limos, no maid service, no room service, but at least I'd be home sweet friggin' home.

Two Weeks Off: Last Chance For Gas

I made a quick trip down to North Carolina during our break to decompress and lick my luxury wounds. I juggled a demanding schedule of home-cooking and supreme laziness, but I did manage to squeeze in one small piece of work-related business: an interview and photo layout for a local publication. It wasn't exactly *GQ*, but I figured my modeling career had to start some-where. And while I knew it would have to eventually end some-where, I didn't anticipate my first fashion shoot would also be my LAST. (Showbiz is one cruel mistress.) The photo session had all the trappings of a high-concept spread: hair and makeup stylist, wardrobe, catering, etc., so I enjoyed a fantasy afternoon of play-ing dress-up. But the best fringe benefit was the up-close-and-personal poses with my attractive female co-model. Big shout-out to my girl, Joy, and the scrappy *Northgate Mall Lifestyle* magazine.

On the subject of media, I'd just assumed I'd be swamped with interview requests—especially from music-centric publica-tions. But that was hardly the case. I ended up amassing a grand total of ONE short interview with ONE magazine over the course of the entire year. (Thank you, *Guitar World.*) I may have thought Jeffrey Lee Campbell was hot copy, but apparently no-body else did. Based on my humbling experience, if the average sideman wants publicity, he's going to have to drum it up him-self...and therein lies the rub. The shameless art of self-promo-tion often sits in direct conflict with the sensitive nature of artists. Time and again, I've seen creative people struggle with tooting his or her own horn; I'm a chronic offender. Lacking enough sav-vy and/or bravado, I failed to parlay my Sting gig into any sub-stantial press. By the time I figured out it was MY responsibility to strike, the iron was ice cold.

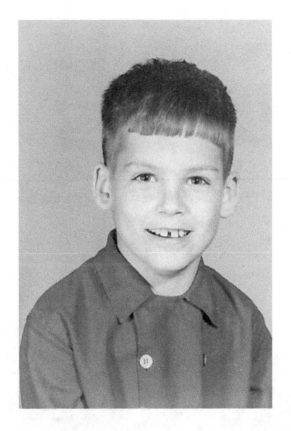

3rd grade school photo. Proudly sporting the double-breasted "Monkee" shirt my Grandmother made for me.

Business card for my first employable band, Lotus. Who needs Helvetica?

Lotus performs at a street fair in Chapel Hill. My life-long co-conspirator
Tony Bowman on the Farfisa Compact Duo.

Rocking a beard, loosened tie and sunglasses with my post-college band, Steps. (L to R: Tony Bowman, Carter Minor, Greg Darden, Morgan Davis)

Bushrock in Paris—"coffee" break in the alley outside our rehearsal studio. (L to R: Jimmy Kovack, Ricky Sebastian, Big Russ, Chulo Gatewood, a distracted Delmar, Serge Fafa—kneeling)

Study materials. My generic, advance copy of Sting's *Nothing Like the Sun* album. Priceless treasure.

Jeff
Pick-up 16:15

NBC SATURDAY NIGHT LIVE
October 17, 1987

4:00 - 5:00 PM	Limosines will pick up band members at their homes.
5:00 PM	Band arrives at NBC - 30 Rockerfeller Plaza, Studio 8H.
5:30 - 6:30 PM	Band Sound Check.
6:30 - 7:30 PM	Dinner @ NBC.
8:00 - 10:00 PM	Dress Rehearsal.
10:00 - 11:30 PM	Break before show.
11:30 - 1:00 AM	Show time.
1:15 AM	NBC BASH - To Be Announced.

"Live from New York . . ." My call sheet for *Saturday Night Live.* They forgot to list: "6pm Building catches fire . . . run for your lives!"

SNL sign-off: Dana Carvey, Steve Martin, Sting, Nora Dunn, Dennis Miller (back) Jan Hooks, Victoria Jackson. I'm tucked behind Jan Hooks—and clearly in HEAVEN. Not so sure about Branford.

Photo by David Allen—TodaysNew.com

LORNE MICHAELS

and the cast and crew of

SATURDAY NIGHT LIVE

invite you to join them on

October 17, 1987

to celebrate the premiere show at

the

CHINA GRILL

60 West 53rd Street

one o'clock am

this invitation admits two

SNL after-party invite. Heady times indeed. I was selling candy in Broadway theaters only two weeks earlier.

With the man who lit the fuse: Delmar Brown.

Ritz dressing room with my hero (and baddest musician I've ever known),
Kenny Kirkland.

Backstage with Trudie Styler in Rio. This photo was clearly taken before I whacked her in the head with a tennis ball.

Percussion tech Nico Wormworth (Tracy's brother), bassist Tracy Wormworth, and the "indispensable" Danny Quatrochi.

Holiday cheer at Sting's 17th century London townhouse with Tom "Tom-o" Herrmann and Sting.

Nico Wormworth with our road manager/drill sergeant,
the incomparable Billy Francis.

The intimidating "Skull and Crossbones" soccer club assembles in Houston for
the much-anticipated Sting Cup. (I'm second from left, front row.)

With Sting's grandmother, "Gram" Agnes in Florence, Italy (while tightly holding on to my "prized English-language newspaper.")

Massage therapy from the benevolent Sandy Aquila; great hands, greater heart. (Mino looks on from the mirror.)

The graffiti-covered Berlin Wall dwarfs Sandy Aquila. Barbed wire looms over Sting's multi-platinum advice, "If You Love Somebody, Set Them Free."

Backstage with "The Man"... and the chest that stopped the show each night during "Don't Stand So Close."

Shoes off, knees covered, rocking a Chuck Berry T-Shirt and MTV cap at
New Delhi's Jama Masjid mosque.

The sultry Dolette McDonald, wearing her heart everywhere BUT her sleeve.

My Amnesty Tour partner-in-crime, E Street guitarist Nils Lofgren

Dad, Mom, and Delmar backstage at Amnesty's Philadelphia stop

An E Street sandwich. Hanging out backstage with Clarence Clemons and Garry Tallent on Amnesty International's "Human Rights Now!" Tour.

The "gentlemen's" dressing room in Sydney, Australia. I couldn't be prouder to be a part of this team (with Kenny, Mino, Branford, Delmar, and JT).

Photo-booth shenanigans with the love of my life, Patty Murray.

Europe

April 15 — July 4 (52 shows in 45 cities)

Three months in Europe with Sting sounds incredibly exciting—
and it was. But it was also a long damn time to be away from home.
Hell, some rock tours don't last three months TOTAL, and if they
do, they rarely go three straight months without some kind of mean-
ingful break in the action. Our just-completed North American leg
had essentially been the same daunting length, but that itinerary
had mercifully steered us back through NYC a couple of times. (An
occasional whiff of home works wonders in the attitude adjustment
department.) But those days were over. Thanks to a little obstacle
known as the Atlantic Ocean, we'd be truly OUT on the road.

I didn't see it coming, but Europe would kick my ass, and, in
the process, teach me the true definition of homesick. Even on
a high-level tour like Sting's, your job sometimes becomes just
that: a job. You're only human, which means—despite being surrounded by luxury and glamour—you're still susceptible to those
pesky laws of human nature. Fatigue, boredom, and loneliness
eventually came calling, and they didn't give a damn about my
substantial salary or the high thread count on my king-size bed.
But I'm getting ahead of myself. Bring on Europe.

Hot off the press came another one of Billy's tour itineraries, complete with scathing commentary. Billy went for the jugular once again, sparing no one. My previous labels of "Rocky" and "womanizer" were yesterday's news, eclipsed by my infamous San Francisco sexcapade. (I told you it was extreme.) The tour personnel page included the following:

> *Jeff Campbell—We will always remember San Francisco, will we not?*

Thanks to our ruthless editor-in-chief, my lewd night by the Bay was now a part of public record. A printed reminder would follow me (and our forty-person entourage) around Europe for the next three months, providing everyone with a handy, reusable punch line.

Meanwhile, on a less humorous note—at least in my opinion—crewmember Ed had the following comment listed beside his name (emphasis mine):

> *"A man of hidden talents, a surprise on the soccer field,* and in his words, a far better musician than a certain band member *(now that would be telling)."*

Billy Francis strikes again. Billy was a pal, but he was also an incorrigible agitator. He loved stirring things up for his personal amusement. Although it was never confirmed by anyone, I had to believe Ed's insult was directed at me. The cheap shot stung, but I can't say I was surprised. If my supporters viewed me as an underdog, it didn't take a genius to figure out how my critics felt.

But what was I supposed to do? Challenge Ed to a duel? Strato-casters at sunrise? No thanks, I took the high road and ignored the remark.

Later in the tour, I mentioned the disparaging "blind item" to our bassist, Tracy. Revealingly, Tracy told me she'd assumed Ed was talking about HER. Isn't that sad? Despite being in one of the best bands on the planet, Tracy and I both worried we weren't as proficient as one of our roadies. Peel back the muso swagger and you'll find insecurity festering just beneath the surface. All aboard the Tortured Artist Express.

Amsterdam, Holland | Statenhal | April 16, 17

I found myself chatting with the hotel bartender after we ar-rived in Amsterdam. (Shocking, I know.) Trying to get a feel for my new surroundings, I inquired about the legal drinking age in Holland. The barkeep gave me a puzzled look. "Age? What do you mean? If someone wants a drink, they have a drink." *Hey Mom and Dad, come on down to Happy Hour. Kids under 12 drink free!* This was my first clue that life in the Dutch capital might be a little unconventional by my buttoned-down American stan-dards.

I soon discovered why booze was considered passé in Am-sterdam: weed was king. The city featured hundreds of "cannabis coffee shops"—local establishments that offered food, drink, and perfectly legal marijuana. Virginia may be for lovers, but Amster-dam is definitely for stoners. However, unlike some of my travel companions, this perk meant nothing to me. A devout non-smoker, I never perfected the art of inhaling. I hated to smoke, LOVED to drink. My hard-partying NYC wingman, Richie Douglas, constantly needled me about my lopsided vices. "Jeff, you have the lungs of [teenage Olympic gymnast] Mary Lou Retton…and the liver of Jason Robards."

But Amsterdam's most provocative feature was its wide-open sex industry. Concentrated in an area known as *De Wallen* (the red-light district), S-E-X was B-I-G business. My prurient curiosity easily outweighed any traces of trepidation, so I hiked over to the Adults Only neighborhood one evening for a firsthand look. I'd braced myself for a seedy vibe à la 70's Times Square, but instead found a non-threatening, almost touristy atmosphere. The well-lit area felt downright welcoming as it bustled with randy sightseers from around the globe.

As I strolled the sidewalks, I was astounded to see prostitutes perched in storefronts. Like human merchandise on display, the girls gave a whole new meaning to the term "window shopping." Store after store flaunted a negligee-clad employee-of-the-week—and each one had the same vacant, thousand-mile stare. Despite repeated attempts, I was never able to establish eye contact with any of the working girls. The lights were on, but no one was home. It was a different story, however, when I revisited the area to take a few photos on a quiet (profitless) Sunday morning. The formerly aloof ladies were all smiles. A couple of go-getters even came out on the street, calling to me, "Hey, Mister! Come back, Mister." No thanks, not my style. Not yet, anyway.

Along with its surplus of brothels, the red-light district also featured a number of nightclubs advertising "Live Sex Shows."

A few of us curious types decided we should investigate these claims—for purely educational purposes, of course. We roamed around *De Wallen* one evening, weighing our sleazy options until we stumbled upon a neon sign boasting: "Real Fucky Fucky!" Gentlemen, we have a winner.

Magnifying the impropriety of our outing, we'd dragged the newest member of our entourage, Ms. Sandy Aquila, along. Sandy, a licensed massage therapist from Nebraska, had been brought on board to help maintain the health and welfare of our Golden Goose. Sting's fitness regimen included a daily massage, and though he'd relied on local professionals for the US tour, he was wary of risking potluck as we navigated Europe. Deciding to hire a full-time "bodyworker" for the European run, Sting recalled an excellent pre-show massage in Omaha, and tapped Sandy for the gig. One little phone call and—BOOM—Sandy's suddenly traveling the world with a huge rock star. I could relate.

Sandy struck me as a sweet, well-adjusted person, so I was surprised she agreed to tag along on our X-rated field trip. But hanging tough with the boys proved to be a savvy move. Sandy's audacity endeared her to the gang, and demonstrated she was up to the challenge of our nomadic cuckoo's nest.

We each paid a forty-dollar cover charge at the box office— and then were mysteriously escorted to a secondary location down the street. (Are we sure this is legal?) We entered a small nightclub and, exhibiting our only good judgment of the evening, chose to sit in the back of the room…a nice, *healthy* distance away from the action. The show quickly lived down to my expectations as a foul-mouthed emcee kicked things off with a monologue filled with raunchy double entendres. Next, two naked—

and clearly undernourished—women drifted out onto the stage and climbed aboard a rickety bed. The bony ladies began writhing around, pantomiming sapphic passion through their suppressed yawns. Things went from bad to worse when some guy dressed in a gorilla suit—sporting a comically large prosthetic "member"—joined the girls to create a bewildering *ménage à Kong*. Last, and definitely least, the show moved on to the audience-participation portion of the evening. We cried "Uncle" and scurried to the exit when some old dude in a trucker's hat made his way up to the stage and began orally sampling the goods. I'd gladly pay another forty dollars to un-see that hour of my life.

After a couple of shows in Amsterdam, we were off to my favorite place on Earth: Italy. I'd fallen in love with the country on my initial visit with Bushrock, and couldn't wait to return—especially with my new-and-improved professional status. Best of all, we were scheduled to perform in eleven different cities across *Italia*.

Milan, Italy | Arena Civica | April 20, 21

Well, that didn't take long. With only one European city checked off our list (and forty-four still to go), we ran into a little problem at Milan's airport. As we made our way through the terminal, Delmar was accosted by an overzealous fan—in the form of a drug-sniffing German Shepherd. Delmar apparently spent his final night in Amsterdam at one of the cannabis cafés, and the herbal scent had followed him all the way to Italy. The moment Rin Tin Tin caught wind of Delmar, things got personal. The nosy canine fell in line behind our procession and buried his well-trained snout deep in Delmar's rear end. Thanks to man's *worst* friend, Delmar was swiftly fingered by customs agents and escorted away.

I was scared straight as a teen by the drug-smuggling film, *Midnight Express*, so I feared Sting's nine-piece orchestra had just been downsized to an octet. My guess was, best-case scenario, Delmar would be denied entry into Italy and sent packing to America (or the next country on our itinerary). Worst-case scenario? Delmar's aromatic ass was going to jail. But after a thorough body search, the agents found no contraband. Despite smelling guilty, Delmar was released. No bud, no foul. Our silver-tongued manager, Kim Turner, was able to mollify authorities with his dynamic personality—and a stack of complimentary concert tickets. With Delmar back in the fold, we were ready to conquer Italy.

Cava Del Tirreni, Italy | Stadio Lamberti | April 23

We knocked out two shows in Milan and then flew south to Naples. As always, once we landed, we were eager to get to our hotel—immediately, if not sooner. The last thing a band ever wants after a long (or short) flight is a lengthy drive. But lengthy is what we got. The troops started getting restless after twenty minutes or so, and, right on cue, began whining, "How much farther?" The local concert promoter urged us to be patient. He was in charge of our accommodations, and assured us we'd be very pleased with our final destination. The bus ride wound up being over an hour long—an eternity in the world of touring. But the promoter was right. The trek was worth every minute.

When we finally reached our journey's end, it was clear why the trip took so damn long. We'd driven all the way to Heaven, or as it's locally known: Amalfi. Our hotel, The Santa Caterina, was built into the side of a cliff overlooking the Mediterranean Sea. After checking into my room, I stepped out onto my private balcony and was met with the most breathtaking view I'd ever seen. The Mediterranean was stunning; deep blue water, dotted with small sailboats and large rock formations jutting from the surface, all beautifully framed by a rugged shoreline that stretched to the horizon.

We set out for work the next afternoon and promptly encountered a traffic jam worthy of any big city. The region's quiet, simple charm became a double-edged sword as its narrow roads choked on the glut of tourist-filled vehicles. Due to the overflow of cars and buses, traffic ground to a complete stop. (Apparently two tour buses met on a hairpin turn and were unable to negotiate their way around each other.) The tie-up was so severe, people began climbing out of their cars and pleading with drivers to back up in hopes of easing the bottleneck. Unfortunately, as we sat in the snarl, our cover was blown.

An eagle-eyed pedestrian noticed our bus contained a certain British rock star, and word quickly spread through the village. In no time flat, our bus was surrounded by excited youngsters, banging on the windows as they shouted Sting's name. Trapped by fame, and an outdated roadway, Sting resorted to hiding on the floor between the seats. Glamorous indeed. Traffic eventually started inching forward, and we finally made it to the venue—albeit WAY behind schedule. I'm not sure anybody noticed. Running late seemed to be a way of life in Italy.

After two glorious days of gazing at the Mediterranean, duty called. Saying goodbye to Amalfi was tough; I didn't want to leave—ever. We departed paradise, motoring along a winding, two-lane highway cut through the hills of Campania. The pastoral setting seemed untouched by modern times. In fact, our bus driver had to stop on a couple of occasions to yield right-of-way to goat herds crossing the road.

We continued by bus to our next port-of-call, enjoying one of those rare travel days that didn't include any airports. I sat back and savored the Italian countryside, perfectly happy to avoid the stress of flying. We drove for several hours, completely crossing the "boot" of Italy—west coast to east coast—to the city of San Benedetto del Tronto. We were scheduled to play an outdoor stadium that night, but, by the time we arrived, weather conditions were horrendous—and ultimately insurmountable. Torrential rains forced the cancellation of our show. I felt bad for the fans, but after chalking up sixty-some concerts since the beginning of the tour, the band's reaction was akin to that of a snow day in grade school. A night off? Awesome! Meanwhile, my immersive geography lesson continued full throttle: wake up on the Mediterranean, go to sleep on the Adriatic. As advertised, the Sting gig was expanding my horizons—literally.

San Benedetto del Tronto, Italy | Stadio Ballerina | April 24 (rainout)
Bari, Italy | Stadio della Vittoria | April 25

Rome, Italy | Stadio Flaminio | April 27

Rome is a truly incredible place, filled with wonder…or so I've heard. Alas, my visit to The Eternal City represents a microcosm of my larger regrets about the Sting tour. Unfortunately, I chose to ignore the classic advice, "When in Rome, do as the Romans do," and instead went with the shamefully apathetic approach, "When in Rome, do jack shit." Despite being in one of the world's most interesting cities, I barely left the hotel. Sadly, I was corroding into an exhausted, jaded traveler with a fading sense of adventure. My daily activities usually fell into the primitive routine of eat/drink/sleep (with a bit of tennis thrown in). I did venture off the hotel grounds one night, tagging along with Branford and a couple of leggy Italian models to some trendy *ristorante*, but God forbid I do anything touristy or educational. And it's not like I didn't have my chances. Sandy (Sting's massage therapist) invited me to join her on a day trip to the Vatican, but I passed. Why? The excursion would require an early morning start. Sistine Chapel? St. Peter's Basilica? Michelangelo? No thanks, I'm gonna sleep in. What a loser.

Sandy was the smart one of the bunch. She explored each stop with gusto, her trusty camera always at her side. Meanwhile, I maybe shot two rolls of film total over the course of the entire year. (Rolls? Film? Yep, no digital cameras back in '88.) Sandy grasped the bigger picture. Instead of treating the tour like work, she recognized the gig for what it was: an all-expense paid, three-month trip around Europe—WITH salary. I could kick myself for taking so much for granted. I just assumed Sting's tour was my first in a long line of musically subsidized trips around the world. But guess what? I've yet to return to Rome. Years after the tour, I got a big dose of reality when my wife and I traveled to London, and Sting wasn't around to pick up the hefty tab...nor hand me a fat paycheck at the end of the week.

Florence, Italy | Stadio Comunale | April 29

It wasn't uncommon to have VIPs at our shows, but we had an extremely special guest in the house in Florence: Sting's grand-mother. Withstanding our high-decibel assault, "Gram" Agnes stuck around for the entire show and hung out with the band afterward. When I asked if she enjoyed the concert, she smiled and replied enthusiastically, "I loved it!" One of my most treasured photos from the entire tour features Sting's lovely grandmother and me, standing arm-in-arm in front of our hotel in Florence. And for the record, she called him Sting, too.

Modena, Italy | Stadio Braglia | April 30
Udine, Italy | Stadio Friuli | May 1
Torino, Italy | Stadio Comunale | May 3
Genova, Italy | Palasport Fiera Di Genova | May 4

Verona, Italy | *Arena di Verona* | May 6, 7

We wrapped up our run of Italy in Verona, playing two nights at the city's historic outdoor arena. Almost two thousand years old, the former gladiator venue stood right in the middle of Verona, co-existing peacefully with the city's modern commercial district. It was wild to wander out of a Roman Empire amphitheater and straight into a United Colors of Benetton clothing store. The ancient arena provided the perfect setting for our Italian swan song. Underscoring Sting's massive appeal in Italy, our final concert was broadcast live to the nation on public television.

Make no mistake, I adore Italy. But after three full weeks in-country, I was ready for a change of pace. The culture's chronic laid-back attitude eventually got under my Type-A skin. If you need something done in Italy, you're often met with a cheerful "*Domani*" (tomorrow) and offered another glass of vino. With that mindset, it's not surprising many of our gigs started much later than scheduled. In the most glaring example of Italian slackness, one of our alleged 8pm shows didn't get underway until almost midnight. And I guess we were lucky the concert happened at all. The original indoor site had to be scrapped at the last minute after the promoter failed to get the necessary permits. Losing his Plan A, the organizer was forced to hastily improvise a new location. When we finally took the stage that night, we found ourselves in the middle of a huge, parking lot—with stacks of metal shipping containers substituting for venue walls. But at least somebody benefited from the impressive ineptitude. Lucky residents in nearby high-rise apartments were treated to a free, unannounced Sting show from the comfort of their terraces.

With Austria and Germany up next, I looked forward to a more efficient and organized way of life. Well, I got what I wished for…and there's a damn good reason why *they* tell you to wish carefully. After a couple days of the stern Germanic vibe—and a few plates of schnitzel—I yearned for my erratic, but passionate ex-lover. Yes, Italy, I'm talking about you. Please forgive me.

Vienna, Austria | Stadthalle | May 9
Munich, Germany | Olympiahalle | May 11, 12

Montreux, Switzerland | MTV Europe taping | May 13

Our cherished day off was gobbled up by a last-minute trip to Switzerland. MTV Europe invited Sting to perform at their multi-artist Montreux festival and, back in the 80's, when MTV said, "Jump"…it was all aboard for Switzerland. The appearance was a straightforward TV taping, so it wasn't necessary to mobilize our entire entourage. MTV crunched the numbers and decided to charter a small plane for our skeletal staff.

Sprinkling a touch of irrational fear on top of my perfectly rational fear of flying, we flew down to Montreux on Friday the 13th. And if that wasn't bad enough, our cozy little airplane carried a grand total of thirteen souls. Double jinx! I gazed out of my cramped window at the jagged, snow-covered Alps below and contemplated, "If the plane crashes in this terrain, who should we eat first?" Fortunately, we reached our destination safely, and I survived my bout with *friggatriskaidekaphobia*. (It's a word, honest.) On a positive note, the trip cured me once and for all of any silly Friday the 13th superstitions. The jury is still out on black cats and ladders.

Switzerland was gorgeous, but the Montreux experience was an artistic bust. Our dubious mission was to videotape lip-synced performances for a few of Sting's new tunes. No LIVE music involved. The lone bright spot of the afternoon was reuniting with Ziggy Marley to mime "One World (Not Three)." But for a band of top-notch musicians (plus me), jetting to another country on your day off to fake your way through a TV show seemed like a joke. And that's exactly how we—OK, *some* of us—treated it.

Predictably, the mock concert bred apathy among the troops. And the generous supply of alcohol in our dressing room only served to fuel our fire—or more accurately, our lack of it. With the musical stakes at an all-time low, the usual suspects got liquored up and clowned their way through the show. (Yes, that would include me.) During one song, a highly animated Mino accidentally knocked over his congas. The tipsy kindergarteners among us burst out laughing as Mino's drums rolled across the stage. The TV crew had to stop tape, wipe up the spilled congas and reset for another take. Despite our immature behavior, Sting stayed calm. Was he vicariously enjoying our punk rock antics? Doubtful. The father of four (now six) was more likely employing child psychology—and a ton of patience. The brats in the band were lucky Sting was usually willing to spare the rod. Thanks, Dad.

Frankfurt, Germany | Festhalle | May 14, 15

In the simplest of terms, the concert promoter makes it all happen. The promoter books the act, secures the venue, advertises the concert, and then, with any luck, makes a little profit on the back end. Another less official, but vital, part of the promoter's job is keeping the band happy. Pampered artists often translate into repeat business on subsequent tours. Accordingly, promoters have been known to lavish musicians with free swag (clothing, caps, bags, etc.), fine dining, and other assorted—and sometimes sordid—entertainment.

Our German promoter went the extra mile in Frankfurt and provided me with a post-gig companion—*all expenses paid*. I was standing in the wings just before showtime, when one of the local honchos pulled me aside, pointed to a group of dolled-up women seated near the stage and told me with a sly smile, "You'll be seeing them again later."

Post-concert, my night of adventure began. Asking no questions, I climbed into the backseat of a Mercedes sedan and was whisked away to an undisclosed location. I had no idea what to expect, so I was a bit surprised when we pulled into the driveway of an upscale house nestled in a residential neighborhood. Walking through the front door, I encountered a bevy of young ladies sipping champagne while music played in the background. The vibe felt like a typical small party, but this wasn't a typical small party at all; this was a business transaction. I grabbed a drink and started mingling, quickly zeroing in on a cute, friendly face. The usual small talk was made, nothing out of the ordinary, just two strangers engaging in the time-honored tradition of flirting. Except, in this instance, there was no mystery as to how my blind date would ultimately play out. We clocked the requisite amount of chitchat, and then my new friend suggested we slip away for a little privacy. But before our rendezvous commenced, I was directed downstairs to a fully appointed locker room (similar to what you might find at a pricey health club). I showered, placed my belongings in a locker, wrapped myself in a towel and headed back upstairs.

After spending some horizontal time with my rent-a-date, I made my way back to the locker room. I took another shower, got dressed, and rejoined the party. Tired, drunk, and bored, I started fishing around for a ride back to the hotel. My earlier driver was long gone, so our hostess volunteered to give me a lift. I bid goodnight to the still-swinging party and wilted into the passenger seat of the madam's late model BMW. The boss lady was a full-figured, mature woman, considerably older than the *sorority* sisters (maybe even pushing FORTY—Gasp!), but I actually found her more attractive than her junior employees. Exhausted, but not dead, I made a halfhearted attempt to hit on my sexy chauffeur. She demurred politely, saying she was flattered, but she'd been "retired" for years.

Despite indulging in an evening of classic male fantasy, I found the experience to be pretty hollow overall. But I guess "meaningless" is the whole point. At the risk of jeopardizing my membership in *Club Macho*, one-night stands have never been my style—or in this case, a one-hour stand. Call me a prude (or a hopeless romantic), but I prefer getting to know a person before wading into such vulnerable, buck-naked waters. Maybe I'm shy, or inhibited, or just plain choosy, but I've never warmed to the concept of sex with strangers. It's advertised as casual—but awkward seems a more accurate description.

Stuttgart, Germany | Schleyer-Halle | May 17, 18

My favorite kind of travel day: NO airports. Our next stop, Stuttgart, was only a two-hour drive from Frankfurt, so instead of hurtling through the skies at 600 mph, I was looking forward to a low-stress commute in a big, comfy bus. But that all changed, courtesy of "Hot Rod" Marsalis.

Branford wanted to experience the legendary *Autobahn* firsthand, so he decided to rent a car and tackle the drive himself. Branford secured a BMW convertible for the trip and invited me to tag along as co-pilot. Some one-on-one windshield time with Branford sounded like fun, so I said yes. But when word spread Bran was driving, Delmar and Mino wanted in on the action, too. Why take a frumpy bus when you can zip through the German countryside in a sleek sports car? Safety Schmafety... to the Batmobile!

The four of us set out for Stuttgart with the top down, but a light rain started to fall almost immediately. We pulled over, put the top up (which definitely lowered the sexiness factor) and then it was back to the races—literally. Despite my uneasiness with flying, I'm well aware driving is a much more dangerous proposition, statistically speaking anyway. And why wouldn't it be? The roads are filled with lead-footed, tailgating bullies carelessly wielding two tons of steel. What could possibly go wrong?

Instead of dozing on a spacious, fortified bus, I wound up crammed into a two-door coupe, white-knuckling it down a rain-slicked highway at 100 mph. And while I considered that to be a pretty significant clip, we were constantly being passed by other drivers. A car would appear on our tail out of nowhere, flash its headlights (apparently the international signal for "get the hell out of my way") and then blow by us like we were standing still. I was totally frazzled by the time we got to Stuttgart. So much for my relaxing day of ground travel.

Zurich, Switzerland | Hallenstadion | May 19, 20
Toulouse, France | Palais des Sports | May 22

Frejus, France | Les Arènes | May 23

After two shows in Zurich, we were off to the South of France. We played in Toulouse, and then, following in the footsteps of other iconic *rockers* like Julius Caesar and Napoleon, we invaded the historic town of Fréjus. Hello French Riviera.

Thanks to savvy scheduling, our concert in Fréjus placed Sting only twenty-five miles from the city of Cannes—which was in the midst of its annual International Film Festival. And since Sting's latest flick, *Stormy Monday* was being screened at the illustrious event, we were all treated to forty-eight hours of elegance à la Cannes. (Perk #279 of working with Sting.) Plenty of artists have no qualms about staying in a luxury hotel while their band languishes at some budget fleabag on the outskirts of town, but lucky for us, Sting didn't roll that way. Instead, the entire band checked into Cannes' posh Hotel Majestic, right alongside our rock-star—and moonlighting movie-star—boss. Whether I was sunning poolside with *la belle élite* or admiring the fleet of private yachts moored along the *Promenade de la Croisette*, one simple thought kept running through my mind: I was a long damn way from Carrboro Elementary School.

My upper-floor hotel room was located directly across the street from the *Palais des Festivals*, affording me a bird's-eye view of the festival's comings and goings. During the closing night ceremonies, I kicked back by my window and ogled the parade of tuxedoes and gowns strolling the red carpet. Tour memories like Cannes always stir up confused feelings of "Did that really happen…or was it just a dream?"

Adding to my overall sense of Riviera wow, our concert in Fréjus was held at an ancient amphitheater that dated back to the first century. Just like in Verona, I found myself rocking a venue that had been serving up entertainment since the early days of the Roman Empire. I stared out into the crowd during our show and struggled to wrap my head around the arena's crazy evolution from gladiators to Stratocasters.

Barcelona, Spain | Plaza de Toros Monumental | May 25

We kicked off Spain with indigenous flair, performing at Barcelona's *Plaza Monumental,* a 75-year-old bullring in the center of the city. (The venue had a rich history of bullfights and concerts, including a 1965 appearance by four lads from Liverpool.) I'd played some interesting joints over the years, but this was my first tango with a *plaza de toros.* The arena's vertical grandstand and compact footprint made it feel like you were inside of a giant bucket—with a dirt floor. Consequently, the audience seemed like it was right on top of us when we took to the dusty stage. After being indoctrinated by the sprawling *football* stadiums of South America, it was strange to be playing outdoors, yet to such an up-close and intimate crowd. On the plus side for humanity, it was reassuring to know the game of soccer commanded a substantially larger fan-base than the thinly veiled animal torture known as bullfighting.

Our bullring performance was indeed unique, but Barcelona had cemented its place in Sting folklore long before downbeat. After soundcheck, the band meandered through the usual backstage maze in search of catering. ("Hello Cleveland!") We followed the posted arrows—and our noses—until we eventually stumbled upon the makeshift mess hall. Typically, our pre-show meal was dished out in some cinderblock hallway located in the bowels of the venue, but our Barcelona supper was served on an open-air concourse, with our picnic tables overlooking the bullpen. And remember, we weren't at a baseball stadium. Living, breathing, snorting bulls stood in a corral just beneath our dinner spread.

As we admired the powerful animals, Mino decided he wanted a photo with the bulls—and I mean WITH the bulls. Mino enlisted Tracy as photographer, before brazenly climbing over the railing and down into the pen. Part matador, part rodeo clown, our fearless percussionist crept toward the animals, trying to get close enough for a memorable—but hopefully not *in memoriam*—photo. As Tracy waited for the perfect framing, Mino began to appreciate the danger of his foolhardy mission. Eyes widening, Mino started softly urging Tracy, "Hurry up. Take the damn picture." Tracy obliged and Mino scurried back up to safety. The daredevil got his souvenir shot; the band got dinner AND a show. Olé!

Valencia, Spain | Estadio Levante | May 27

Sting was sick. Reminiscent of our Miami stand in January (which seemed like two lifetimes ago), Sting's pipes were shredded. Being a trouper, our leader was determined to soldier on, but I learned that decision didn't rest entirely with Sting. Turns out, Lloyd also had a say in the matter...as in Lloyd's of London, underwriters of Sting's world tour.

Stating the obvious, rock 'n' roll at the Sting level is BIG business. Accordingly, major tours carry insurance policies to protect against financial loss due to injury, interruption, or cancellation. So, as the band cooled its heels in the Mediterranean, Lloyd's of London dispatched a doctor to assess the state of Sting. After a checkup, the verdict was in: stop singing—or else. I was told if Sting ignored doctor's orders, he ran the risk of having his tour insurance cancelled. Clichés be damned, the show *mustn't* go on. Of course we were sympathetic to Sting's health problems, but no one was complaining about a little time off on Spain's gorgeous eastern seaboard. Alas, our mini-vacation was cut short when the iron man returned after missing just one concert. We snapped to attention and cranked out a couple more shows in Spain before heading back to France.

Madrid, Spain | Auditorio de la Casa | May 28
Zaragoza, Spain | Romareda Stadium | May 29
Bordeaux, France | Patinoire | May 31
Montpelier, France | Zenith | June 1
Grenoble, France | Palais des Sports | June 2

The French may have a reputation for sophisticated elegance, but their domestic airline sucked. After being spoiled by our private plane in the US, France's Air Inter was a rude awakening. Incredibly, the flights offered NO reserved seating; first come, first served. This guaranteed all hell broke loose each time "now boarding" was announced. The chaotic free-for-all provided a perfect illustration of man's inhumanity to man. I'm confident *Titanic* passengers displayed more decorum as they climbed into the lifeboats. Meanwhile, it was a sight to see Sting join in the fray, throwing elbows like the rest of us as he jockeyed for a desirable seat on the plane. I know we are all God's children, but watching the King of Pain tangle with the unwashed masses (present company included) just didn't seem right. Tossing the tiniest crumb to their customers, Air Inter allowed people traveling with small children to pre-board. That being the case, our battle cry at the gate quickly became, "Somebody loan me a baby!"

Leading up to our three-night run in Paris, Sting informed the band he wanted to record the shows. There was ongoing talk of releasing a "Live in Europe" album; unfortunately, that project never saw the light of day—at least, not officially. But bootleg recordings always seem to leak out into the world. Years after our tour, I was walking down the stairs in my apartment building when I heard a neighbor's stereo blasting "Tempted" by Squeeze. I eavesdropped through the door, thinking, "Wow, Squeeze is rockin'." I lingered in the hallway, enjoying the performance, when it hit me: "Hey wait a minute, that's not Squeeze…that's ME." Sting never released our version of "Tempted," so I had no idea how the guy got his hands on the track. I guess I could have asked but, like a typical New Yorker, I didn't know my neighbor's name.

After learning our Paris concerts might be released commercially, I did what I do best: worry. What if I had an "off" night? I was terrified by the thought of having a bad show preserved for posterity. (I was too naive to realize you were allowed to fix mistakes on live albums. Welcome to the sneaky world of post-production.) Determined not to leave anything to chance, I started secretly honing my big feature, the "Little Wing" guitar solo, note by note.

I hid out in my hotel room, tinkering under the radar as I methodically built the perfect beast. When I felt my creation was finally ready for prime time, I quietly inserted the prefab *improvisation* into our show. I was pleased with the results, but a certain co-worker smelled—or more accurately HEARD—a rat. After a couple of concerts, Branford recognized I was repeating myself and proceeded to call me on it...without saying a word. Branford let his horn do the talking by incorporating *my* themes into *his* "Little Wing" solo. When I noticed my guitar licks coming out of Branford's saxophone, I glanced over at him. He was staring back at me with his classic smirk, while quoting lines from MY solo—intertwined with SPONTANEOUS bursts of Marsalis genius. Message received; lesson learned. First, never attempt to sneak anything by Branford's ears. Second, do not play scared. So what if you fall on your face? Our band's musical style was built on taking risks and trying to have a little fun along the way. Kenny's explicit pre-show mantra summed it up perfectly: "Take your dick out!"

Paris, France | Palais Omnisports de Paris-Bercy | June 4, 5, 6

My return to Paris stood in stark contrast to my initial visit with Bushrock less than a year earlier. This time around, instead of *tripling* up in a cramped room at a cheap hostel (with a communal bathroom down the hall), I checked into the exquisite Royal Monceau hotel. The Monceau is, without a doubt, the most luxurious place I've ever laid my head. In fact, the hotel was so plush (read: pricey), Sting's accountant vetoed staying there on our subsequent trips to Paris. But like the poet says, "'Tis better to have loved and lost..."

* * *

There's no way I could've ever achieved my crazy dream of becoming a professional musician without my parents' unwavering faith in me. My dad, Jim, helped me buy my first electric guitar—and shaped my work ethic in the process—by matching my lawn-mowing proceeds dollar-for-dollar. *Earning* that Fender Mustang made it all the sweeter. Meanwhile, my mom, Nancy, dutifully served as my chauffeur AND roadie. She not only delivered me to my lessons/rehearsals/gigs, she also helped hoist my unwieldy Twin Reverb amplifier in and out of her car on countless occasions. I sure as hell couldn't lift that monster by myself at the tender age of thirteen…and that might still be true today.

Attempting to honor a lifetime of support and sacrifice in some small way, I treated my parents to a Parisian getaway with *Cirque du Sting*. Our European family reunion required a bit of strategic planning (and some cold, hard cash), but it was well worth the effort. Sharing the glamorous combination of Sting AND Paris with my folks remains one of my most treasured memories of the tour.

The band lit up when I surfaced at our lobby call with my parents in tow. Jim and Nancy's familiar faces were a welcome sight for the troops' homesick eyes. Smiles and hugs flowed as we filtered out of the hotel and climbed onto the bus. Shortly after settling into our seats, a visibly upset Sting stormed aboard spouting a string of obscenities—completely unaware of any *civilian* presence. I felt bad about putting Sting in a potentially awkward situation and delicately pointed out my folks tucked in the back of the bus as soon as he came up for air. I was afraid I might have stoked Sting's anger even further, so I was relieved when he abruptly changed gears. Sting morphed into the quintessential host, welcoming my parents to Paris while apologizing for his colorful language. A true gentleman, and a respectful son, in action.

Arriving at the venue, I watched with joy as Sting and my father walked down the loading dock side-by-side, laughing and chatting like old pals. That image will never fade. Our ordinarily salty crew rolled out the *rouge* carpet for Mom and Dad, giving them a behind-the-scenes look at how the magic was made. Come showtime, instead of putting my folks out in the audience, I persuaded them to watch from the wings. The exclusive vantage point provided my parents an up-close-and-personal perspective to the loud and sweaty action.

Meanwhile, I wasn't the only one who'd successfully coaxed family members to Paris. (The City of Light isn't exactly a hard sell.) Sting's partner, Trudie, and their two young children, Mickey and Jake, were also on hand. At one point during the show, I glanced over to see my mom perched on a road case, smiling broadly as she held little Jake in her lap. (Jake's birth was the climatic ending of Sting's documentary, *Bring on The Night*.) Sting and Trudie's hospitality made my parents feel like a part of the family. It meant the world to them—and me.

With the folks in town, I needed some inspired sightseeing advice. No problem, I went straight to our resident Francophile, Mino. He didn't give my query a second thought, enthusiastically recommending the bohemian district of Montmartre. Armed with our insider tip, the Campbell clan hit the streets, destination Sacré-Cœur. We exited the hotel and noticed a commotion heading in our direction. The advancing sidewalk cyclone turned out to be The Family Sting, surrounded by a swarm of paparazzi. Sting and Trudie's faces were etched with resignation as they pushed through the photo mob while lugging their two crying toddlers. The scene provided a sobering look at the price of fame. When I mentioned the incident to Sting later, he shrugged and acknowledged it came with the territory. But Sting did confess to teaching his young son a trick for dealing with obnoxious photographers. If any of the cameramen became too pushy, three-year old Jake had Dad's green light to let fly with an emphatic, "Fuck off!"

Mino's suggestion was spot on. Montmartre was the perfect call. Located on a hill overlooking the city, the charming neighborhood (and one-time home to Picasso, Renoir, and Matisse) was filled with quaint cafes and sidewalk artists. We stopped in a restaurant for lunch, and were fortunate to snag a window table with a magnificent view of the Parisian skyline. After finishing our meal, I politely signaled our waiter for the check. He nodded, and then proceeded to ignore us completely. The French are notorious for their surly attitude toward tourists (especially us "ugly Americans"), but the wait eventually became ridiculous.

After repeated requests for the check, I finally gave up and told my parents we were leaving. I assumed once we rose from the table, we'd receive our bill *tout de suite*. We stood and started for the exit. Nothing happened; it was like we were invisible. We strolled right out of the bistro without ever raising a single eyebrow. Who says there's no such thing as a free lunch? My parents and I had one in Paris. Hounded by her guilty conscience, my mother spent the rest of the afternoon nervously looking over her shoulder, certain we'd be arrested by a local *gendarme*.

* * *

As we were putting the final touches on our second sold-out night at Bercy, tennis ace Mats Wilander was across town putting the final touches on his third French Open title—and setting the stage for yet another *glamtastic* footnote in my global fairytale. The celebrity worlds of music and sports collided later that evening as Team Sting and the newly crowned tennis champ partied aboard a boat moored on the River Seine. How the hell did I end up on a private yacht in Paris, sharing a crowded dance floor with Sting, Mats Wilander…and my mother? My childhood imagination had proven to be no match for reality. I'd exceeded my wildest dreams—exponentially.

The next day, Sting (frustrated tennis star that he was), told me he'd struck a late-night, champagne-fueled deal with Wilander (frustrated rock star that he was). Coveting each other's glory, the two champions agreed to swap some surplus hardware: a Grammy for a French Open trophy. Chalk up another life lesson. The "grass is greener" syndrome extends to ALL income strata. People with the most fantastic lives in the world still have their fantasies.

Offenburg, Germany | Oberrheinhalle | June 8
Dortmund, Germany | Westfalenhallen | June 9

Bidding adieu to Paris—and my homeward bound parents—the tour caromed from the romance of France to the rigidity of Germany. We knocked out scheduled shows in Offenburg and Dortmund, before making a last-minute detour to London. Our itinerary had originally promised a day off in Berlin, but that precious downtime had been sacrificed for the greater good. Instead of lounging around the Iron Curtain, we'd be performing at the Nelson Mandela FreedomFest—an all-day, all-star extravaganza at London's Wembley Stadium. The concert was organized to celebrate Mandela's 70th birthday, while simultaneously raising public awareness about his ongoing political imprisonment (twenty-seven years and counting, at the time).

The high-profile FreedomFest would clearly be an epic event, but with two strenuous months of Europe already under our belts, the band was less than thrilled about heading to London for an extra show—and then rushing back to Germany for a performance that same evening. As our whining reached a crescendo, Sting mockingly urged us to keep our fingers crossed. "Maybe South African authorities will decide to release Mandela before Saturday and the concert will be cancelled."

London, England | Wembley Stadium

+

Berlin, Germany | Waldbühne | June 11

As they say in baseball, "Let's play two!"

In order to honor our 8pm downbeat in Berlin, we had to take the opening slot at *Mandela-palooza*. And even then, we'd have to bolt immediately after our set, completely missing out on a momentous day/night of music. The FreedomFest was broadcast in 67 countries to an estimated audience of 600 million—and featured a veritable Who's Who of Pop. The lineup of performers included mega-artists Whitney Houston, Phil Collins, The Bee Gees, and Stevie Wonder. The backstage hang alone would have been a once-in-a-lifetime experience, but Berlin beckoned. We'd be long gone before the party really got cranking.

Being the first act of the day meant we were the last act to soundcheck. This pragmatic reverse order at multi-artist events leaves the stage preset for the top of the show. When our turn finally came, we dragged our butts out on stage for the quickie midmorning run-through—which felt more like the middle of the night to us rock 'n' roll vampires. As the band sleepwalked through one of Sting's requests, I glanced up to see a human stampede barreling across the massive soccer field. Ready or not, stadium officials had decided it was time to open the gates. (So what if we were still sound checking?) As a result, hundreds of die-hard fans were racing toward us, eager to stake out primo front-row real estate.

I assumed Sting would shut things down when he saw the invaders. Nope. To my groggy dismay, he went in the opposite direction. Instead of waving us off, Sting rewarded the early birds with a command performance; leading his bewildered band through the entire Mandela set (mercifully, only four songs), before winking at the lucky mob. "Now when we come back in an hour, pretend like you're hearing these songs for the first time today…and go crazy!" The bite-sized crowd let out a cheer as we shuffled off the stage—temporarily. Our demanding two-performance/two-country day had just become a three-performance day. One down, two to go, with a flight to Berlin sandwiched in between.

We played our *second* Wembley show around noon, before dashing out of the stadium, airport bound. I felt something beneath my feet as I rode along in the back of the van, and leaned over to discover a cloth bag shoved up under the seat. I took a peek inside and froze. The French Open tennis trophy was staring back at me. Mats Wilander had obviously made good on his end of the swap, I assume Sting held up his part of the bargain as well. Contemplating the years of hard work and dedication required to capture a French Open trophy, I had to chuckle at the current status of the coveted prize: dumped unceremoniously on the floor of a rental van.

Our private plane touched down in Berlin and we headed straight to the *Waldbühne* (The Forest Stage). The amphitheater, constructed for the 1936 Olympics, sat just down the hill from Olympic Stadium—the historic venue where African-American track and field star Jesse Owens captured four gold medals, and infuriated host Adolf Hitler in the process. (So much for that Aryan superiority thing.) Entering the stage door, we were led through an odd, curved tunnel to our dressing rooms. When I asked about the peculiar hallway, a staffer told me it was designed to thwart assassination attempts on Hitler. In theory, the bending corridor would make it difficult to get a straight shot at Der Führer. Wow.

The silhouette of Olympic Stadium loomed over us as we launched into our third show of the day. We rocked the *haus* as usual, but I never shook the creepy feeling I was performing in a space once occupied by one of history's most evil characters. Sharing the stage with Nazi ghosts of the Third Reich was pretty intense.

I finally crashed in my hotel room, and turned on the TV to see Eric Clapton standing in the same spot I'd stood just twelve hours earlier. The Mandela marathon was still going strong. Two concerts (and countries) later, I was in a Berlin bed watching the finale of a London show I'd kicked off that morning. It was quite a memorable day, bookended by two extremes of humanity—Mandela and Hitler.

At the time, Berlin was still divided into East and West by the infamous Berlin Wall. The iconic symbol of Cold War oppression stood only a couple of miles from our hotel, but true to lazy form, I failed to take advantage of a significant sightseeing opportunity yet again. What the hell was I thinking? (That was the problem, I wasn't.) A year later, I threw another log on my fire of road regrets as I watched The Wall come tumbling down on the Nightly News. It haunts me to this day that I couldn't summon a shred of intellectual curiosity in amazing places like Rome or Berlin. I just didn't get it.

Meanwhile, Sandy was out exploring with her usual zeal—and snagged maybe the best photo of the entire tour. The shot features Sandy standing in front of the graffiti-covered Berlin Wall, strategically positioned beneath the large, spray-painted plea, "If You Love Somebody, Set Them Free." Now where had I heard that before?

Hamburg, Germany | Sporthalle | June 12, 13

We continued to cut a rock 'n' roll swath across Europe. It'd been two months since we'd seen the good ol' US of A, and the cracks were beginning to show. Non-smokers had started smoking; non-drinkers had started drinking. Meanwhile, others had gone in the opposite direction and made laudable efforts to clean up their act. I even buckled down at one point and logged ten CON-SECUTIVE days without a single drop of booze. (Trust me, if you knew me back then, you'd be very impressed right now.) As Kenny deadpanned, "Desperate times, desperate measures."

Touring spawns a fascinating social experiment. You're thrown in with a group of random strangers, and required to navigate a high-pressure, emotionally charged situation in unfamiliar (and ever-changing) surroundings. It's challenging, to say the least. We traveled together, we ate together; some of us fought, some of us loved. At times, I felt like I was in the Army, but thank God, I didn't have to deal with live ammo whizzing past my head. Staying sane was proving to be tricky enough—even without the threat of mortal danger. (My fear of flying notwithstanding.)

As my homesickness intensified, I realized my constant scrutiny of the remaining itinerary was beginning to overwhelm me. On paper, three more weeks looked like three more years. Out of desperation, I swore off my long-standing habit of thinking multiple chess moves ahead and vowed to only look at the current day on our schedule. As the saying goes, "When eating an elephant, take one bite at a time."

Despite being an official member of the glamorous life, I still wrestled with recurring bouts of melancholy. And although I knew alcohol was playing a huge role in my despair, I made little, or no, effort to reel things in. It sounds cliché, but being cut off from friends and family made it extremely difficult to stay grounded. There were essentially no rules and no boundaries—but there were plenty of starstruck enablers hanging around to help grease the skids. If you wanted, every night (and/or day) was a party. My dream job had revealed its insidious dark side.

There was one saving grace throughout my downward spiral: my dear friend, Sandy Aquila. While her skilled hands were busy rescuing Sting's muscles from the ravages of the road, her kind heart was preserving what was left of my dwindling sanity. Sandy possessed a peaceful, enlightened energy, and her companionship most likely kept me from a complete meltdown. After eight taxing months of trying to act cool, emotional exhaustion was as big a problem for me as physical exhaustion. Sandy's gentle spirit was an oasis. I could drop the rock-star pretenses around her and simply be my insecure, vulnerable self.

Sandy and I grew closer as we traipsed around "the continent." Meanwhile, the entire entourage was running on empty. Everybody was attempting to survive by whatever means necessary as the European finish line came into view. In Sting's case, he wisely took advantage of our proximity to London and started jetting home on his days off. Unfortunately, Sting would drag Sandy along on these junkets—and inadvertently twist the knife into my gloom.

One afternoon, after a soundcheck somewhere, Sandy gently informed me she and Sting were heading to London post-show. Something inside of me snapped and, lacking any better options (or moral fiber), I embraced the *adult* equivalent of pouting: drinking. I consumed a massive amount of dressing room booze, and was completely sloshed by the time we took the stage. I sulked my way through the whole concert, hiding behind my "leave me the fuck alone" sunglasses like a spoiled brat. Sting picked up on my unsteady (and unprofessional) behavior, but chose not to reprimand me. Although I deserved a swift kick in the ass, Sting charitably cut me some slack. The General seemed to grasp the fragility of his troops at that late juncture.

That said, compassion has its limits. Sting couldn't resist taking a justified potshot at me as he reintroduced the band at the end of the night. "And on guitar, we have MOST of Jeffrey Lee Campbell." Touché. Thanks to Sting for maintaining a sense of humor (and humanity). And extra special thanks to Sandy for helping me get through those dark days so far away from home.

Bremen, Germany | Stadthalle | June 15

Pent-up aggression finally reached critical mass, and an unlucky dressing room paid the price. Ripping a page from the rock-star playbook, we trashed the joint. What started out innocently enough with a few thrown grapes quickly escalated into a full-blown food fight. Snack trays were tossed against the wall, beer was sprayed, tables were overturned, and a tub of ice was dumped on the floor.

It was pure, uncut juvenile delinquency and, I must confess, it felt great. Our cathartic tantrum definitely scratched an itch.

But every action creates a reaction. Sure enough, post-show, our tour accountant "reacted." After the German promoter angrily vowed to bill Team Sting for the damages, The Goon stormed into our dressing room (or what was left of it) and let us have it. The red-faced Goon called us every name in the book while threatening to dock our pay. We just shrugged. "So dock us already." We were past the point of caring. (The Goon followed through on his threat. The next paycheck was a little light.)

If the band's disaffection seems somewhat overblown, it's important to remember there was no Internet in 1988. Let me repeat: NO INTERNET. No real-time global news, no real-time sports scores, no email, no Skype or FaceTime. The telephone was as modern as it got. And thanks to extortionate rates and whacked-out time-zone considerations, international phone calls were few and far between. I was disconnected—physically and spiritually—from all things "home" for the better part of three months. I might as well have been on the moon.

It's hard to imagine now, but, at the time, there was only one way to catch up on *semi*-current events: the humble newspaper. Therefore, *USA Today* or *The International Herald Tribune* became my lifeline. I was like a dog with a bone whenever I got my hands on one of those prized English-language newspapers. Borrow my paper? *"No, my brother, you've got to buy your own."*

There was one thing even more coveted than the printed word: The Armed Forces TV Network. It was rare for our hotels to carry the American-friendly channel, but I felt like I'd hit the lottery when they did. The network, created to entertain US military abroad, was a godsend for this homesick *soldier*. I'd hunker down in my room for hours of sweet—if not bittersweet—Yankee diversion, watching anything and everything. News, talk shows, game shows, cooking shows, soap operas, you name it. The mindless American fare freed me from the lonely shackles of the road and temporarily transported me back to my cozy NYC couch.

In addition to the absence of Internet, there were no laptop computers or iPods/smart phones. This inconvenient truth made traveling with a personal music library quite cumbersome. CDs were just starting to appear on the scene (the mighty mp3 was still only a twinkle in some scientist's eye); so analog cassettes ruled the day. My low-rent, portable stereo system consisted of a Sony Walkman, two battery-powered speakers, a tattered GAP shopping bag full of bulky lo-fi tapes, and a generous supply of AA and C batteries. (Batteries became a hot commodity on long flights. The man with the extra AA's could name his price.)

I'm fully aware this all sounds like Grandpa's "I walked five miles to school in the snow" sermon, but I'm only trying to put things in context. Life on the road is grueling in any era, but if we'd had access to iPods, smartphones, and the Internet, it would've seemed like an episode of *The Jetsons*.

However, there was one considerable upside to touring in the technological Dark Ages. With no cellphone cameras around to document our *sometimes* questionable conduct, and no social media available to impulsively upload compromising photos/videos, we were free to misbehave with impunity. Compared to today's TMZ/Instagram world of 24/7 scrutiny, we lived like JFK in the laissez-faire days of Camelot.

Copenhagen, Denmark | Brøndbyhallen | June 16
Stockholm, Sweden | Isstadion | June 18
Helsinki, Finland | Jaaihalle | June 20
Oslo, Norway | Drammenshallen | June 22

After playing four shows across Scandinavia, we collapsed into the only three-day break of the entire European run. My bandmates took advantage of the extended lull and escaped to London or Paris, treating themselves to a well-deserved getaway—but on their own dime. Meanwhile, exhibiting a rare flash of restraint, I stuck with the itinerary and moved on to our next stop: Frankfurt, Germany. Not the most enchanting of places to spend my long weekend, but at least Sting Inc. was picking up the tab.

As my co-workers were living large, I was holed up at the Frankfurt Holiday Inn, entertaining myself with a three-month pile of tax-deductible receipts. Huh? Yep. For better or worse, I'm one of those guys who is obsessed with crossing things off his to-do list. (I'm the polar opposite of a procrastinator.) In this specific flare-up of my OCD, I'd decided to get a head start on my globally complicated tax returns. After all, April 15 was *only* ten months away.

I'd amassed a sizable collection of crumpled sales slips in varying currencies as our European campaign unfurled. The bulging envelope of receipts in the bottom of my suitcase had started gnawing at me, and something just clicked in Frankfurt. I resolved to decode my foreign itemized deductions, then and there. How hard could it be? (Answer: hard.) This was long before the Euro standard existed, so I was faced with converting lire, francs, pesetas, marks, etc., into the corresponding dollar amounts. It was a damn good thing I had three full days at my disposal, because unlocking the financial Tower of Babel turned out to be a hell of a slog. On the upside, battling unfamiliar currency humbled me for life. Today, I have nothing but patience for confused foreigners as they struggle with American legal tender at my neighborhood Starbucks.

Smoke poured from my calculator in Frankfurt, but I eventually planted a flag atop my mountain of receipts. And along with my sense of accomplishment, my tedious *staycation* yielded an unforeseen bonus: solitude. The break from my beloved bandmates was extremely therapeutic. After seven months of touring, I was learning to appreciate the advantages of flying solo. Isolation equaled self-preservation. The road taught me how to keep myself company, molding me into the contented loner I am today.

St. Goarshausen, Germany | Freilichtbühne Loreley | June 26
Brest, France | Parc de Penfeld | June 28

With a day to kill before returning to Denmark, management shipped us back to Paris. *C'est la guerre.* It wasn't unusual to bump into other bands out on the road, especially in the sexier locales. And with Paris being one of the sexiest locales on the planet, the place was practically a revolving door of rock stars. Our previous visit dovetailed with George Michael's "Faith" Tour; this time around we crossed paths with Michael Jackson's "Bad" Tour. Unfortunately, Michael had just wrapped his two-night stand, so I missed out on seeing The Gloved One perform (with his up-and-coming background singer, Sheryl Crow).

On our afternoon off, Branford invited me to tag along for a power hang with Michael Jackson's musical director/keyboardist, Greg Phillinganes. Greg's brilliant fingerprints were all over my record collection (with artists including Stevie Wonder, Eric Clapton, Chaka Khan, Anita Baker, etc.), so I jumped at the offer.

It was impossible to ignore the elephant in the room as we walked into Greg's suite. A giant road case sat in the middle of the floor, completely devouring any nominal *feng shui*. The rolling boxcar housed an allegedly "portable" recording studio. Greg's mobile setup included a reel-to-reel tape recorder, full-sized keyboard, preamp, mixer, vocal mic, drum machine—plus storage space for his ten-speed bicycle. Considering the footprint of the massive, but painfully limited, studio-on-wheels, it's hard to be too nostalgic for those analog 80's. With today's digital technology, an iPad and a usb microphone would *virtually* blow Greg's travel rig out of the water—except for his racing bike of course. There's not an app for that…yet.

The three of us sat around Greg's room, sharing and comparing tales from the road. Surprisingly, Greg seemed somewhat blasé about his golden gig with The King of Pop. I'd been a huge Michael fan since The Jackson 5 first burst onto the scene, so I was baffled by Greg's indifference. But the devil is in the details. Greg confided that after committing to Michael's tour, he'd been approached by Eric Clapton about joining *his* upcoming world tour. Greg wanted to say yes to Clapton, but he wouldn't—or couldn't—bail on Michael. Wow, talk about luxury problems. And while I empathized with Greg, I can't say I agreed with him. I understand how most players would probably prefer Clapton's musical spontaneity to Jackson's choreographed precision, but faced with the same choice, I'd have to go with my man Michael. I'll burn in Guitar Hell for saying this, but if I had to play a song night after night, I'd choose "Billie Jean" over "Layla." Sorry Eric, I'm a soul man.

Hearing war stories from other touring musicians reinforced just how good we had it on Planet Sting. While many of his rock-star brethren were known to rule with a moody, iron fist, Sting's manner was calm and self-assured. Sting chose inspiration over intimidation, treating his musicians as peers worthy of his respect. Sting's detractors love to bitch about his perceived lack of modesty, but I believe our leader's healthy ego actually made our lives easier. Unlike some of the insecure divas that litter the rock 'n' roll landscape, Sting isn't threatened by sideman virtuosity. To the contrary, he demands it. But Sting can afford to be deferential. NOBODY is going to make that guy look bad, he's too good at what he does. Sting gave our band an incredible amount of leeway to stretch out, experiment, and most importantly, shine. He was generous, and in my opinion, *that* is the true measure of a musician.

People always ask me, "Was Sting a nice guy?" Absolutely. Sting was a very nice guy, especially for being an international superstar. I think it's unrealistic to expect celebrities to be "normal"—their crazy, fishbowl lives are anything but. And the fact they're artists suggests they probably weren't ever normal to begin with. Creative people are a little nutty. (I'm Exhibit A.) Take the inherent wackiness; add heaping helpings of power, big money, and stress...you've got a volatile brew. With my insider's perspective, I quickly recognized the pressures of being Sting. Rock star might sound like an attractive career choice, but I'm here to tell you: showbiz is a meat grinder.

Roskilde, Denmark | Roskilde Festival | June 30

Skipping all over the place by this point, we headed to Denmark for the Roskilde Festival. We landed at Copenhagen Airport, collected our luggage, and walked outside to meet the bus. But there was no bus. Achieving a tour first, we'd beaten our local driver to the designated spot. Restless musicians abhor a vacuum, so Delmar, Mino, and I decided to go back inside the airport for something to drink. We alerted Billy before wandering off; assuring him we'd be right back. Eyebrow raised, Billy warned the bus would be arriving any minute and encouraged us to stay put. We ignored our road manager's sound advice—and stupidly played right into his hand.

One of Billy's favorite tricks was stranding tardy band members. If you were late for an appointed departure time, Billy had no qualms about leaving you high and dry. He loved making transportation your responsibility. Sure enough, by the time we made our way back from the concession stand, Team Sting was in the wind. This created a problem, a REAL problem. We'd missed the bus, but our luggage had not. And our dearly departed bags contained our itineraries, which held a vital piece of information: the name of our hotel. There we stood, marooned at the airport, in need of a ride—but more importantly, in need of a destination.

We'd played Copenhagen only two weeks earlier, and luckily I'd overheard Billy mention we'd be staying at the same place as before. Armed with that tidbit, we hailed a taxi while desperately trying to recall any distinguishing details about our previous hotel. (The road becomes such a blur. Want to play "Stump the Band?" Ask a touring musician where he was yesterday.) We wracked our brains, but the only thing I could come up with was a vague recollection of a fountain in front of the hotel. Thankfully that single clue was enough to crack the case. Our sympathetic cab driver deduced the location and delivered us to the correct doorstep. Entering the lobby, we were greeted by our old pal Billy, smiling from ear to ear as he savored our self-inflicted drama.

* * *

We took the stage at Roskilde and slowly climbed to cruising altitude on "The Lazarus Heart." The band toyed with the bubbly intro as anticipation grew for the guest of honor. When Sting appeared, the crowd erupted. Our leader grabbed his microphone to welcome the adoring masses … and nothing. There was no sound. Assuming the dead mic was just a momentary setback, the band plowed forward. But the stubborn glitch refused to play nice. Sting continued to bark into his mic sporadically, only to be met with the same result: silence. Crouching roadies scrambled back and forth across the stage, frantically trying to rectify the problem as the song rolled onward. Sting jived around in the interim, doing a few dance steps while wailing away on his tambourine. But thanks to the ongoing technical difficulties, the star of the show had been reduced to bystander status. After what seemed like an eternity, Sting's mic finally came to life. Sting belatedly screamed, "Hello Denmark!"—and the crowd re-erupted. Granting ourselves a "mulligan," the band went back to the top of the tune and started over … this time, WITH our lead singer. Longest Lazarus ever.

Sting seemed to take the microphone fiasco in stride, giving his usual killer performance. But as we decompressed in our dressing room post-show, it was impossible to ignore the commotion coming from Sting's inner sanctum next door. Sting launched into an unprecedented tirade. He was out for blood—and apparently lamps and dishes as well. Items crashed against the wall as a livid Sting screamed for the head of the guilty party. Tom-o—good crew captain he was—insisted on shouldering the blame for the audio shipwreck. Tom-o contended if anybody was going to be fired, it should be him. Fortunately, Sting eventually calmed down and nobody lost his job. I assume Tom-o was gambling (and/or praying) his years of dedicated service would shield him from Sting's angry axe. Luckily, Tom-o was right.

Torhout, Belgium | Torhout-Werchter Festival | July 2

We closed out our European tour in Belgium with a unique, two-day, two-city festival near Brussels. Day One of the event was held in Torhout. (Overnight, the whole kit and caboodle would move ninety miles east to the city of Werchter for a second day of rock 'n' roll.) Other acts on the migratory bill included 10,000 Maniacs, INXS, and Bryan Adams.

Hungover as usual, I slumped on a couch in the run-down trailer that was masquerading as our dressing room. I was in desperate need of a nap, but there'd be no snoozing. Our singlewide sanctuary was parked right behind the stage—and its flimsy aluminum walls were proving no match for the festival's thundering

PA system. Like it or not, my pre-show chill-out would include *foreground* music, courtesy of Canadian rocker Bryan Adams. But my blahs slowly lifted as Adams kicked off one catchy hit after another. The playlist included platinum classics like "Cuts like a Knife," "Run to You," "Heaven," "Somebody," and "Summer of '69." The set was impressive, and ultimately irresistible. Adams not only wowed the fans, he wowed me. I'd never really appreciated the scope of Bryan Adams' catalog until that afternoon. No wonder the dude ruled MTV back in the Big 80's.

Werchter, Belgium | Torhout-Werchter Festival | July 3

V-E Day! After playing fifty-one shows across Europe, we were one concert away from going home. I was wandering around the backstage area before the show when I spied Sting huddling with Branford and Kenny. The power trio saw me and waved me over. Kenny took a quick peek over his shoulder and then asked in a hushed tone, "Do you know JT Lewis?" The answer was no. Kenny and Branford proceeded to enlighten me, singing the praises of the Brooklyn drummer. Drummer? Could it be? Was there another execution in the offing? I wouldn't have described our band chemistry as perfect, but I had no idea Sting was mulling a change. Jean Paul had logged six months with the band, but I suddenly got the feeling he wasn't going to see month number seven. Kenny and Branford continued to champion JT until a somber Sting uttered two words: "Call him."

While we were busy toasting the end of our European tour,

tragic news trickled in from the Middle East. Earlier that day, the US military accidentally shot down an Iranian civilian airliner over the Persian Gulf, killing all 290 people on board. The horrific incident shocked the world and stirred fears of retribution against American interests.

Homeward bound: Brussels to NYC | July 4

Brussels Airport was in a state of total chaos when we arrived. Security measures had been ramped up to the highest levels, with airport agents personally interviewing every single traveler. The intense scrutiny was a welcome sight, but it succeeded in creating major delays...and major jitters. I was an anxious flyer on the best of days, so I felt an overwhelming sense of dread as I boarded the plane. I kept telling myself retaliation wouldn't—or couldn't—happen literally overnight. But then again, July 4 seemed like the perfect date to make an anti-American "statement." The good news: we made it home safely. The bad news: retaliation eventually occurred.

Six months later, Pan Am Flight 103 exploded over Lockerbie, Scotland, killing all 243 people on board. Terrorists claimed the bombing was revenge for July's Iranian Air disaster. The doomed aircraft was traveling from London's Heathrow to New York's JFK, a very familiar route for me at the time. "There but for the grace of God..."

USA/Canada

July 9 — August 28 (31 shows in 29 cities)

After three exhausting months overseas, I was thrilled to be home. But before I could catch my breath, I was on my way to Milwaukee. Six days removed from Europe, we kicked off a two-month summer tour of the US and Canada. On the bright side, at least we were back to traveling on our private plane. No more elbowing French grannies out of the way for one of those coveted aisle seats.

Climbing aboard our cherished plane, the mood quickly soured when Sting discovered a personal message crudely carved into one of the cabin's tabletops:

"STRING [sic]—get a sense of humor"

Turns out, while we were crisscrossing Europe, Rod Stewart had been gallivanting around the US in *our* plane. When Rod learned the aircraft would be reverting to Sting, he decided to leave a little memento for our boss. The flight crew evidently thought Sting would find the inscription amusing. He didn't. (I'm guessing Sting didn't fancy the slightest whiff of disrespect at private charter prices.) Management conveyed Sting's displeasure, and a brand-new, pristine tabletop was in place when we boarded the plane the following day. There were rumblings about payback for Rod's smart-ass whittling, but like Sergeant Schultz from *Hogan's Heroes*, "I know nothing."

Our punishing schedule continued to demand its TWO pounds of flesh. Examining the latest itinerary, it was clear even our road manager was wearing down. Unlike previous editions, our tour personnel page did not contain one single snide remark. Over the span of six months, I'd gone from being *Rocky* to *San Francisco deviant* to just plain old *guitarist*. Times were indeed tough if Billy was too tired to bust chops.

Although the pace did seem extreme, I was still more than happy to be a part of the *abuse*. Meanwhile, a couple of the more jaded employees had quietly rechristened the relentless tour "Nothing Like the *Greed*." Not to be outdone, the always-candid Branford upped the rhetoric in an interview with *Rolling Stone* magazine, bluntly describing the tour as "terrible." Just getting started, he continued his rant:

> *"It's just too damn long. Everybody's burned out. I have a tre-mendous amount of loyalty to Sting, so I'll stick it out, but anybody else, anybody else, I would have quit. It's impossible to give your best when you're doing seven shows in eight days, and the day off is a travel day followed by nine shows in ten days. The only thing more absurd than this schedule is Michael Jackson's schedule. They perform one day and then they're off three days. The band spends all of their money out of boredom."*

As the old joke goes:

Q: How do you make a musician complain?

A: Give him a gig!

Milwaukee, Wisconsin | Milwaukee Summerfest | July 10

Despite Billy's uninspired itinerary, tour personnel was in fact THE headline. I spied an unfamiliar face as I boarded our flight to Milwaukee. Suspicions confirmed: Sting had hired another new drummer.

> *Drummer #3—Come on down. You're the next contestant on Nothing Like the Sun!*

As I settled into my designated recliner, I was introduced to my new co-worker, JT Lewis. JT's credits included Tina Turner, Lou Reed, and Herbie Hancock, so I was excited about the infusion of fresh (but experienced) blood into our road-weary band. There was just one *minor* issue. We were scheduled to perform in a few hours, and JT had never played a single note with us. Probably fearing a revolt, management had wisely avoided calling any rehearsals during our painfully short vacation. But as a result, our new drummer was staring at a fiery baptism. I assumed JT had received live recordings of our show and had done his homework. I'd learned to take things in stride by that point. Not my problem.

We touched down in Milwaukee and drove straight to the venue for an extensive soundcheck/rehearsal. We reviewed the "tops and tails" for every song on the setlist, hastily assembling our new rhythm section on the fly. That evening, my oft-ridiculed traits (overly conscientious, co-dependent, too damn uptight) came in quite handy. I hovered around JT's drum riser most of the concert, feeding him subtle cues throughout the show. A grateful JT pulled me aside after the gig and thanked me for the help, labeling me "a real pro." Excuse me? A pat on the back? Stop the presses!

Accolades had proven to be scarce in the big leagues, so I embraced JT's compliment and held on tight. I'd initially been frustrated with the lack of positive feedback from my fellow musicians, but Branford had set me straight early on. I was moaning one afternoon about not knowing where I stood when Branford interrupted and looked me squarely in the eye. "Don't worry, I'll tell you when you're fucking up." And that was that.

St. Paul, Minnesota | Riverfest | July 11

Falling right back into the groove of pillaging our way across the land, the traditional late-night hang wound up in my hotel room. My mini-bar was quickly depleted, so lacking any good sense, or fiscal restraint, I called room service and ordered a fifth of vodka. Hotel liquor by the bottle is a guaranteed budget buster, but what the hell, we were looking at a day off; there wasn't any reason to hold back. (Actually, there never seemed to be any reason to hold back. THAT was the problem.) The party raged and supplies dwindled again. Oblivious to the hour, I put in another call for liquid reinforcements. This time, I was politely rebuffed by room service. "We're sorry sir, but it's past 4am; the hotel is no longer allowed to serve alcohol." We thumbed our noses at the curfew (courtesy of other illicit substances), and pressed onward.

The sun was peeking through the curtains by the time our party finally dissolved. Drunk and exhausted, yet completely wired, I was crawling into bed when my telephone rang. Foolishly, I answered. It was the Devil—posing as room service. Satan cheerfully informed me it was after 7am, so my earlier request for a bottle of vodka could be filled... "if I still wanted it." Rationalizing a *nightcap* might help me fall asleep, I slurred, "Send it up."

Knock Knock. My liquid breakfast arrived and I poured myself another drink. I lay in bed, grinding my teeth while I waited for the Russian sedative to kick in. But before sleep came, the phone rang again. It was Billy, asking if I was interested in an early morning game of tennis. Way past crazy, I said, "Sure, why not?" There were plenty of reasons "why not," but none of them stopped me.

I stumbled downstairs to the tennis courts and proceeded to give it the old college try. But since I was literally seeing double by that point, I didn't fare too well. No kidding, unless I kept one eye closed, I saw two yellow tennis balls coming at me. After a couple of lopsided games, Billy invoked the mercy rule. He humanely called off the match and suggested we grab some water, and a much-needed seat. Billy, a seasoned veteran of the road, had seen it all, but my heavily compromised state had his full attention... and/or pity. Billy sighed as he looked at me drooped in my chair. "Jeff, you're as bad as Jimmy Page" [guitarist for Led Zeppelin]. And since Billy's resumé included the notoriously debauched Zeppelin, he knew of what he spoke. I stupidly construed the unflattering comparison as some kind of lifetime achievement award, and pumped my fist in the air. "Yeah baby!" I was such a fucking idiot.

Winnipeg, Manitoba | The Arena | July 13
Calgary, Alberta | Olympic Saddledome | July 15
Edmonton, Alberta | Northlands Coliseum | July 16
Vancouver, British Columbia | BC Place Stadium | July 18

Portland, Oregon | Oregon Sate Fairgrounds | July 19

We cranked out four shows in Canada (including a hoedown at the Calgary Stampede), before heading back to the motherland. We touched down at a small airport outside of Portland, and were promptly met on the runway by Uncle Sam's Welcome Wagon—aka US Customs. I guess the prospect of a degenerate rock band entering the country on a private plane had the border patrol tingling with excitement. The no-nonsense Feds herded our group off the aircraft and told us to wait on the tarmac. Adding to the unexpected *pleasure*, the Pacific Northwest was in the grips of an extreme heat wave—effectively turning the runway into the world's largest griddle.

The agents pulled our luggage from the cargo hold and spread it across the scorching concrete. They instructed us to stand beside our respective bags—and then the treasure hunt was on. The G-men rifled through our personal belongings, trying their damnedest to make headlines as we sizzled like human bacon. Fortunately, I had nothing to worry about. My sweaty brow was exclusively heat-related. Unlike certain daredevil band members, I wasn't crazy enough to risk sneaking illegal substances over international borders. I don't know if we were completely innocent, but we were innocent enough. The search came up empty and we were sent on our way.

A physician showed up at our Portland gig to administer vaccinations for the next item on our macro to-do list: Amnesty International's "Human Rights Now!" World Tour. The Amnesty itinerary included exotic destinations like Africa and India, so various immunizations (yellow fever, hepatitis, typhoid, etc.) were required before traveling. Billy gathered the entourage in the catering area before the show and introduced us to our Heineken-swigging, ponytailed doctor—and his arsenal of hypodermic needles. I put on a brave face, but in truth, I was somewhat skittish about being inoculated by some tipsy dude who looked more like a rocker than an MD.

After receiving my shots, I asked the hipster doctor if I should expect any side effects. "Not really," he replied, "possibly a low-grade fever or some anxiety." I just laughed and wondered how I'd ever notice the difference; that pretty much described my daily condition. But Dr. Ponytail was wrong.

The entire group was down for the count by the time we piled into our van after the show. Performing in Portland's triple-digit heat probably didn't help, but it was like we'd been slipped a communal mickey. The ride to the airport was dead silent as we nursed our vaccination hangovers. I tried to suppress my nausea but, thanks to our moving vehicle, I lost that battle. In dire need of a barf bag, I grabbed the closest thing available: the plastic grocery bag that contained my sweaty stage clothes. Not the ideal choice, but I was desperate. Unfortunately, I forgot to alert Fiona.

Fiona Williams, our lovely wardrobe person—and proper British lass—had one of those proverbial "dirty job, but someone's got to do it" jobs. Fiona was an unsung hero of the tour, tasked with keeping us crisp, clean, and sewn up for every performance. (She also graciously braided my regrettable "rat tail" on numerous occasions. That alone made her eligible for sainthood.)

After each concert, we'd stuff our sweaty stage wear into individual bags and pass the smelly buck to Fiona. With momlike superpowers, Fiona would magically transform our balled-up, dirty laundry into freshly pressed, neatly hung clothes by the next gig—which was usually the following day, and usually in a different city. But there were a few isolated instances where Fiona was unable to get our stage clothes dry-cleaned by showtime. On those rare occasions, I'd see her standing in the wardrobe area, spritzing and ironing the "used" clothing with one hand—while she held her nose with the other, as the noxious funk steamed out into the air.

We pulled up to Portland's airport around midnight and oozed out of the van. Our next gig was in San Francisco, but, with a day off first, Team Sting was LA bound. (Los Angeles would serve as our adopted home for the next few weeks.) Meanwhile, I'd decided to break ranks and head directly to San Francisco to spend the downtime with my brother. I was booked on a commercial flight the following morning, so it was me against the world as I checked into the airport hotel for the night. Holed up in the no-frills lodge, my vaccine demons really kicked in. The violent chills and nausea normally would've scared the hell out of me, but thankfully I knew why I was "dying." I felt like a poor, helpless junkie—sweaty and delirious, lying all alone in some cheap hotel room. After a long, restless night of detox, I woke up feeling almost human and boarded my flight to SFO.

I reconnected with my bandmates a couple of days later in San Francisco. They all laughed—sympathetically, of course—as they brought me up to speed on Fiona's Portland trauma. Apparently, when Fiona reached in to my combination laundry/barf bag, the soiled garments caused her to shriek and recoil in horror. Her stiff upper lip had met its match. Feeling guilty, I immediately tracked Fiona down and apologized for my unpleasant, yet unavoidable, booby trap. At least I could profess innocence in the matter. For once, I could blame my affliction on mandatory toxins.

Concord, California | Concord Pavilion | July 21

Mountain View, California | Shoreline Theater | July 22

Assigning all rock guitar duties to yours truly, Sting stuck to his nylon-string classical guitar, plus the occasional flourish of synthesizer…when his keyboard was working. In Mountain View, Sting's Roland D-50 synth was giving him trouble from the first downbeat. The dicey keyboard snapped, crackled and popped—but Sting was unflappable. Being an old pro, he deftly spun the technical glitches into entertainment gold. After wrestling with the unit for two or three songs, Sting threw his hands in the air and shouted into his mic, "Anybody want a synthesizer?" The crowd laughed, but Sting wasn't joking. He unplugged the keyboard, tucked it under his arm and walked to the front of the stage. Sting leaned over and handed the defective souvenir to a stunned audience member. Meanwhile, by the time Sting made it back to center stage, a new instrument was already in place. Big budget rock tours have redundancies that would make NASA proud.

Heading to our van after the show, I saw the beneficiary of Sting's largess waiting by the loading dock. I recognized the guy immediately; he was the only person in the crowd cradling a Roland D-50. The fan doubled down, asking Sting to sweeten the deal further by autographing the bulky memento. Sting chuckled at the fan's chutzpah, shrugged, and scribbled his name across the keys. The twice-lucky guy walked away with a unique, signed keepsake—suitable for boring future grandchildren. (*Granddaddy, What's a Sting?*) But, a couple of months later, I was leafing through *Musician* magazine when a classified ad caught my eye:

> *"One-of-a-kind Roland D-50 synth for sale to the highest bidder. Autographed by Sting."*

So much for sentimentality, but who am I to judge? Maybe the baby needed shoes.

* * *

During our West Coast swing, we enjoyed an amazing three-week residency at The Four Seasons Hotel in Beverly Hills. On gig days, we'd caravan over to nearby Burbank airport, jump on our plane and blast off to the city du jour. We'd bang out a quick show and then zoom back to our idling airplane. Before I knew it, I was crawling into the same king-size bed I'd woken up in that morning. Three straight weeks of no packing or unpacking, no checkouts, and best of all: Beverly Hills. Life was sweet.

Despite being a bona fide Beverly Hillbilly, I did my best to blend in with the beautiful people. I'd hang out by the "cee-ment pond" during the day, covertly ogling the parade of celebs from behind my Ray-Bans. (*Hey, there's Courtney Cox. Look, it's Hall and Oates. Wow, is that Sting over there? Oh wait, never mind.*) Surrounded by extreme indulgence, the lines of reality were easily blurred. One lazy day, I was lying by the pool, sipping a frozen concoction, when I caught myself complaining about having to trudge upstairs for my in-room massage And no, I wasn't joking. Even I was disgusted to hear the whiny words pass from my lips. I swear if I ever get my hands on a time machine, I'm teleporting back to that very moment and giving myself a good smack in the head.

Tackling yet another lost afternoon, a few of us delinquents loitered by the pool. We engaged in the typical, mundane chit-chat; familiar topics like sports, movies, "that blonde chick over there"…or the pending score with our Hollywood drug dealer. But like all good gangsters, we made sure to speak in code whenever we discussed lawless activities.

Our nickname for cocaine was "deska."This nonsensical word was a bastardized version of the Japanese expression *"desu ka"*—a formal phrase that often occurs at the end of a question in Japan. For example, in this felonious context: "*Anata wa kusuri o motte iru nodesu ka?*" (Loosely translated: "Hey Dude, got any blow?")

Kenny was the point man for our illicit transaction that day, so he'd stayed behind in his room to wait by the phone. He said he'd let us know when the deal came through, but with no handy cellphones back in those days, letting us know involved a coordinated, if not convoluted, effort. In order to contact a Four Seasons guest poolside, you had to call the front desk, and then endure the "please hold" Muzak while an operator sent out a search party. A bellhop would roam the pool area, carrying a gilded dry erase board with your name scrawled on it. "*Mr. Big Shot, you have a call on the courtesy phone.*" Whew, what a production; was that really in my lifetime? Sounds more like something from *The Flintstones*.

We were worshipping the late afternoon sun, when along came one of the switchboard's foot soldiers, tinkling his tiny hand bell as he hunted his mystery prey. Like Pavlovian dogs, we glanced up from our deck chairs in unison—and immediately fell out laughing. According to the bellhop's sign, there was a call holding for "MR. DESKA." There was no need to answer the phone, we got the message. It was party time. Yabba Dabba Do!

(Despite the humorous anecdotes, I don't mean to glamorize or trivialize drug use. Sadly, ten years after our tour, my dear friend—and musical hero—Kenny Kirkland died from an apparent drug overdose. RIP Kenny, I'll never forget you.)

Los Angeles, California | Wiltern Theater | July 27

In an effort to shake things up a bit, Sting put together a special "invitation only" concert at LA's cozy Wiltern Theater. The show represented something of an artsy detour from our usual arena-sized offering. Underscoring the evening's upscale vibe, management opened their wallet and rented a concert grand piano for Kenny (candelabra not included). Kenny was grateful, but circumspect. Is bigger better? Kenny conducted a side-by-side comparison between his tour-issue, digital piano and the luxury rental—and surprisingly wound up preferring the sound and touch of his electric "acoustic" keyboard. The swanky 9-foot grand was relegated to elegant furniture status.

Sting expanded our repertoire for the exclusive event; sprinkling jazz standards, show tunes, and even some original compositions by his band members across the three-hour concert. But the bonus material wasn't randomly pulled out of a hat. As always, there was a method to our leader's urbane madness. Sting performed a haunting rendition of the Gershwins' "Someone to Watch Over Me"—echoing his contribution to the recent Ridley Scott film of the same name. We also played "Mack the Knife" from *The Threepenny Opera*, which served as a teaser for Sting's upcoming role in the Broadway revival. Sticking with the sophisticated theme, Sting, of course, included our cerebral Frank Zappa cover, "Idiot Bastard Son." (I'm happy to report no audience members sustained any narcolepsy-related injuries that night.)

Sting also showcased his unselfish nature by elevating three of his sidemen to featured artists. Our boss humbly disappeared into the wings as Dolette stepped into the spotlight to belt out her song, "I Don't Wanna Be." Delmar took the reins next, leading the band through his majestic anthem, "The Promise." Kenny and Branford topped things off with Kenny's instrumental composition, "Blasphemy." I rest my case: "generous."

The concert was recorded with an eye toward commercial release, but, just like our European project, the album never hit the streets. However, for those with larceny in their heart, a high-quality recording of the show is apparently available on various bootleg websites. Hmmm, maybe *that's* how my anonymous NYC neighbor got his hands on our live version of "Tempted."

An overflow crowd of VIPs and scenesters crammed into the Wiltern's downstairs lobby to eat, drink, and be schmoozy after the show. My weary legs were in desperate need of a seat, so I wriggled out of the fray and claimed an unoccupied square inch on the staircase. I was chatting with some LA cutie when actor/comedian Tracey Ullman climbed through our conversation toward the exit. Passively eavesdropping as she squeezed by, Tracey did a double take and stopped dead in her tracks to inquire about my accent. Ms. Ullman, known for her wide array of zany characters, had obviously honed in on my Carolina drawl and wanted to pinpoint the exact geography. She blurted out, "Where are you from? Talk to me." I could almost see the wheels spinning in her head as she catalogued my Tar Heel inflection. Creativity never sleeps *y'all*.

Los Angeles, California | The Forum | July 28
Costa Mesa, California | Pacific Amphitheater | July 30

San Diego, California | Devore Stadium | July 31

Happy Birthday to me! I can't think of a better way to spend a birthday than rocking out under the stars in climate-controlled San Diego with my good pal Sting…and 15,000 of my closest friends. I'd persuaded my girlfriend, Denise, to schlep cross-country to join in the festivities, but I'd had to pull a few strings to keep her by my side. As a rule, personal guests were not allowed to travel on *Air Sting*. (The official excuse was "insurance considerations.") Nevertheless, I worked up my nerve and asked Billy for a birthday dispensation. He surprisingly granted my request, permitting Denise to tag along with us to San Diego.

In hindsight, Billy probably regretted extending the unprecedented courtesy. Dolette followed my lead less than a week later and asked for the same "significant other" exemption. Fearing a trend, Billy said no. It was a ballsy ruling, but that's our Billy. The flagrant double standard ended up putting him—and me—in Dolette's doghouse for a stretch. (She had a point.) Meanwhile, Denise's presence on the plane ultimately turned out to be a zero-sum game. As we took to the air that afternoon, we were one band member light.

When New York musicians visit LA, renting a car is practically a sacrament. And not just any car, mind you; it should be a sports car, and if at all possible, a convertible. Who can blame us? After enduring stinky subways and freezing cold winters, there's nothing more exhilarating than cruising down Sunset Boulevard in a late-model ragtop. Personally, I had no interest in the ritual—I'd much rather drink than drive. But following muso protocol, Delmar rented a sexy ride for the LA duration.

As the band climbed into our airport-bound van on my birthday, Delmar announced he was going to follow along in his car. Billy's veteran nose smelled trouble, but he shrugged and sighed, "OK, whatever." Always the cutup, Delmar couldn't resist engaging in a little highway hijinks as we convoyed to Burbank, repeatedly pulling up beside the van to honk and wave. It was all fun and games until the freeway split and Delmar found himself trapped in the wrong lane. Bye-bye, Delmar.

Our van went one way, Delmar went the other. When we arrived at the airport, Delmar was nowhere to be found. Cue Billy's evil grin. As I mentioned, Billy loved abandoning wayward musicians. Even if you were only a couple of minutes late, Billy would turn to the driver (or in this case, the pilot) and say, "Time's up. Let's go." That day, staying true to form, Billy pulled the trigger and we took off for San Diego sans Delmar.

We did our usual soundcheck—minus one keyboardist—and then sat down to dinner. Still no sign of Delmar. I was just beginning to wrap my head around the concept of doing a show without our flamboyant synthesist, when I heard that distinctive laugh echoing down the hallway. I looked up and there he was: Delmar Brown, the crazy cat with nine (or now maybe eight) lives. After getting stuck on the wrong freeway, Delmar drove on to LAX, bought a plane ticket, flew to San Diego, grabbed a taxi, and voilà. With the Sting squad back at full-strength, we took the stadium stage and rocked San Diego on that picture-perfect evening. It still rates as my coolest birthday ever.

Paso Robles, California | Mid-State Fair | August 2

I suffered pangs of withdrawal as we closed out our Beverly Hills residency. After three sun-drenched weeks of utopia, the dreaded day of exodus arrived. Playtime was over. I stood at the checkout counter in a daze, watching the hotel printer spit out page after page of my itemized overindulgence (room service, poolside service, restaurant, lobby bar, mini-bar, valet parking for friends, long distance phone calls, pay-per-view TV, laundry, etc.). Ouch! The eventual four-figure tally on my incidentals bill was quite sobering...but only in the figurative sense, of course.

Englewood, Colorado | Fiddlers Green | August 4

Kansas City, Missouri | Starlight Amphitheater | August 6

Another humid night, another sweaty "shed"—the less-than-endearing term for the amphitheaters that make up a good chunk of the summer touring circuit. After an uninspired visit to catering, I decided to go for a walk. (Killing time is elevated to an art form on the road.) Our latest venue was located in the middle of a sprawling park, so my stroll lacked any real points of interest—unless you consider grass and trees interesting. I grew bored with my nature hike and corrected course for the air-conditioned comfort of our dressing room. I was cutting through the backstage parking area when I noticed an odd-looking fellow wandering between the tour buses. Sporting a long black coat and a wide-brimmed hat, the guy looked totally out-of-place, yet eerily familiar. I scrolled through my memory banks and made it all the way back to my 6th grade musical production. That's it! I was staring at "Fagin"—the evil ringleader from the musical *Oliver!* (A touring company of the show was moving into the amphitheater after our departure.)

I took a closer look at the Dickensian dude, and my jaw dropped. The ominous man in black was none other than Davy Jones, lead singer of the 60's supergroup, The Monkees. I'd been a tad too young to develop full-blown Beatlemania, but I was right in the demographic crosshairs for the subsequent Monkee-mania. (My Grandmother even made a red double-breasted shirt for me so I could dress like a Monkee.) I stood motionless in that gravel parking lot, thrilled by the sight of my one-time idol. But, at the same time, my heart sank. How could it be? Superstar Davy Jones…*reduced* to doing musical theater in Kansas City.

Being naive and, even worse, a despicable "gig snob," I was disillusioned by what I perceived to be Davy's humiliating fall from grace. How the hell do you go from being a big-time TV/recording star to doing piddly bus-and-truck theatrical tours in the flyover states? But have no fear; the cocky kid from Carrboro would eventually get the answer to his smug question—in spades. Come to find out, King of the Hill isn't a tenured position.

Today, with substantially more perspective (and humility), I understand just how difficult it is to carve out a lasting career in "this business called show." Very few people get to spend the bulk of their lives in entertainment…but Davy Jones was one of them. Davy got his start on British TV in his teens before transitioning to the theatrical stage. (Ironically, Jones starred as the Artful Dodger in the original West End and Broadway productions of *Oliver!*)

At the ripe old age of 21, Davy conquered the pop music world as frontman for The Monkees. By the time our paths crossed in Kansas City, Mr. Jones was 43 years young and still getting it done—thirty years into his allotted "fifteen minutes of fame." The showbiz vet had clearly figured out the secret to being a lifer: don't ghettoize job opportunities, a gig is a gig. That being said, if you're really in it for the long haul—buckle up! Some *decades* are going to be better than others. Tragically, Davy died of a sudden heart attack at age 66. Rest in peace, Davy Jones. Wish I'd said hello.

Atlanta, Georgia | Southern Star Amphitheater | August 8

An outdoor gig in Georgia…in August…at the Six Flags Amusement Park. *Oh, the humanity!*

Nashville, Tennessee | Starwood Amphitheater | August 9

I was excited, but not really surprised, when I wandered out on stage for soundcheck and saw Sting chatting with "Mr. Guitar," Chet Atkins. We were in Nashville after all—plus Sting's exclusive weapon of choice was Gibson's Chet Atkins CE guitar. I'd actually performed with Chet many years earlier in North Carolina, so I was eager to reconnect with the Nashville legend and dazzle him with my impressive success. (It sounded good on paper.)

During my senior year of high school, I was hired to be in the house band at *The Duke Children's Hospital Classic*—an annual charity event held in nearby Durham, NC. Our mission was to provide musical accompaniment for the gala's celebrity performers, and although crooner Perry Como was the evening's headliner, I was much more psyched about sharing the stage with world-class picker, Chet Atkins. Chet introduced himself to the band at our haphazard rehearsal, before passing out the sheet music for his featured tune. I took a look at the page and saw nothing but gibberish. Instead of a traditional chord chart, the arrangement was written as a "Nashville Number Chart." (A shorthand system that uses numerals—rather than the alphabet—to indicate a song's chord progression.) Obviously noticing the confused look on my face, Chet asked if I understood the notation. When I sheepishly confessed, "No," Chet smiled, picked up a pen, and translated the chart for me. A gentleman, and a gentle man.

Unfortunately, this is where my heartwarming tale grinds to a halt. I approached Sting and Mr. Atkins at our Nashville soundcheck, and politely interrupted the pair to reintroduce myself to Chet. When I excitedly reminded "Mr. Guitar" of our history together, he responded with a blank stare. Chet grunted a disinterested "Hello," and immediately turned back to Sting, making it quite clear I was no longer a part of the conversation. I retreated to my workstation halfway dejected and halfway pissed. (*How dare he blow me off? I play guitar with Sting.*) Ah, dumb bird of youth. Despite my thoughts to the contrary, I wasn't famous—I simply worked for somebody who was. Today, I understand the laws of the jungle. Sidemen come, sidemen go. The interchangeable little guys all start to look alike to the big shots.

Chicago, Illinois | Poplar Creek Music Theater | August 11

Departing Nashville after the show allowed us to wake up in Chicago to a true day off—NO gig, NO travel. I knew exactly where I wanted to waste my summer afternoon: the friendly confines of Wrigley Field. A few of us made our way out to the revered ballpark to partake in America's pastime, and, as an added bonus, the Cubs were hosting our beloved hometown Mets.

During a break in the beer-fueled action, I was standing in a long line for the men's room when I felt a tap on my shoulder. I turned to see my good friend—and fellow North Carolina guitarist—Scott Sawyer. What were the odds? How many toilets does Wrigley Field have? Scott, a native Chicagoan, happened to be in town for a visit, so we made plans to hang out later.

Knowing my tastes (or more accurately, my thirsts), Scott took me around to a few of the Windy City's classic watering holes. We ultimately landed at the renowned blues club, Kingston Mines, where we unexpectedly ran into Mino. We joined forces, grabbed a table, and settled in for some authentic, deep-dish Chicago blues. Club management discovered we were members of Sting's band, and urged us to get up and play a number for the crowd. Needing no arm-twisting, we threw together a makeshift power trio: Scott on guitar, Mino on drums, and me on...BASS. (Duck!)

Searching for a something to play, we agreed upon "Jean Pierre" by Miles Davis. And with Mino being an alumnus of the legendary trumpeter's band, the selection gave our *Kingston* trio a little extra gravitas. I enjoyed myself as we jammed away, but I'll be the first to admit our performance didn't exactly rival Miles's version. When we left the stage, a frustrated Mino didn't pull any punches. He accused me of being musically sloppy, fuming we had professional reputations to protect. Mino had a valid argument, but I'd been under the impression we were just trying to have a little fun. And in my defense, I'd been drinking for hours. Maybe more importantly, I'm not much of a bass player, even when I'm sober.

My hotel room was designated "party central" the following night. As the liquor flowed, Mino began busting my chops (again) about the previous evening's jam session. He derided me, which I was more or less used to by that point, but then he started dogging my pal, Scott. Scott wasn't around to defend himself, so I felt compelled to stick up for my homeboy. (Mino was way off base, Scott is a heavyweight.) After hearing enough of Mino's bullshit, I drunkenly challenged him to a fight. Mino chuckled. That just made me madder. I continued to throw down the gauntlet, but Mino refused to take the bait. Thank God, he would have killed me. Kenny was an eyewitness to my boozy bluster, and took great pleasure in mocking my wobbly boxing stance and slurred threats over the next few days. ("*Shtand* up, Mino, I'm gonna kick your *ash.*") Based on Kenny's hilarious imitation, I was doing some serious bobbing and weaving that evening—all involuntarily.

I awoke from my Chicago coma with a raging case of cottonmouth. I fell out of bed and literally crawled toward the refrigerator, desperate for any cold, wet relief from my booze-induced dehydration. Dragging myself by my elbows, I groaned when I rounded the corner and saw my fridge door standing wide open. But it didn't matter; the damn thing was completely empty. Now *that's* what I call a party. To the bathroom sink!

I slurped tepid water from the faucet while contemplating the financial ramifications of my barren icebox. Ransacking a mini-bar does not come cheap—especially at The Ritz-Carlton. I approached the front desk at checkout time, gave them my room number and braced myself for the damages. The perky clerk brought up my account. "That will be eleven dollars please." Well, I knew that was wrong. Preferring to stay on karma's good side, I encouraged the receptionist to have housekeeping re-check my mini-bar usage. Head pounding, I propped myself up against the counter and awaited my amended verdict. Suzy Sunshine eventually looked up from her computer and smiled. "Thanks for waiting, sir. That will be one hundred and seventy-eight dollars please."

Charlevoix, Michigan | Castlefarms Music Theater | August 12
Auburn Hills, Michigan | The Palace | August 13

Cuyahoga Falls, Ohio | Blossom Music Festival | August 15

The Blossom Music Center was quite a few cuts above the typical "shed" on our itinerary. Maybe it was because the venue also served as the summer home for the Cleveland Orchestra, but the modern, well-appointed facility was first-class all the way. Unfortunately, the same could not be said for our hotel. *The road giveth, the road taketh away.* We were seasoned enough travelers to smell the impending boredom as we checked into our bland corporate lodging on the outskirts of Akron. And thanks to a scheduled day off, we were facing a double dose of suburban purgatory.

I awoke the following morning to find one of Billy's daily sheets unexpectedly slid beneath my door. (No gig/no travel usually meant no missive.) I broke into a smile when I saw: "Pack your bags. We're leaving." Lucky for us, Sting had thought the better of wasting his precious day-off gazing at a dreary stretch of I-77. Making good use of our standby flight crew, the boss called an audible, and we were NYC bound. *Sting giveth.*

How I loved that chartered plane. It was like having our own private social club—at fifteen thousand feet. The cushy cabin was ideal for lounging, reading, sleeping, and when the mood struck, poker. A friendly little game of cards made for the perfect in-flight activity, especially after a show, when the adrenaline—and beer—was flowing. But I did learn one valuable, if not obvious, lesson at our mile-high casino: The rich guy ALWAYS wins. (At least in the long run, anyway.)

With Sting faithfully abstaining from our macho communion, Kim Turner was the game's default fat cat. Accordingly, in the spirit of Robin Hood, I enjoyed taking our well-to-do manager's money most of all. I derived great pleasure from the sour look on Kim's face whenever I raked in a sizable pot. Then one day it hit me: I was merely inflicting flesh wounds … at best. No matter how much money I took from Kim, it'd never amount to more than chump change in his big-boy world. Even after a substantial loss, Kim's frown was fleeting. He'd curse me, and then break into a grin as he casually dug another crisp hundred out of his wallet. I finally grasped that a twenty-dollar loss was hurting my pocketbook way more than it was hurting Kim's, so I proposed a new system. In an effort to distribute the financial pain evenly, I suggested we replace our dollar-for-dollar wagers with bets based on percentages of our respective incomes. (One percent of my weekly salary was $25. Wonder what one percent of Kim's was?) Kim's eyes flashed fear when he heard the radical idea, before dismissing my pitch out of hand. He had no desire whatsoever to level the playing field. "No fuckin' way, deal the cards."

Boston, Massachusetts | Great Woods | August 17, 18

Our private plane afforded us the luxury of returning to New York between our two-night stand in Boston. But despite the theoretical allure of home, in reality my NYC standard of living was not nearly as nice as the road. Sure, it was comforting to be in my own apartment during the Northeast stretches, but on the downside, fresh sheets and clean towels suddenly became *my* responsibility. A night or two at my amenity-free abode always provided a humbling reminder of my not-so-distant past...and, as it would turn out, my not-too-distant future.

I opted out of the trip home after our first show in Boston, staying behind to catch up with one of my closest friends—and fellow transplanted Southerner—Greg Darden. Greg and I went WAY back, playing in bands together since some of my earliest days of strumming. Remember my adolescent "Sex Machine" recording? Greg was the other guitarist in that band.

Our private plane had introduced me to the rock-star ritual of "doing a runner." Whenever we were scheduled to fly right after a show, the band would literally "run" straight from the stage to an idling van. No showers, no change of clothes, just "Thank you, goodnight!"—and the next thing we knew, we were speeding down the highway to the airport. The mad dash enabled us to get a jump on post-concert traffic jams, while also helping our pilot beat any local airport curfews. Always a participant in the runner, I'd never really considered our finale from the fan's perspective…until Boston.

My bandmates scrambled out the backdoor as I cracked open a couple of beers. Greg and I kicked back in the deserted dressing room, sipping and smiling as we toasted the crowd's muffled chant of "One more! One more!" But then it dawned on me: this boisterous public display of affection was not going to have a happy ending. After Team Sting had a sufficient head start, the house lights blazed on, confirming there would, in fact, be no "more." The pro-Sting cheers quickly morphed into a big, angry "Boooooooooo" that echoed throughout the venue. I guess Greg and I could have gone back out on stage and attempted to placate the masses. We knew "Sex Machine," but I doubt that's what—or WHO—they wanted.

I was back on the passenger manifest after our second show in Boston. We touched down in New Jersey around midnight, but instead of heading home to our respective pillows, we were off to NYC's famed Hit Factory recording studio. Tonight, it was Sting who wanted to hear "one more." A third encore of sorts, except two hundred miles later.

Sting was still toying with the idea of releasing a concert album, but after scouring his extensive collection of road tapes, he'd been unable to find a suitable take of our Squeeze cover, "Tempted." Sting was determined to get a solid version of the tune for our projected "Live in Europe" disc—even if it meant using a

Manhattan studio to do so. But at least we weren't starting completely from scratch. One crucial element was already in place: applause. Sting had reels and reels of enthusiastic crowd noise. He simply needed better music to go along with it.

We hit a snag just shy of our destination: West 54th street was closed. The Hit Factory shared the same small but vibrant block as the Ritz nightclub (which had recently moved uptown to the former address of the infamous disco, Studio 54). Thrash-metal's Megadeth had headlined The Ritz that night, and their raucous post-show crowd had spilled out into the street just before our arrival, prompting cops to shut down the block.

Traffic barricades and the NYPD Mounted Unit forced us to complete the last hundred yards of our Boston commute on foot. We grabbed our instruments and abandoned ship, falling in behind Sting. We waded into the melee, but the sea of humanity miraculously parted as our rock 'n' roll Moses led us to the Promised Land. I got a kick out of watching the wave of stunned faces ripple through the crowd as the metal-heads (and cops) slowly recognized the famous Police-man walking among them. The Hit Factory, The Ritz, Megadeth, Sting, and a team of horses— just another run-of-the-mill Thursday night in Manhattan. And that was only on one tiny block.

Like every other recording session since the beginning of time, boredom set in as the band waited for the engineer to fine-tune the drum sounds. Delmar and I seized our opening and snuck out to the nearby muso bar, Possible 20. The notorious saloon, located just around the corner from the studio, served as a magnet for the city's incorrigible musicians. (In fact, the bar's name was derived from musician slang for overtime, which our union measures in twenty-minute increments. "*The gig is three hours long… with a possible 20.*") Delmar and I slammed down a couple of shots, powdered our noses, and then raced back to The Hit Factory.

Fortunately, it only took a handful of takes before Sting was satisfied. Mission accomplished; we finally had a strong *live* performance of "Tempted." Apologies if I've burst any bubbles, but odds are there's a little, if not a lot of, post-production smoke and mirrors on your favorite concert recordings. One rocker confided to me that ALL the vocals on his (ostensibly) live album had been recut in the comfort of a recording studio.

Along with his misgivings over "Tempted," Sting also had concerns about my guitar solo on his preferred take of "King of Pain." He wondered if *we* could possibly make it "sing a bit more." As our late-night session wrapped, Sting asked if I could meet him back at the studio the next day to take a look at the issue. Of course, I said yes.

But when tomorrow rolled around, I was the proud owner of yet another world-beater hangover. "King of Pain" indeed. Regrettably, by that advanced point in my drinking career, I'd turned pro. And professional drinkers know there's only one sure-fire fix in hangover emergencies: the proverbial "hair of the dog." On really rough mornings—or depending upon how late I slept, afternoons—the only effective remedy for my toxic condition was a stiff drink.

I felt like total shit as I limped to meet Sting. I wrestled with stopping by a pub for a quick bracer, but thank God I had the wherewithal to hold off. Sting and I wound up working together one-on-one in close proximity, and while I'm sure I reeked of stale vodka, at least I didn't reek of fresh vodka. Kim handled the engineering duties as Sting and I searched for some new and improved guitar magic, but it became obvious rather quickly that none of our hearts—hungover or not—were in the session. We tried various approaches for an hour or so, but nothing clicked. We finally surrendered and stuck with my original guitar part (which, in my opinion, sounded fine to begin with). We called it a day and went our separate ways. My "way" was a beeline for the neighborhood pharmacy—aka Possible 20.

"King of Pain" was the only recording from our tour that was released commercially. Sting included it as a bonus track on his CD single "All This Time" (from his next album, *The Soul Cages*).

Portland, Maine | Ball Park/Old Orchard Beach | August 20

I hobbled aboard our midday flight to Maine, reeling from another night of being over-served by my NYC enablers. I headed straight for the ice chest, shoved Sting's carrot juice out of the way and grabbed a bottle of Corona. I slumped into my recliner, and chugged the Mexican antidote as we waited for takeoff. Unfortunately, the mild brew didn't begin to dent my fuzzy condition. The moment we reached cruising altitude, I retreated to the bathroom. I dropped to my knees and hugged the toilet, praying for my nausea to subside—or a quick death.

I felt horrible at soundcheck, much worse than usual for some reason. With no appetite come dinnertime, I tried going the liquid route. I downed a couple glasses of red wine for medicinal purposes, but the cure didn't take. Branford picked up on my shaky status and suggested we go for a walk. I jumped at the offer; I'd try anything for relief.

I gulped sea air as we strolled Portland's waterfront, listening quietly while Branford lovingly told me to get my shit together. Branford wisely steered clear of the road's unchecked debauchery, so he didn't suffer drunken (or hungover) fools gladly. He deemed the band's drawn-out, boozy dinners and late-night drug hangs as a big waste of time and energy—and money. Branford's idea of a good time was a sweaty pickup game of basketball and a quick bite to eat at the nearest fast food joint. It would've behooved me to take a page or two from his playbook, but I was too far gone by that point. I wasn't living it up; I was self-destructing.

Bristol, Connecticut | Lake Compounce Park | August 21

Columbia, Maryland | Merriweather Post Pavilion | August 22

Two of my dearest friends from North Carolina, Keith Crittenton and his wife, Elaine, made a road trip to Maryland to catch our show. Keith and I grew up together on the same street, and formed my very first band: The Trek. Our prepubescent power duo featured Keith on guitar and me on DRUMS! (We had The White Stripes and The Black Keys beat by decades.) My paper-headed Sears drum set was basically a toy, but Keith had real deal, big-boy gear: a red Fender Mustang guitar (with snazzy white racing stripe) and a blue tuck-n-roll Kustom amplifier.

I was a goner the moment I laid eyes on that rig. It was my first encounter with a Fender, and I was never the same. I can still smell the fuzzy red lining in that guitar case. I've always heard, "You don't choose music, IT chooses you." I agree wholeheartedly. While all my *normal* peers were busy fantasizing about the opposite sex, I was busy dreaming about electric guitars. (OK, I thought about girls, too. Otherwise, why even bother with learning how to play the guitar?)

I wanted to make sure Keith and Elaine got a chance to meet Sting, so I invited them backstage before the show. (Afterward wasn't an option; the band was doing a runner.) We canvassed the area and eventually tracked down my boss. I excitedly handled the introductions, gushing to Sting, "Keith was my very first guitar teacher." Sting shook Keith's hand and frowned. "Oh, so it's YOUR fault."

* * *

Sting performed solo versions of "Roxanne" and "Message in a Bottle" for the second (and final) encore each night. The band would rejoin Sting onstage toward the end of "Message" for a foot-stomping, hand-clapping, sing-along on the song's closing vamp, "*Sending out an SOS, Sending out an SOS.*" Over time, a few of us began ditching our sweat-drenched suit jackets for the official goodnight, returning to the stage in our casual, but retro-trendy, wife-beater T-shirts. Unfortunately, the excesses of the road had wreaked havoc on some of our waistlines, and the skintight tees weren't doing our budding love handles any favors. Word eventually came down via Fiona that Sting was banning uncovered tank tops from the stage. A few of us protested mildly, but Sting held firm, contending "certain people" were getting too flabby for the clingy look. I jumped to my own defense, playfully arguing I should be exempt from the rule because my midsection was covered by a guitar. Without missing a beat, Sting sniffed, "Well then, Jeff, you need to get a bigger guitar."

Sting owned the high ground in the band's battle of the bulge. Between a strict regimen of yoga and his disciplined diet, Sting stayed in top physical shape. But then again, he needed to. HE was the one who voluntarily peeled off his shirt every night during the last verse of "Don't Stand So Close." (Sting's sexy strip show echoed the original "Don't Stand" music video by The Police.) Hey, if you got it, flaunt it.

New York, New York | Madison Square Garden | August 24

We were back on our home court, ready to prove ourselves to Madison Square Garden once again—and this time we had a little something extra up our sleeve: Mr. Bruce Springsteen. Sting and Bruce might have seemed like odd bedfellows, but there was a completely logical explanation for the alliance. In a little over a week, we'd be kicking off the multi-artist Amnesty International "Human Rights Now!" World Tour—a massive undertaking that included Peter Gabriel, Tracy Chapman, Senegalese superstar Youssou N'Dour, and Sting's new pal, Bruce Springsteen.

Before the first note of the Amnesty tour was ever played, industry wags were sniping that the stage might not be big enough to hold both Sting and Bruce...and their super-sized egos. In an effort to neutralize some of the pre-tour snark—and grab a little ink along the way—Sting invited Springsteen to join us at Madison Square Garden. (We worked up a version of Bruce's "The River" for his cameo.)

I was futzing around onstage before soundcheck when I glanced up to see "The Boss" stroll out of the shadows. Not my boss, mind you, THE Boss—and I'll admit my heart skipped a beat. I'd logged almost a year in the big time, but I still found myself awed by Springsteen's aura. And, truth be told, I'm only a casual fan at best. (Although I do think "Born to Run" is one of the greatest tunes ever.) Personal tastes notwithstanding, Springsteen is a HUGE rock star—and you could smell it on him. We all exchanged brief hellos and then got down to business. We ran through Bruce's number a couple of times and, before I knew it, Springsteen was gone, exiting as inconspicuously as he'd entered.

Meanwhile, I'd added a brand-new, state-of-the-art digital reverb to my rig and I was eager to take it out for a test drive. My plan was to stick around after soundcheck and do a little tinkering, but I forgot to factor the Garden's union protocols into the equation. Disregarding Billy's call for dinner, I started fiddling with my latest gadget. Bad idea. Sting was up in my face within seconds. "Jeff, shut the fuck up RIGHT NOW. If you make one more sound, you're gonna cost me ten-thousand dollars." I thought Sting was kidding at first, but then I saw the fire in his eyes. Nope, he was dead serious. Madison Square Garden is a strict union hall, and NYC's all-powerful stagehand local (Local

One) does not mess around. According to union regulations, if the band made ANY noise on stage during the mandated dinner break, the arena crew would be considered back "on the clock" and paid at a premium. With Sting making his point so persuasively, I put down my guitar. My new plaything would have to wait until a later, less-expensive time.

That night, once the crowd was good and lathered up, Sting cryptically invited a "friend" to join him on stage. As Sting's mystery guest sauntered out into the spotlight, a massive roar rose from the belly of the arena. And I mean MASSIVE. I'd played in front of much larger audiences, but the Garden's thermonuclear reaction was unlike anything I'd ever heard. It felt like the ceiling might cave in. The tag team of Sting and Bruce pushed the already hyped-up fans into an all-out frenzy. The overwhelming moment gave me chills—and a sneak preview of what the Amnesty tour held in store.

After the show, Sting's record label, A&M, hosted an intimate, downtown bash for the band and the usual VIP suspects. But we'd been warned in advance: "Absolutely NO guests!" Duly noted, count me out. I'd invited Bill Covington (my Delmar matchmaker) and his wife, Custis, to join me at the concert and we had plans to hang afterward. If my pals weren't welcome at the party, I had no interest in attending. Choosing the warmth of close friends over the chill of powerful strangers was a no-brainer by that late point of the tour. Plus, let's face it, without Bill's kindness and support, MY name would've never been on that exclusive guest list in the first place. My priorities were straight.

Wantagh, New York | Jones Beach Amphitheater | August 25

As the band fell in for soundcheck, it was clear the previous evening's party had been a knockdown, drag-out affair. I'd NEVER known Sting to overindulge, so I could hardly believe my eyes: he looked like shit. Getting up to speed on the juicy details, I heard the highlight of the party was a drinking contest between Sting and Madonna—with Sting downing twelve shots of tequila. TWELVE?!? My boozing skills were formidable, but there's no way I could have kept up with that kind of pace. Tequila ain't no plaything; a dozen shots seemed borderline suicidal for a casual drinker like Sting.

Halfway through the world's least-inspired soundcheck, a green-gilled Sting succumbed to his injuries and disappeared into the wings. I wandered backstage a few minutes later and saw Sting laid out on a slab of cement—eyes closed, arms folded, seemingly in need of an undertaker. (I wonder how Madonna felt?) But come showtime, Sting rose from the dead and delivered his usual dynamite performance. Being something of an expert on hangovers, I was quite impressed by Sting's resurrection. As a buddy of mine used to say, "Rock 'n' roll will either kill you…or cure you." It seemed to be doing a bit of both to Sting at Jones Beach.

Syracuse, New York | New York State Fair | August 27
Saratoga, New York | Performing Arts Center | August 28

We wrapped our North American summer leg with two shows in upstate New York, and then collapsed into a generous, well-earned…two-day break. After six weeks of hitting it hard, we had forty-eight measly hours to convalesce before heading off to London to begin yet another six-week leg of concerts. On deck: a whirlwind trip around the globe with Amnesty International's "Human Rights Now!" Tour. Despite my chronic battle fatigue, I was psyched. I still had a few drops of rock 'n' roll left in the tank. Between Amnesty's all-star lineup and its exotic itinerary, I knew I was in for the ride of my life. Africa with Springsteen? Let's go!

Amnesty International "Human Rights Now!" Tour

With Bruce Springsteen and the E Street Band,
Peter Gabriel, Tracy Chapman, Youssou N'Dour
September 2 — October 15 (20 shows in 19 cities)

Seemingly overnight—when it was actually TWO overnights—I was right back on the launching pad. I sat on my couch in a daze, waiting for my here-we-go-again ride to the airport. But my late-afternoon pickup time came and went with nary a peep from my apartment buzzer. As the wait grew, it became obvious I was a forgotten man. (The limo driver was responsible for securing three Upper West Side passengers: Delmar, Fiona, and me. Somehow, he botched the headcount.)

Instead of panicking, I slowly grasped my good fortune. So what if I missed my flight? I could just as easily leave the next morning and still make it to London with time to spare. Most importantly, I'd get one more glorious night at home. Oh, hell yeah! Surprising even myself, I heeded my inner bad boy and decided to sit tight. I did the backwards math and waited until there was absolutely NO way I could make my flight...and then I called to inquire about my missing ride.

Patty LaMagna—the main cog at KRT management—answered the phone. When I gave her my *bad* news, an exasperated Patty groaned, "Jeff, why didn't you call me earlier? There's no way I can get you to JFK in time now." I played dumb as Patty sighed, "Oh well, you'll just have to go to London tomorrow." The little devil on my shoulder beamed with pride as I offered my (insincere) apologies. For what it's worth, I did feel guilty about complicating Patty's chronically complicated job, but when opportunity *doesn't* knock, you have to listen. We hung up so Patty could get started on my new travel plans—and I could get started on my NYC dinner plans.

My front door buzzed bright and early the next morning. I was exhausted, but so was my margin for error; thank God my driver didn't stand me up again. Transatlantic sailing was smooth and, in spite of toying with the Travel Gods (and Ms. Patty La-Magna), I made it to London in time. So what if it was twelve hours later than originally scheduled? Pulling up to the hotel in the late evening, I climbed out of my taxi and into the eye of a muso hurricane. It looked like a Shriner's convention of rockers had descended on the lobby. *Wow, there's Clarence Clemons. Damn, it's Peter Gabriel. Look, Nils Lofgren. This is going to be fun.*

Amnesty International mounted the ambitious and aspirational "Human Rights Now!" World Tour in order to commemorate the 40th anniversary of the UN's Universal Declaration of Human Rights. The watchdog organization had sponsored a smaller, six-city, "Conspiracy of Hope" tour two years earlier, featuring Sting, U2, Peter Gabriel, and Lou Reed. But this time around, Amnesty had decided to go BIG. Our tour was budgeted at a cool twenty-two million dollars, and boasted an entourage of approximately two hundred people (with legendary rock promoter Bill Graham at the helm). We were scheduled to hit nineteen cities on five continents in the span of six short weeks, and factoring in TV syndication deals, it was estimated the humanitarian juggernaut could potentially reach over a billion people.

London, England | Wembley Stadium | September 2

I had some time to kill before heading out to Wembley, so I wandered over to the mega HMV record store in Piccadilly Circus. I was browsing the aisles when I glanced up to see an unexpected, and definitely unwelcome, face. Yes, the same flirty face that launched a thousand jokes—and one infamous Heathrow punch—was staring right at me. Time had healed nothing. Nine months later, I was still pissed off about ending up as collateral damage in some imaginary lover's triangle. The femme fatale approached after our eyes met and offered a nervous hello. My chilly response obviously found its mark as she meekly added, "I owe you an apology." I replied without hesitation, "And I owe *you* a punch in the mouth." Conversation over. (Calm down, I wasn't really going to hit her.)

* * *

Other than your passport, your laminate may be your most important companion on the road. That little plastic rectangle that dangles from the neck of every touring musician/roadie serves as their omnipotent ID, providing "All Access" at each concert stop. But there's one catch: the golden hall pass will only work its magic when you actually remember to carry it with you. Arriving at Wembley Stadium, I realized I'd committed a cardinal sin. I'd left my laminate back at the hotel. Dammit! The perfectionist in me hated making such a rookie-like mistake, especially in front of all the cool new kids.

As always, in time of crisis, I ran straight to "The Fixer" (Billy). I confessed my blunder and braced for impact. Billy sighed, rolled his eyes, and reached in his briefcase for a "stickie"—a disposable, adhesive backstage pass that screams "non-VIP" (or in this instance, "flaky musician"). But I wasn't getting off the hook that easily. Before handing over the stopgap ID, Billy whipped out a Sharpie and wrote across my pass in bold print: "I am the FIRST musician to forget my laminate." Billy slapped the amended sticker on my chest and tossed me out of the production office. Emblazoned with rock's version of The Scarlet Letter, I was forced to spend the rest of the day advertising my incompetence to all my new co-workers.

The Amnesty tour was one big happy (albeit slightly dysfunctional) family, but the pecking order was clear: Springsteen and Sting were the patriarchs. And although the concert's "order of appearance" was shuffled on a regular basis, Bruce or Sting was usually in charge of closing out the evening. However, the rock-star hierarchy was put on ice at the top of each show as all five headliners gathered to sing the tour's official theme song, Bob

Marley's "Get Up, Stand Up." After the Million Dollar Quintet wrapped up their opening call to arms, a local—but regionally significant—artist would play a few tunes, priming the crowd for the main event(s). With six different bands and numerous impassioned speeches, each concert was a marathon.

Paris, France | Palais Omnisports de Paris-Bercy | September 4, 5

Let the record show we made it *all* the way to the second stop on our itinerary before dissension developed in the ranks. Tour planners definitely fumbled the ball when selecting our Parisian lodging: the spartan (and remote) Orly Airport Hilton—located fifteen LONG miles outside of Paris. The musicians on the Amnesty tour were all seasoned travelers, and accustomed to staying in the heart of their host cities. Being well acquainted with the charms of Paris, nobody was happy about being stranded that far from heaven. In fact, Sting was having none of it. In an uncharacteristically tone-deaf move, Sting abandoned the troops and personally moved to the luxurious Royal Monceau in central Paris. (The same pricey digs where Team Sting stayed—once—before The Goon issued his accountant kibosh.) I was surprised Sting would risk possible resentment from his tour mates, especially so early in the run, but a man's got to do what a man's got to do. Meanwhile, Bruce Springsteen and Peter Gabriel toed the blue-collar line and toughed it out in solidarity with us little guys. I guess we all have our limits. Apparently for Sting, it was the Orly Hilton.

Delmar followed Sting's lead—but on a smaller scale. With

no intention of wasting his night off pining for Gay Paree, Delmar decided to rent a car and head for the city. When word leaked out that Delmar was going over the wall, Garry Tallent (E Street bassist) and I eagerly chipped in a few francs for a slot in the getaway vehicle. Believe it or not, I actually had a date. Masquerading as an international playboy, I'd made dinner plans with a cute acquaintance from LA, who just happened to be in Paris. Can I get an *Ooh La La?*

We set out for Paris proper with the fearless Delmar Brown behind the wheel. I foolishly climbed into the passenger seat and wound up holding my breath for the entire, terrifying trip. (An ashen Garry Tallent sat frozen in the back.) Delmar's aggressive driving techniques rivaled any New York cabbie I'd ever encountered, but we somehow cheated death and made it to the city in one piece. Garry and I kissed the ground as we exited the car—and assured Delmar we'd find alternate transportation back to Orly. That turned out to be a little easier said than done. After a cozy, extended dinner with my California girl, I asked our waiter for advice on catching a cab back to the distant hotel. The server shrugged and said it would probably be impossible at that late hour. Uh oh. Despite being a hardened NYC pedestrian, a fifteen-mile midnight hike was clearly a non-starter. Luckily, the waiter's dire prediction was overblown and we eventually found a taxi driver willing to take us back to the hinterlands.

My LA arm candy joined me at our show the following night. After Sting's set, she batted her eyelashes and asked if we could stick around to hear a couple of tunes from Springsteen. I had other *activities* in mind, but being a gentleman, I deferred to the lady's wishes. We were hanging out in the backstage concourse, awaiting Bruce's downbeat, when one of Springsteen's beefy security guards approached. Without a hint of respect or diplomacy, he insisted we'd have to clear the area before The Boss made his way through. Oh really? The guy could have torn me in half like a small-town phone book, but I ignored his bullshit directive. I've never been one to challenge authority, but this demand was ridiculous. I was a performer on the tour just like Bruce Almighty (income brackets notwithstanding), and I was not going to be treated like a security threat—or even worse, some kind of fanboy. I stood my ground and the tough guy eventually backed off. A few minutes later, Bruce and his entourage came strolling down the hall. The security goon lobbed dirty looks in my direction as the procession neared, but his evil eye came to an abrupt halt when Bruce waved and shouted, "Hey, Jeff!" From that moment forward, I was a "made man." I never heard another peep from Springsteen's secret service.

Budapest, Hungary | Népstadion | September 6

Amnesty International was committed to visiting countries where human rights were a tangible, if not pressing, issue. (Russia and Poland rejected our overtures. The Philippines, Nicaragua, and Senegal were deemed problematic or outright dangerous.) The goal was to spread the message to as many people as possible, so tickets prices were kept amazingly low at our economically challenged stops. To that end, admission for the show in Hungary was only about two dollars, resulting in a crowd 80,000 strong. Unfortunately, our trip to Budapest was a brief one. We flew in from Paris on the day of the show, and then departed for Italy immediately after the concert. Due to the tight scheduling, I missed out on a chance to ignore another historic and fascinating city.

Unlike the Sting tour, where we were often airborne within minutes of our last note, Amnesty's escape from Budapest was more of a rolling process. Springsteen had been charged with closing out the Hungary show, so the bulk of us were already settled in for the flight by the time Bruce's gang started straggling on board. I watched discreetly from my seat as a hunched-over Clarence "Big Man" Clemons squeezed down the aisle to his probably unfamiliar coach-sized accommodations. Large humans and airplanes are a marriage made in Hell, so the six-foot-five Clarence had my complete sympathy. (We eventually acquired a couple of spacious jumbo jets, but we used smaller planes for the first batch of short flights inside Europe.) Continuing my subtle stargazing, I couldn't help but smile when I noticed Clarence's payload. In addition to his horns, the world-famous saxophonist was also clutching a bag of McDonald's. *Et tu, Budapest?* Seeing Clarence Clemons as a normal dude with a taste for fast food helped put me a little more at ease. Being surrounded by a planeload of MTV super heroes was still a bit unnerving at that early juncture.

Turin, Italy | Stadio Comunale | September 8

Capping off a day that saw breakfast in Paris and dinner in Budapest, I finally crawled into an Italian bed at some godforsaken hour. I awoke around the crack of noon to the faint but distinct sounds of cheering. Confused, I pegged the noise as probably coming from a nearby sporting event. I dragged myself to the window and raised the glass to investigate. The mystery was instantly solved. A large crowd of people were gathered in front of our hotel chanting, "Bruce! Bruce! Bruce!" Wow. Until that moment, I'd always considered Sting to be "as big as it gets." But I bore witness to a whole new level of adulation as I stood there in my boxers. Sorry Sting, but I'd never seen a rally like that at any of our hotels. To quote a wise friend, "There's ALWAYS a bigger club."

At the risk of sounding partisan, I didn't share the public's fierce obsession with Bruce. I appreciated Springsteen's work, but I was a much bigger fan of Sting's music—and that was true even before he hired me. Nevertheless, maybe those pre-tour gossip-mongers were on to something. Maybe we did have the makings of a juicy rivalry. I was tempted to stick my head out of the window and loyally counter: "Sting! Sting! Sting!"

Invigorated by my favorite country on the planet, I ventured out beyond my customary two-block radius from our hotel. I spent my afternoon wandering around the magnificent city, admiring the architecture, the piazzas, and the *almost* annoying surplus of pretty people. I returned to the hotel feeling quite cultured—and thirsty—so I decided to duck into the bar for a quick drink. Entering the lounge, I saw our drummer, JT, sitting with a certain New Jersey deity. I sidled up to the bar, ordered a cocktail, and copped a seat beside my tour mates. I tried to act naturally, but COME ON...I was hanging out with a guy who had hundreds of fans surrounding the hotel, rabidly chanting his name.

Shooting the breeze over our adult beverages, the topic eventually drifted to music. Springsteen and I reflected on our lifelong love affairs with rock 'n' roll, laughing about the "good old days" when we drooled over guitar catalogs like they were girlie magazines. Expanding on that theme, we agreed the final frontier for a professional musician was to somehow reconnect with that original youthful exuberance; when music was purely a passion—untainted by skinny paychecks, shitty contracts, and hard-knock cynicism.

As the conversation (and whiskey) flowed, I noticed an attractive young woman sitting alone at the end of the bar. She was trying her best to appear disinterested, but she obviously had her eye on *one* of us. Seizing a lull in the shoptalk, the lady cleared her throat and—with all the innocence she could muster—asked Bruce, "Excuse me, but do I know you? You look very familiar. What's your name?" JT and I sat in silence as the dubious question hung in the air. Springsteen let out a chuckle, and then replied with warranted skepticism, "My name?...Frank...Frank Sinatra." The boys had a good laugh, while the rebuffed stranger shrugged and went back to her drink. Rude? Maybe. Necessary? Probably. I guess there's a slight chance the woman honestly didn't recognize one of the biggest rock stars in the world—but Bruce's gut evidently told him otherwise.

I tagged along on an impromptu Miles Davis alumni dinner with Mino and bassist Darryl Jones on our night off in Turin. (Darryl was onboard the Amnesty tour as a member of Peter Gabriel's band.) I approached the evening with requisite cool, but secretly I was thrilled. I'd had a "man crush" on the ultra-hip Darryl for years. Matter of fact, I still do today. I covet Darryl's groove, his swagger, and his unparalleled résumé. Darryl's remarkable career includes stints with Miles, Sting, Herbie Hancock, Peter Gabriel, and Madonna. And then there's his current employer...a little outfit known as The Rolling Stones.

Mino—our undisputed food and wine expert—took Darryl and me on a foodie pilgrimage to Turin's La Prima dal 1979 Moreno. We were greeted in typical Italian fashion when we arrived at the world-renowned eatery: like long-lost family. We were led to the bar for a quick apéritif before being escorted to our table for an unforgettable gastronomic journey. The experience was more akin to dining in someone's home than a restaurant. There were no menus to pore over, no entrées to debate. We just sat back as course after delicious course appeared at our table. Each time I thought the meal was finished, the chef would re-emerge from his kitchen and beg us to try "just one more" of his delicacies. And with each new dish, came a different, yet equally exquisite, wine pairing. We finally reached our breaking point after sampling two desserts and surrendered. Supremely satisfied, we thanked our doting hosts, paid our hefty—but worth every *lire*—tab, and waddled out of the Italian house of pleasure. Best. Meal. Ever.

My small-town taste buds certainly received a thorough education as I circled the globe. Unfortunately, my newly acquired palate craved attention on occasion. A few months after the tour, I was dining at my favorite NYC haunt, the West Bank Cafe, and decided to spring for an expensive bottle of wine. (*Châteauneuf-du-Pape, he sniffed haughtily.*) The waiter poured a small portion for my approval and I proceeded to play the role of jackass to the hilt. I swirled, I smelled, I stared, and finally—as the world collectively rolled its eyes—I took a sip. Then for the first time in my life, I deemed a wine unsatisfactory. My best friend, Richie Douglas, was tending bar that night, so the wine was replaced; no questions asked. But Richie couldn't resist busting my chops as our Hell's Kitchen Rat Pack boozed it up later at the bar. "A year ago, Jeff was drinking Budweiser. Now he's sending back hundred-dollar bottles of French wine." The shoe fit.

* * *

In my limited—yet paradoxically vast—travel experience, European hotels had always been beautiful, but not necessarily the most contemporary. Turin was no different. The lodging was elegant, but old. On the plus side, staying in these venerable structures usually meant my room was accessible by stairs. As an avowed claustrophobe, I welcomed any opportunity to avoid using "the lift."

The afternoon of our concert, I made my way down the hotel's marble staircase, wanting nothing to do with the *charming* antique elevator. I'm no fan of even the most modern designs, so I sure as hell wasn't going to board that cramped relic. I reached the lobby—and stumbled into the middle of a rock-star emergency. The elevator was stuck between floors (I told you), and among its hostages was the King of New Jersey. Selfishly, my first thought was "better him than me," but my palms got sweaty just thinking about Bruce's confinement. As tour minions scrambled for a solution, the elevator suddenly lurched back to life.

When the car reached the ground floor and the doors opened, the problem was obvious: Bruce and his hefty bodyguards were packed into that tiny elevator like black-denim sardines. No wonder the old-timey thing had given up the ghost. The former captives seemed in pretty good spirits, save for one burly security guy who made a dash for the front door. He was clearly eager to reacquaint himself with sweet freedom … and fresh air. I felt his pain.

That evening, we performed to a crowd of 58,000 passionate Italians. (Is "passionate Italians" redundant?) The fans went crazy, but considering the Springsteen vigil outside of our hotel, I can't say I was surprised. The audience couldn't get enough of Sting, Peter Gabriel, and their *favorito*: BRUUUUUUCE!

Barcelona, Spain | Camp Nou Stadium | September 10

After rocking Barcelona, we bid farewell to the relatively familiar bosom of Western Europe, and settled in for an eleven-hour jaunt to Central America. Fortunately, for the first lengthy flight of the tour, we'd graduated to our official mode of travel: two World Airways DC-10 jumbo jets. One for the people; one for the gear. The charters were typically used to ferry US soldiers between the States and various military destinations around the globe, but the planes would be "at ease" for the next five weeks as they transported a less clean-cut—and much less lethal—army.

San Jose, Costa Rica | Estadio Nacional | September 13

Amnesty was the first major rock tour to hit Costa Rica in over fifteen years. (Santana was the last big act to perform there—in 1973.) And while the government was supportive of our efforts, the country's Catholic Archbishop condemned the concert. The religious leader feared our presence would "encourage drug use." (Hey, wait a minute, I *resemble* that remark.) On top of our mixed reception, Mother Nature also weighed in, sending Hurricane Gilbert to the party. The massive storm threatened to cancel the show altogether, but in spite of the heavy rains, we managed to pull it off.

Reminiscent of Brazil, I found Costa Rica to be lush, mysterious…and a bit unsettling. Between the stifling humidity and dense forestation, I felt like I needed a machete and a pith helmet just to navigate the hotel grounds. Plus, like South America, I couldn't shake the nagging feeling a coup d'état might breakout at any moment. I learned a lot about myself during my year on the road. Among those revelations? I prefer urban jungles to real ones.

Augmenting my uneasiness, Costa Rica was the first stop on our itinerary deemed to be a health risk. The local mosquitoes were known to be toxic little buggers, so malaria pills had joined vodka on my list of required daily medications. But despite my pill-popping diligence, I was still on edge as we sweated through our muggy, morning game of tennis. I kept one eye on the ball, but the other trained on the sky for any incoming, bloodthirsty kamikazes.

Jungleland did have a silver lining: the exchange rate was super friendly. Without earning an extra dime, I was suddenly in the chips. Prices were not only reasonable—they were INSANE! Drinks? One dollar. Meals? Five dollars. Most exciting of all, our hotel's laundry service was only seven dollars. That same wash/dry/fold amenity at a London or Paris hotel would easily run thirty dollars (or more). I flexed my newfound wealth and washed every stitch I owned. It was wild to watch my net worth fluctuate by simply changing time zones. I felt like a hobo in Beverly Hills, but a tycoon in San Jose.

The strong Costa Rican dollar also came in handy for our road manager. After a heated, long-distance argument with his fiancée, Billy retreated to the hotel casino to blow off some steam. By the time I caught up with him, he was pounding drinks while making (and losing) large bets on blackjack. Billy was burning through stacks of twenties like it was Monopoly money. It was disconcerting to see the normally even-tempered Billy lose his cool. He reminded me of me.

Toronto, Canada | Maple Leaf Gardens | September 15

Switching gears *slightly*, the tour bounced from a Central American rain forest to the Great White North. We deplaned in Toronto and fell into formation for the well-worn customs drill. Mr. Border Patrol gave me the usual once-over, before reeling off his standard litany of questions. I answered politely and waited for my green light. Think again, Cowboy. I was stunned when the agent singled me out and pointed me down a nearby hallway. Gulp. I wasn't stupid (or brave) enough to risk carrying contraband through customs. Nevertheless, despite being guilty of nothing, my heart was pounding. I'd make the world's worst criminal.

I took a deep breath when I reached the end of the hallway and knocked on the door. A disembodied voice growled, "Come in." I entered to find a lone uniformed officer sitting behind a desk. He looked up from his paperwork and sighed, "What the hell are you doing here?" I replied I was just following orders. He cut to the chase. "Do you have any drugs on you?" I responded, "No." He rolled his eyes and barked, "Then get the fuck out of here!" I happily obliged.

Montreal, Canada | Olympic Stadium | September 17

Montreal's Olympic Stadium has the largest seating capacity of any venue in Canada, but after ten months on the road, gigantic stadiums had become somewhat old hat. People often ask me if it was scary to play in front of such huge crowds. No way! It was fun. Ironically, it was the smaller crowds that made me nervous; specifically, the eight other people ON stage beside me. That *audience* intimidated the hell out of me. Trying to keep up with Sting and his group of world-class musicians—now THAT was scary.

On the upside, as a member of Sting's band, I was able to measure my skills against the *creme de la creme* of the industry. I never had to worry about being a big fish in a small pond; I was swimming in one of the biggest, baddest ponds in the business. Sharing the stage with those guys (and gals) was an honor. I might not have been an all-star, but at least I can say I made the team.

* * *

I never sensed any negative or competitive energies between the bands on the Amnesty tour. The environment was entirely collegial and supportive. In fact, it wasn't uncommon to see fellow musicians hanging out in the wings, grooving to our set. (Springsteen watching ME play? Crazy!) Of course I made a point to check out my fellow artists as well. Taking full advantage of my "All Access" credentials, I'd simply flash my laminate and wander into the concrete moat that separated the stage from the audience. The barricaded security area afforded me the ultimate front-row seat.

I finally got a chance to catch Tracy Chapman's set in Montreal. Her solo performance was mesmerizing, but it made me wonder: how does it feel to face such a massive crowd all by yourself? I'd always enjoyed the insulation of a band, so I had no point of reference. Being in a band is like being in a gang; it's nice to know someone's got your back—especially when the crowd starts booing (or throwing things). But Tracy had no such fraternal buffer, it was just her and her guitar. Magnifying the isolation, the introverted Chapman barely spoke between songs. I found the lack of stage patter refreshing; the awkward silence added a beautiful tension to the show. During Tracy's final tune,

I slowly panned my view from the lone player on stage to a stadium packed with 60,000 people. Tracy was seriously outnumbered, but the audience was hanging on her every note.

Courtesy of the fine folks at Amnesty International, I made a long-overdue trip down to "E Street." For years, true believers had urged me to check out one of Bruce Springsteen's live shows, rhapsodizing over his dynamic—and lengthy—performances. (Sorry, you lost me at "lengthy.") With my pop-centric attention span, a three-or four-hour concert was far from a selling point. Quite the opposite, it sounded like a perfect reason to stay away. But thanks to Amnesty's mandated time limits, I finally got to see what all the fuss was about…in an easy-to-swallow, one-hour dose. It did not disappoint. Condensing Bruce's fire and brimstone into a sixty-minute stick of dynamite made for a helluva show. His passionate, evangelical delivery lived up to every ounce of the hype. Hallelujah! I once was blind, but now I see.

Every act on the Amnesty tour was incredibly talented; there were no weak links. But if forced to choose a favorite, Peter Gabriel would get my vote. Peter's music was powerful, yet sensitive—and his stellar band blew me away. (Darryl Jones: bass, David Sancious: keyboards, David Rhodes: guitar, Shankar: violin, Manu Katché: drums.) Interestingly, Manu Katché had played drums on Sting's *Nothing Like the Sun* album, but he'd passed on an offer to do the subsequent tour. Apparently, Manu's calendar stayed full with top-call session work, so he didn't need—or want—to be out on the road. But Peter Gabriel had somehow coaxed Manu to participate in Amnesty's limited six-week run. I'm guessing in addition to the amenable time frame, a big part of Peter's pitch came down to two little words: "Darryl" and "Jones."

Each night, if I was in the building, I made sure to be front and center for the downbeat of Gabriel's smash hit, "Sledgehammer." Chills ran down my spine as Darryl and Manu played the ever-loving shit out of that groove. I've never heard a more impressive rhythm section.

* * *

Reebok was the exclusive sponsor of the Amnesty tour, underwriting the enterprise to the tune of ten million dollars. And with a sports apparel company as our sugar daddy, we were rolling in swag. Reebok showered us with shoes, shirts, caps, socks, and best of all, a hip, black leather tour jacket. The coats were quite popular with the entourage, making our hotel lobbies look like they'd been overrun by a giant motorcycle gang, hell-bent on achieving "Human Rights—NOW!"

Each tour member also received a large Amnesty/Reebok duffle bag; a generous gesture that inadvertently caused a logistics nightmare for our baggage handlers. The luggage crew had their work cut out for them as they sorted through a couple hundred identical black canvas bags at every hotel check-in. ID tags notwithstanding, delivering the look-alike luggage to its rightful owner proved to be an ongoing challenge. Ever the pragmatist, Billy grouched, "If they'd had any sense, Amnesty would have waited until the end of the tour to give us the damn bags."

Philadelphia, Pennsylvania | JFK Stadium | September 19

Philadelphia was Amnesty's only East Coast stop in the US, but public enthusiasm was surprisingly muted—relatively speaking. (Never thought I'd use the word "muted" to describe a football stadium filled with 75,000 people.) Despite our Dream Team line-up, the Philly concert still fell short of a sellout. Stymied scalpers were left holding the bag, reportedly dumping tickets for as little as ten dollars each. Amnesty's executive director, Jack Healey, was not happy about the lukewarm reception, and he didn't mince words at our local press conference. Claiming it was outrageous that thousands of tickets were still available on the day of the show, a frustrated Healy went as far as to accuse American fans of apathy. Who knows? I won't speculate whether the other countries on our itinerary were more socially conscious than America. Maybe they were just more entertainment-starved? Remember, Costa Rica hadn't seen a significant rock concert in over fifteen years. For the Northeastern United States? It had probably been about fifteen *minutes*.

Los Angeles, California | LA Coliseum | September 21

I snagged the coveted front passenger seat for our commute to the Coliseum, but riding shotgun wound up being a little too literal for my liking. As we rolled through the streets of LA, I asked our van driver about the city's well-publicized gang problems. (It seemed like the Bloods and Crips were in the national news every other day.) Our chauffeur confirmed gang violence was indeed a problem in Los Angeles, before adding, "Matter of fact, in this part of town, you're a potential target right now." He had my undivided attention. The driver explained if a gang member mistook my black baseball cap for dark blue: bang bang, hello drive-by. He suggested I might want to remove my hat just to be safe, but I was already one step ahead of him. My MTV cap was in my lap and, for good measure, I slouched down in my seat for the rest of the trip.

As always, LA lived up to its glitzy reputation. Our backstage compound looked like an "Oscar meets Grammy" party. (A-listers included Bono, Barbra Streisand, Jon Bon Jovi, Daryl Hannah, Whoopi Goldberg, Michael J. Fox, and Rob Lowe.) I shook my head in disbelief as I watched the Tinseltown elite roam around our makeshift village. It blew my mind that THEY were the audience—and Jeffrey Lee Campbell was the performer. Compared to just one year earlier, my universe had been turned completely upside down.

After LA, the tour was set to steer north to Oakland, before crossing the pond to Tokyo. But the Tokyo show had created a dilemma for Team Sting. In a mere three weeks—at the conclusion of the Amnesty tour—Sting was scheduled to crank right back up in … (you guessed it) Japan. And with a four-night stand in Tokyo on tap, Sting was justifiably concerned that a September appearance with the Amnesty all-stars might cannibalize his October ticket sales. Sting certainly didn't want to undermine his Japanese draw (or promoter), so the decision was made to skip Amnesty's Tokyo concert. Claiming "previous commitments," Sting bowed out temporarily.

In addition to Tokyo, Sting also scrapped the Oakland date. I'm not sure why we bailed on the Bay Area, but you didn't hear any complaints from our band of weary warriors. The net result was a full week off in New York City. I made the most of my much-needed break from the world at large, being as lazy as humanly possible during the hiatus.

I was channel surfing from the comfort of my couch one evening and stumbled upon a news story about the Amnesty tour. I perked up when I heard ABC's anchorman report Sting had "quit" the human rights campaign. Say what? Until that moment, I'd always regarded network news as accurate and trustworthy. Silly me. The report claimed ongoing ego problems between Sting and Springsteen had finally boiled over—and Sting had walked out. What a complete load of crap. Minimal investigative reporting would've uncovered the real reason behind Sting's absence: his upcoming shows in Japan. Come on ABC, follow the damn money.

Not surprisingly, my spontaneous vacation flew by. In two blinks, it was time to rejoin Amnesty's rock 'n' roll circus, which was now parked halfway around the world in India. No problem; just a matter of jumping on British Airways: NYC to London…London to Dubai…Dubai to New Delhi. Whew! Thankfully, it was a direct flight with no transfers or long layovers, but it still left a bruise.

Our seven-hour flight to London barely registered; we were just getting started. But cabin fever had officially kicked in by the time we landed in the United Arab Emirates (another seven hours later). With a brief stopover in Dubai for routine maintenance, passengers were permitted to deplane if they desired. I'd

achieved peak restlessness hours earlier, but didn't feel motivated (or adventurous) enough to trek to the distant terminal. As a
compromise, I decided to poke my head outside for a quick breath
of fresh air. This seemed like a good plan until I stepped through
the plane's doorway and Dubai's oppressive heat punched me in
the gut. The Persian Gulf clearly didn't give a damn it was the
middle of the night—it was still hot as hell.

I gazed out across the darkened Middle Eastern landscape
in awe. I was attempting to process my latest latitude and longi-
tude when I felt a tap on my shoulder. I turned to find a smiling flight attendant, who politely informed me I needed to come
back inside the airplane, or proceed to the terminal—but I was
not allowed to stand pat. The hostess spelled out the international chain of custody, explaining I was protected by Great Britain
inside the aircraft, or by the United Arab Emirates inside the
airport. But on the jet's stairway, I was a man without a country.
She ominously trailed off, "And if anything was to happen…" I'd
heard more than enough. I scurried back to the security of my
seat, ready for India. Or so I thought.

New Delhi, India | Nehru Stadium | September 30

After almost twenty-four hours of captivity on British Airways,
Team *Stung* finally touched down in India. We dragged our depleted asses through customs and collapsed into the waiting van.
Dawn was breaking as we pulled up to our hotel—just in time
to collide with a well-rested, enthusiastic gang from the Amnes-

ty tour. The unbearably chipper group was heading out on a day-trip to the Taj Mahal, and they urged us to join them. Yeah, right. I'd just spent an entire day on an airplane, now I was supposed to endure a three-hour bus ride to look at some white building? Even the fabled Taj Mahal couldn't compete with the thought of a shower and a twelve-hour nap. No thanks; I wasn't going anywhere but to bed. I may never get another chance to see the Taj Mahal, but for once in this story, I have no regrets.

I slept on and off for a day before finally rejoining the human race. I met up with Delmar and Mino in the hotel lobby, and we set out to see at least a sliver of India. Our taxi driver gave a cursory tour of a few points of interest, before ultimately delivering us to the ancient section of New Delhi—cleverly known as *Old Delhi*.

I felt like a time traveler as we wandered through the slums of Old Delhi. I halfway expected to see Indiana Jones leap from the shadows and brandish his bullwhip to clear the chaotic crowds. The setting simply did not compute with my Western sensibilities. Scores of ragged, malnourished people lived in shanties and cardboard boxes alongside open sewers. It was a disturbing image I'll never forget. Curious locals gathered around as we walked the squalid streets, reaching and grabbing at us, obviously eager to touch the opulent strangers. Despite my deepest sympathies, I was concerned about my exposure to the extremely unhygienic conditions. I'm no germaphobe, but when I got back to the hotel, I took the longest, hottest shower of my life.

The highlight of Old Delhi was our visit to Jama Masjid, one of the largest mosques in India. Over three hundred years old, the massive structure was big enough to hold twenty-five thousand worshipers. As we attempted to enter, we were met with "no shoes allowed." We respectfully removed our Air Jordans and tossed them onto the pile of footwear outside the gate. (Local kids hanging around the entrance assured us they'd keep an eye on our sneakers while we were inside.) We hit yet another roadblock when we stepped into the mosque's archway: short pants were also considered a no-no. In spite of the searing heat, men weren't allowed to bare their legs inside the temple. But unlike our shoes, removing our shorts would've only made matters worse. Luckily, Jama Masjid was on the case, providing burlap wraps to cover our blasphemous knees. We obviously weren't the first clueless pagans to visit the holy site.

I stood in the middle of the historic shrine, sporting white athletic socks, a sweaty Chuck Berry T-shirt, a beat-up MTV baseball cap, and a filthy horse blanket wrapped around my waist. *Ladies and Gentlemen, please welcome the newest member of Jama Masjid's Dress Code Hall of Shame.* We roamed the courtyard wide-eyed, taking in the exotic sights and sounds before eventually being led to an area that housed a collection of religious artifacts. A feeble gentleman with a long white beard moved in quasi-slow motion as he showcased the Islamic treasures. The most intriguing antiquity in my opinion was a glass vial containing a strand of hair from the prophet Muhammad's beard. (That's a thousand-year old whisker!)

The geriatric curator closed his presentation by asking if we'd like to make a donation to the mini-museum. I responded with my ingrained NYC panhandler shrug, trotting out the "Sorry, no change" excuse. Our turbaned guide didn't bat an eye. He whispered, "No problem," and pulled back his robe to reveal a shiny, belt-mounted coin changer. I did NOT see that one coming. Granted a do-over, I contributed a handful of rupees to the cause. We encountered more of the same entrepreneurial spirit as we exited the mosque. The formerly easy-going kids at the gate were now demanding "two dollars a pair" for the safe return of our hostage shoes.

After witnessing the inhumanity of Old Delhi, I couldn't help but feel guilty as I returned to my posh accommodations. Our hotel was modern and comfortable, with a sprawling rear lawn that featured tennis courts and a swimming pool. Adding to the country club vibe, a tall, manicured shrub surrounded the recreational area. The wall of greenery provided a lush veil of privacy for hotel guests. But if you viewed the backyard from the hotel's upper floors, you realized the towering bushes served a dual purpose. The foliage not only kept prying eyes out, it kept prying eyes IN. With a higher vantage point, you got the full, unvarnished picture: affluent guests frolicking about while homeless people lived in cardboard boxes right across the street. India's brutal juxtaposition of the haves and the have-nots was on graphic display from up above.

We piled into our bus the next evening and began making our way to the stadium. After a few miles, the well-lit, paved city streets of Delhi suddenly changed into dark, dirt roads. The dividing line between modern and primitive was stark, and practically instantaneous. I was peering out my window when the bus jerked to a stop. I had to rub my eyes to confirm I wasn't hallucinating. Like I'd always heard—yet found a bit hard to swallow—cows were wandering freely in the street. The four-legged pedestrians jaywalked at will as drivers patiently navigated the bovine obstacle course.

Athens, Greece | Olympic Stadium | October 3

The tour threw a big 37th birthday bash for Sting in Athens. His previous birthday party (on the day I'd been hired) seemed like a million years ago—or at least a million miles ago. Amnesty honchos reserved a large chunk of tables at a local restaurant, and the *lucky* proprietors were all smiles as we invaded the establishment. Tsk tsk. Little did they realize, a Trojan horse was rolling through the gates. Do the math: the only thing more volatile than a party involving a rock band is a party involving multiple rock bands. The joint was doomed.

Maybe the size of our group simply overwhelmed the restaurant, but, for whatever reason, the service was horrible. We placed our orders and then waited...and waited for the food to arrive. Not a good plan on our host's part; no chewing meant more drinking. Our dinners finally started appearing, but many of the meals were undercooked and inedible, or delivered to the wrong guest. In all the confusion, things started getting out of hand.

We'd been told in advance the restaurant encouraged the celebratory Greek custom of plate smashing. As the ouzo continued to flow, one drunk and disorderly member of our party (not me, honest) decided it was time to get the ball rolling. The instigator rose from his seat, screamed *Opa!* and slammed his plate to the floor. One shattered dish was all it took to light the fuse. In the "monkey see, monkey do" world of musicians, plates started flying everywhere. The air was filled with whoops and hollers—and the wails of dying china. A flood of waiters rushed to our area, desperately trying to put an end to the carnage. The staff pleaded for us to stop destroying their fancy dishes, explaining the restaurant used specific, inexpensive plaster plates (sans food) for the actual smashing ritual. *Oops-a!*

Pouring gasoline on the fire, the restaurant's belly dancer started flirting with our fearless leaders. The sexy tummy set her sights on Springsteen first, toying with The Boss as she playfully tried to unbutton his shirt. Birthday boy Sting seized the moment and, without any prodding, removed his own shirt. (There he goes again.) Even the mild-mannered Peter Gabriel was ultimately dragged into the fracas. Pretty soon, the whole gang was up on their feet, dancing around the room behind the silky provocateur. It was an epic blowout.

As we finally staggered out of the restaurant, I noticed E Street back-up singer Patti Scialfa giving her boss an angry earful. Hmmm. Springsteen had recently filed for divorce from Julianne Phillips, and gossip rags were buzzing that Bruce and Patti's relationship had escalated from business to something a little more pleasurable. In light of Patti's fiery outburst, I wondered if the rumors might just be true. I guess they were. Three years later, Bruce and Patti were married.

We dusted ourselves off the next night and served up some American-British-Senegalese rock 'n' roll stew to over 70,000 hungry Greeks. I returned to the hotel after our show, grabbed a quick shower, packed for the following day's departure, and then headed down to the hotel bar for my usual round of nightcaps. I stumbled back up to my room after closing the joint, placed my duffle bag outside my door for early morning pick-up, and crashed into bed. Rising a few short hours later, I was packing my carry-on when I had a terrifying realization: I couldn't find my passport.

If a Ten Commandments of Touring existed, "Thou shalt protect thy passport" would be at the top of the list. From my very first trip abroad (with Bushrock), veteran band mates had repeatedly warned me to safeguard my travel papers. I took the sound advice to heart, making a point to never carry my passport on me unless I was specifically en route to the airport. Whenever I ventured out into the world at large, I'd leave my passport behind in my hotel room. And as an added precaution against theft, I'd stash the booklet deep inside my suitcase. This was a solid strategy— provided you remembered to extract the hidden passport BEFORE relinquishing your bag to the luggage crew. Being pampered rock stars, we weren't personally responsible for schlepping our belongings to and from the airport. On travel days, I'd simply place my luggage outside my door and, like magic, I wouldn't see the bag again until I walked into my next hotel room. But guess what I forgot to "extract" in Athens? Need I go on?

Yep, it was time to depart Greece—for Africa, no less—and I didn't have my passport. The only good news? I knew exactly where it was. Stuffed deep in my airport-bound duffle bag. Code Red!

Trying not to freak out, I called Billy and gave him my bone-headed news. Billy knew he didn't have any time to waste berating me, so he just groaned, "Meet me in the lobby." The plan was to rush to the airport, intercept the baggage truck and recover my passport before the luggage was buried in the bowels of our jumbo jet. Further complicating my self-inflicted emergency, the city of Athens was in the middle of a taxi strike. But the battle-tested Billy stayed calm under fire. He flagged down a private citizen—an opportunistic cab "scab"—and bribed him to drive us to the airport.

Billy explained my dilemma to the authorities at the terminal, and was whisked away to meet our baggage truck, already on the tarmac. (Being undocumented, I wasn't allowed to take part in the scavenger hunt.) Billy's needle-in-a-haystack mission was to locate my bag—hiding among the luggage of two hundred other people—and then dig through my dirty laundry in hopes of finding the wayward passport. And don't forget, Reebok had gifted the entire tour with identical duffle bags, so describing my luggage to Billy was pointless. He already knew what it looked like: everybody else's. Faced with a truckload of indistinguishable black canvas bags, Billy's only search method was to manually check ID tags—one by one.

Powerless to help, I was reduced to pacing back and forth on the Greek side of customs. My imagination ran wild as my fate hung in the balance. What if Billy struck out? I felt a surge of panic as I contemplated the burden of navigating Athens on my own. I'd need to find the American consulate and apply for a replacement passport. (How long would that take? Days?) And even after I obtained my new papers, I'd have to fly commercially—and unaccompanied—from Greece to Africa. That sounded like the perfect route for aspiring hijackers to me. Slamming the brakes on my racing thoughts, I vowed to ignore the scary voices in my head. But the machine guns slung over the airport guards' backs weren't exactly helping matters.

On a positive note, as I was coming unglued in my designated corner, I was befriended by two young ladies. Presented with four pretty Greek shoulders to cry on, I shared my tale of woe. The cute locals were sympathetic to my predicament and offered to help in ANY way possible. (*Bow-chick-a-wow-*

wow.) I was a desperate man—but still a man—so I clung to their sexy, smiling faces as a potential bright spot in my hour of darkness. Meanwhile, I started seeing members of the Amnesty tour making their way through the terminal. Shit! Time was getting tight. Word of my plight had obviously spread, as I received numerous compassionate smiles and waves from my Africa-bound comrades. Springsteen even gave a kindhearted nod as he passed, acknowledging the poor loser who'd stupidly packed his passport.

I was beginning to lose hope when the cavalry appeared on the horizon. Relief washed over me as I saw Billy rushing in my direction, waving that little blue book in the air. Praise the Lord, I'd been rescued by the crusty, but chivalrous, Billy Francis. (Semper Fi, leave no man behind.) All kidding aside, Billy went above and beyond the call of duty that day, and I'll never forget it. He saved my absent-minded ass from God-knows-what. Thankfully, this scared little boy would not have to make his way to Zimbabwe all by his lonesome. My tour mates cheered sarcastically as I boarded the plane, but the catcalls were sweet music to my ears. I was ecstatic to be back among two hundred of my closest friends—and on my way to Africa.

With my fears of abandonment safely behind me, and my passport tucked securely in my pocket, I enjoyed every single minute of our flight to Africa. We touched down in Zimbabwe eight hours later—and pillows started flying through the cabin, right on cue. Yes, pillows. We'd developed a steadfast tradition as the tour *matured*. Every landing was celebrated with a massive pillow fight. The flight attendants had initially protested the rowdy ritual, citing a slew of FAA violations, but since it was "our" plane, most of the regulations had dissolved into mere suggestions.

Our childish battle was always waged in the spirit of good clean fun…until Zimbabwe. Things took an ugly turn that afternoon when one of Sting's roadies got carried away and flung a hard-bottomed seat cushion through the air. The flying weapon nailed Delmar in the head and a heated war of words ensued. The eyeball-to-eyeball showdown was ultimately diffused, but as we deplaned, I saw Delmar's assailant sitting on the tarmac with tears streaming down his reddened face. I totally identified with the roadie's frayed emotional state. The sight of a grown man sobbing in broad daylight underscored just how fragile we'd all become.

Despite a year filled with one unreal experience after another, setting foot on the continent of Africa was awe-inspiring. My guitar had taken me many incredible places, but I never dreamed I'd play a gig (or two) in Africa. Rock tours tend to hit the same cities—leg after leg, tour after tour—so the life of a sideman can often feel redundant. But even the most jaded members of the Amnesty entourage were psyched about seeing Africa, with one notable exception: my man Branford.

Back when Team Sting took its weeklong breather from Amnesty—to avoid double-dipping Tokyo—Branford decided to go for the gold and stretch his break by an additional two weeks. (Marsalis clout in action!) But Branford's extended hiatus meant he'd miss out on three of Amnesty's more exotic stops: India, Greece, and Africa. The timing was purely pragmatic, but Branford caught some flak from pal, and fellow African-American, Darryl Jones nonetheless. Citing cultural pride, Darryl contended Branford should jump at a chance to visit ancestral Africa. But

Darryl's attempted guilt trip was DOA. If I learned anything on Sting's tour, Branford Marsalis is his own man. Impervious to the peer pressure, Branford stuck to his guns, telling Darryl, "I hear you bro, but I need a break." (During his absence, Branford recruited Miles Davis's saxophonist Kenny Garret to fill his shoes. Kenny sounded amazing—and I'm happy to report he didn't take a single swing at me.)

Harare, Zimbabwe | National Sports Stadium | October 7

My first taste of Africa was remarkably unremarkable. I'd looked forward to discovering a whole new world, but Harare felt more like a quaint Midwestern city circa 1965. Uninspired by the bland surroundings, my burnout re-reared its apathetic head. I hated feeling this way. I wanted to share the energy and enthusiasm of my colleagues. But, in my slight defense, none of the other bands were in the late throes of a yearlong tour. My fellow travelers all seemed pretty gung ho about the condensed, six-week global adventure. Me? I was running on fumes—and had PLENTY of Sting miles still left ahead. Matter of fact, in just a little over a week, I'd be barnstorming my way around Japan. Meanwhile, my Amnesty pals would be back home and gainfully unemployed. Those lucky bastards.

Similar to the Taj Mahal junket in India, tour management organized a field trip to Africa's Victoria Falls. Twice the height of Niagara Falls, Victoria Falls is the largest waterfall in the world. But despite the rare opportunity—surprise, surprise—I passed on the outing. I have some regrets about it now, but at the time, my decision was very easy: the expedition involved an airplane. Thanks, but no thanks. After ten months of relentless air travel, I had no interest in ANY nonessential flying…not even to see one of the Seven Natural Wonders of the World.

As a Sting employee, my job description entailed at least three or four flights a week. That was more than enough takeoffs and landings for my frazzled nervous system. (At a certain point, you begin to think you're pushing your luck.) I actually suffered a couple of borderline meltdown days during the tour where I truly felt I couldn't face one more flight. But what was I supposed to do? Hitchhike home from Brazil? Having no choice, I dug deep and climbed onboard anyway. Sucking it up definitely took its toll.

Instead of joining the intrepid Victoria Falls explorers, I fell in with a few equally unadventurous types and spent the afternoon playing tennis at our promoter's country estate. (Breaking a sweat had become one of my primary salvations as I struggled to maintain what little bit of sanity I had left.) As we served and volleyed in the hot African sun, a groundskeeper cleared our empty water bottles and asked if we'd like something more to drink. We chimed, "Absolutely," but with a justified fear of foreign tap water, we specifically requested bottled water. I'd already been forced to raid the tour's Imodium supply once, so I was the poster boy for "Don't drink the water." (Damn you, Barcelona.) Leery of local H_2O in any quantity, I was hyper-vigilant. I kept my mouth closed tight while showering, and only brushed my teeth with bottled water—or whatever toothpaste-friendly beverage happened to be left in my mini-bar.

We took a break from our sticky tennis match and grabbed

a seat to await our refreshments. Thank God, Kim happened to glance over and catch our water boy in action. Kim let fly with an expletive, as we turned to see the well-meaning kid crouched down on the lawn, refilling our depleted Evian bottles with a garden hose. We yelled, "Whoa, not water in a bottle—bottled water!" The startled youngster froze, dropped the hose and disappeared inside the house. Dodging a major bullet, we were relieved when the worker returned carrying factory-sealed bottles from our host's trustworthy stock.

That evening, I bumped into a couple of the Victoria Falls day-trippers back at the hotel. I inquired about their excursion and learned it had been an adventure from the get-go. The hotshot charter pilot had unnerved the group with his daredevil maneuvers, repeatedly swooping over and around the falls for up-close and nausea-inducing views. Fortunately, once the gang was reunited with *terra firma*, they enjoyed a relaxing afternoon—for the most part.

One of Sting's roadies, affectionately known as "Duds," decided to go for a swim and unwittingly provided the heart-stopping highlight of the day. The gang was watching Duds paddle along when, out of nowhere, a hippopotamus rose to the surface. Cartoon hippos may be cute and friendly, but real hippos are considered one of the most dangerous animals in Africa. Luckily, the deadly predator was feeling charitable—or full—because *Tarzan* lived to tell his tale.

Our tour physician caught wind of Duds' daring swim, and immediately voiced concern about possible exposure to harmful bacteria. (Yes, we had a doctor traveling with us full-time.) The medic strongly urged Duds to be checked for infection after the tour ended. We all howled when the doctor informed Duds a proper biopsy would require a procedure known as a "rectal snip." Yikes! That sounded more like sadomasochism than medicine to me. Poor Duds, his ass may have avoided "death by hippo," but it didn't escape completely unscathed.

Suppertime in Zimbabwe…now what? Finding a decent meal in uncharted cities (or uncharted continents) could sometimes be an iffy proposition. But my world-wise mentor, Billy Francis, taught me a reliable workaround for sketchy locales. Never ask for a "good" restaurant, ask for "the most expensive" place in town. The blunt question removes all subjectivity. Our latest port-of-call seemed like a prime candidate for price profiling, so we put the squeeze on our hotel concierge. Armed with the answer, Billy, Nils Lofgren, and myself set out for Harare's finest—or at least, priciest—dining.

We surveyed the high-end menu and settled on our orders. We were laughing and chatting away when Nils suddenly fell silent. With a horrified look on his face, Nils pointed to the large column beside our dimly lit table. Billy and I turned to see a monstrous African beetle slowly making his way up the nearby pole. (It's still the largest bug I've ever seen.) We debated on bailing, but our growling stomachs persuaded us to hang tough. Meanwhile, the quick-thinking Nils devised a plan to insect-proof our dining experience. Following Nils's inspired lead, we stuffed our pants legs into our socks and sat crossed-legged for the rest of the evening—hoping our defensive measures would protect us from the roving Bugzilla (or any of his cousins).

Abidjan, Côte d'Ivoire | Stade Géo André | October 9

Our second stop in Africa was more in line with my original, exotic expectations. I felt like I'd landed in a different century as I gazed out our bus window to see a group of colorfully dressed women washing clothes in the river alongside the highway. One team scrubbed, while another team spread a patchwork of wet laundry across the sunlit banks to dry. Laying the freshly cleaned items so close to a bustling freeway seemed to kind of defeat the purpose, but I got the feeling there weren't any self-serve laundromats right around the corner. (I didn't even see any corners.) It was a perfect illustration of how America's common conveniences aren't "common" everywhere. On the bright side, the ladies didn't need rolls and rolls of quarters to feed ravenous clothes dryers. Come to think of it, maybe *they* were the modern society. They were the ones employing cutting-edge solar power.

* * *

Children swarmed around us as we exited our bus at the venue. The excited youngsters were obviously eager to show off for their out-of-town guests, and began flinging rocks up into the surrounding trees—trees that just happened to be filled with bats. (For the record, I don't like bats. Who does?) Whenever one of the rocks found its mark, an unlucky bat would come tumbling to the ground. The boys would race over, grab the stunned creature by its wing and whip it against the curb before proudly holding up the motionless beast for our approval. Umm—cool? The violent display seemed strange at first, until I thought back on my childhood. Growing up, we loved to hang out under the streetlight on summer nights…and throw rocks at bats. Africa and Carrboro may be worlds apart, but I guess kids are kids.

The local bats—the conscious ones, anyway—provided spontaneous bursts of aerial choreography throughout our set. Roused from their roosts by certain frequencies, the colony would dart up into the air and start circling the stadium, swooping up and down to our thumping beat. In the middle of "One World (Not Three)," Sting couldn't resist and segued into an impromptu jam on Neal Hefti's iconic *Batman* TV theme. "*Nana Nana Nana Nana—BATMAN!*"

Unlike our typical audiences, the Abidjan crowd was overwhelmingly male. It was wild to gaze out into the mass of humanity and see hardly any female faces. (And while we're on the subject, even fewer white faces. As Clarence Clemons said to Springsteen, "Now YOU know what it feels like!") Despite the gender imbalance, Sting still unleashed his trademark "Don't Stand so Close" striptease. Sting peeled off his sweaty shirt as he crooned about forbidden schoolgirls, but rather than letting his shirt fall to the stage floor as usual, Sting impulsively tossed it into the crowd. The article of clothing might have sparked a brief, good-natured tug-of-war at a more conventional concert, but on that muggy afternoon in Côte d'Ivoire, a small riot broke out instead. Men started fighting over the souvenir and the skirmish quickly turned violent. As we soldiered on with the tune, I was shocked to see one of the moshers whip out a blackjack and start beating another man over the head. All for a stupid shirt.

Crowd control, especially in less-regulated parts of the world, could sometimes be a nightmare. I'd watch in horror as hemmed-in audience members fought, puked, fainted, or cried for help as they were crushed against the barricades near the front of the stage. Instincts told me to put down my guitar and aid my fellow man. But what the hell could I do? Crowd safety was the venue's responsibility. Nevertheless, continuing to strum through the pandemonium always felt cold-hearted.

São Paulo, Brazil | Estádio do Palmeiras | October 12

Certain repeat destinations started to seem downright familiar after almost a year on the road. The notion I could loosely find my way around world cities like Paris, London, or Los Angeles made me feel so cosmopolitan. Along those lines, I immediately recognized my surroundings as we pulled up to our hotel in São Paulo. (Add another city to the list.) We were back at the swinging São Paulo Hilton, home of the infamous high-pressure water massage. Without thinking, I blurted out, "Hey Sting, this is the place where you and I got hosed down last year." Sting responded with a chilly stare, playing dumb in front a busload of suddenly intrigued tour mates. My bad. I guess I didn't have that "cosmopolitan" thing figured out after all.

I couldn't wait to check out our locally added act in São Paulo: singer-songwriter Milton Nascimento, aka "the Stevie Wonder of Brazil." I'd become a fan of Nascimento's work through his collaborations with Wayne Shorter, George Duke, and my

R&B idols, Earth, Wind & Fire. Fueling my anticipation further, rumor had it jazz guitar great, Pat Metheny, would be sitting in with Nascimento's band. Welcome to my world—another day, another superstar (or two). But by that point, hobnobbing with big name celebs was old news; or at least that's how I tried to play it.

I'd learned early on to hide any traces of awe in the big leagues. Acting excited was a dead giveaway: rookie on board. Accordingly, I dug deep and presented the best poker face I could muster. I tried—with varying degrees of success—to take all things in stride, no matter how mind-blowing they might be. Fortunately, the statute of limitations on mandatory cool expired long ago. Today, I'm free to openly marvel at the all-star company I was keeping. Day in and day out, I was surrounded by some of the finest talent in the world.

Meanwhile, Sting had a special guest up his sleeve as well. In his ongoing efforts to shine a light on the rainforest crisis, Sting had asked his Amazon pal, Chief Raoni, to join us at the São Paulo concert. The Kayapo leader accepted Sting's invite and negotiated the grueling thousand-mile journey from the deep Xingu jungle to the throbbing metropolis of São Paulo. I can't imagine a more mind-bending case of culture shock.

Sting brought the Chief out on stage during our set and introduced him to 70,000 screaming fans. The juxtaposition between aboriginal Raoni and our band of hipsters was jarring, to say the least. In addition to his tribal attire, Raoni's physical appearance was dominated by a symbolic "lip plate"—a large wooden disc embedded in his lower lip. (I'd tried not to stare when I first met Raoni, but the flapping protrusion was pretty hard to ignore.) The São Paulo crowd stood transfixed as Chief Raoni applied war paint to Sting's face, before the two performed a traditional Indian song together. I've played a lot of interesting gigs over the years, but this one was in a class of its own.

Mendoza, Argentina | Estadio Mundialista | October 14

The Republic of Chile ranked high on Amnesty's list of human rights abusers, but with no expectations of a Chilean welcome mat, the tour settled for shouting distance and parked itself right next door in the western reaches of Argentina. The two countries were separated by the imposing Andes Mountains, but a nearby pass allowed thousands of Chileans to make their way to our concert. Score one for the human spirit. In spite of their oppression—or maybe because of it—the people of Chile were willing to travel hundreds of miles to hear our message of freedom.

To keep things loose, the Amnesty bands would often mix and match musicians. But unfortunately, I wasn't famous enough—or bold enough—to get in on the action. Like the nerd at the playground, I always wound up watching from the sidelines. Self-doubt and fear of rejection made me gun-shy. I didn't want to ask, I wanted to be asked. And we all know how that usually turns out.

Wallflower status notwithstanding, I desperately wanted to play at least one song with the E Street Band before the tour ended. But my window of opportunity was closing fast. I worked up my nerve in Mendoza and asked my pal Nils to put in a word with his/The Boss. Carrying my water, Nils lobbied Bruce … and it worked. Bruce granted my wish, agreeing to let me sit in on "The River" that night. When Nils told me I'd been green-lighted, I gave him a bear hug and spent the rest of the day eagerly anticipating my five minutes of E Street glory.

But just before the show, Bruce mysteriously reversed his decision and declared, "No guests tonight." I was bummed. Nils sensed my disappointment and attempted to shore up my ego by labeling Bruce's flip-flop "bullshit." I appreciated Nils's kind-hearted gesture, but the damage was done. Springsteen's last-minute veto stirred up all my feelings of inadequacy. Even from my lofty perch as Sting's guitarist, the rejection hurt.

The highlight of our set that evening was "They Dance Alone"—Sting's protest anthem inspired by the country just over the mountains. As the song climaxed, we were joined on stage by members of the *Mothers of the Disappeared*, the group founded by women who'd lost loved ones under Chilean dictator Augusto Pinochet's murderous regime. (Sting's poignant lyrics explicitly address Pinochet by name, taking the evil leader to task for his wanton brutality and corruption.) The scene was powerful and heartrending, but I must confess I was a little distracted. Performing in the shadow of the Andes, my overactive imagination kept drifting to paranoid visions of Chilean sniper squads. I felt like a sitting duck out there on that brightly lit, stadium stage— standing a mere twenty-feet from General Pinochet's *least* favorite pop star. Matter of fact, I may have inadvertently created a new dance step that night: "The Funky Moving Target."

Buenos Aires, Argentina | Estadio River Plate | October 15

35,000 miles later, Amnesty crossed the finish line in Buenos Aires. A year after my first visit to the Argentinian capital, I was back at their huge soccer stadium, once again preparing to strum my guitar for 60,000 hot-blooded music lovers. I never thought I'd experience something like that once in my life, much less twice. Elevating my festive mood, I'd received the ultimate graduation gift: an invitation to sit in with Bruce Springsteen and the E Street Band.

For the tour's finale of finales, Bruce presided over an all-star jam of "Twist and Shout"—and I got to go along for the ride. Sting and Peter Gabriel ramped up the traditional closing-night hijinks, reappearing for the last number dressed as Springsteen clones. (The dapper Brits shed their designer threads in favor of Bruce's official uniform of black jeans and shirtless black vest.) Sting and Peter egged Springsteen on as the jam unfurled, encouraging him to escalate his already over-the-top antics. The marathon three-chord rave-up eventually devolved into a sloppy game of "Follow the Leader," with the trio of superstars chasing each other around the stage, turning somersaults and spewing streams of bottled water high into the air. The song was one big mess…but what a beautiful, joyous mess it was. As musical moments go, it left a lot to be desired; as lifetime achievements go, I was in heaven. Honorary members of the E Street Band that night included Sting, Peter Gabriel, Youssou N'Dour, Branford Marsalis, David Sancious, Springsteen's manager Jon Landau, Amnesty director Jack Healey, and all the way from Carrboro, North Carolina—ME!

The next day, two hundred hungover rock 'n' roll refugees boarded *Amnesty Air* for the trip home. Everyone cheered—and threw pillows, of course—when we touched down at JFK. Ahh-hh, my cue to exhale. I'd developed a superstitious ritual throughout my year of near-constant flying: I never adjusted my watch to our new time zone until we were safely on the ground. Even on the pilot's final approach, I refused to touch that dial. My Swatch was officially off-limits until I felt the jet's wheels bump the runway. It was my nutty little signal to God I took nothing for granted.

A flight attendant announced the local time as we taxied to the gate. Our lengthy flight had basically been due north, so the time-change only amounted to a one hour difference. The whole cabin burst into laughter when Bruce's drummer, Max Weinberg, groaned, "Oh come on! If I'm going to fly for ten hours, I want to move my watch more than THAT."

A year or so later, I bumped into E Street pianist Roy Bittan in Los Angeles. We gabbed about current events for a few minutes before setting sail for memory lane. Roy summed up our global adventure perfectly. "Jeff, the Amnesty tour was LITERALLY a once in a lifetime experience." That was a powerful statement coming from a super-successful, seasoned veteran like Roy Bittan. Around the world in 40 days.

Japan

October 19 — November 3 (9 shows in 5 cities)

After wrapping our six-week, five-continent sprint for human rights, I had ONE single day in NYC to catch my breath—and do laundry—before jumping on a plane to Japan. (Maybe I should've contacted Amnesty International about my questionable treatment. Article 24 of the Universal Declaration of Human Rights guarantees "reasonable limitation of working hours.") The brutal dovetail between the two legs resulted in a personal *best*, establishing a travel record I hope to never break. In a period of less than seventy-two hours, I was in Buenos Aires, New York City, and Tokyo. I hit all four hemispheres—Southern to Northern, Western to Eastern—in under three days. And keeping with our merciless travel demands, when we landed in Tokyo (after clocking thirteen hours in the air), we immediately boarded another flight to Nagoya. By that point of my crazy year, I simply kept my head down ... and the bottle up.

There's no doubt in my mind those harsh stretches of travel helped cement my chronic homebody status. Every musician should be lucky enough to tour the world—ONCE. But wanting to do it more than once depends on your constitution. Life on the road is not for everybody (and that list would include me). On the upside, my year of furious globetrotting cured me of any and all wanderlust. Today, despite *loving* ridicule from my friends, I barely leave my Hell's Kitchen neighborhood. And when I do, my preferred mode of travel is by foot.

* * *

I absolutely loved Japan. The faraway land was exciting and unique. In fact, so unique we required the services of a full-time translator. Until Japan, I'd been able to semi-communicate in most of our foreign ports of call. Thanks to dusty remnants from Mr. Dewey's high school Spanish class, I could usually string together enough cognates to get by. But Japan's inscrutable language had rendered all of my fallback tricks useless. (My Japanese vocabulary consisted of two words: "domo" and "arigato"—both courtesy of Styx.) And as far as deciphering their written word? Impossible!

Or as the sign in a Tokyo window would read:

無理

Enter Koko—our smart, cute, and indispensable translator. (Coincidentally, my brother, Will, toured Japan with Harry Connick Jr.'s Big Band a few years later, and Koko handled translation duties for them as well.) Koko stayed by our side throughout Japan, helping us bridge the insurmountable communication gap.

I kept her quite busy, constantly asking how to say certain words and phrases. But despite Koko's patient repetitions, I'd often end up begging her to "just write it down." I've always been a visual learner, so if I actually saw the words, I had a fighting chance of retaining the phonetics. Meanwhile, Branford usually grasped Koko's lessons with a single listen. This didn't surprise me in the least; great musicians have great ears. While I was dependent on my "left brain" to process the information analytically, Branford thrived on the purely aural. That dude made me so damn jealous. Forget about the more provocative body parts, most musicians wish they were endowed with *bigger* ears.

Nagoya | Rainbow Hall | October 20
Sapporo | Makomanai Open Stadium | October 22

After playing Nagoya and Sapporo, we made our way to the mighty beast of Tokyo. And just like Manhattan had done a couple of years earlier, the electrified metropolis swept me off my feet. I can't help it; I'm a sucker for big cities. They seduce me with their promise of limitless opportunity, while cleverly using their hustle and bustle to drown out my small-town inferiority complex.

I realize it sounds superficial, but important cities make *me* feel important. They appeal to my ego's lust of grandiosity. But in my defense, they also appeal to my passion for exceptionalism. Big cities sizzle with the prospect something "big" can happen at any moment — and Tokyo definitely held up its end of the bargain. (Stay tuned.) Places like NYC, Paris, and London can be incredibly intoxicating, and, for some of us, habit-forming. I've long contended by the time you're sick of living in New York City, you're also hopelessly addicted to it.

Tokyo's fast-paced intensity resembled Manhattan more than any other stop on our tour. The city's pulse actually eclipsed the breakneck tempo of NYC in certain respects. The screaming neon billboards in Shibuya Crossing made Times Square seem almost quaint by comparison. Meanwhile, the crush of commuters at rush hour would force mild-mannered subway workers to morph into human battering rams, aggressively shoving overflow riders into the already jam-packed cars. But for my money, Tokyo's vending machines said it all. City sidewalks featured self-serve, coin-operated machines stocked with bottles of whiskey. Now *that* is hardcore, even by my rock 'n' roll standards.

Tokyo | Tokyo Dome | October 24, 25, 26, 27

We played four sold-out shows at the massive Tokyo Dome, performing to approximately 50,000 fans each night. And while I'm no accountant, that kind of business obviously translated into some serious yen. *Somebody* was raking in the big bucks that week…but it wasn't me. That said, let me make one thing clear: I'm eternally grateful to Sting for hiring me. I would've done his tour for peanuts—literally. But by Japan, it was late enough in the game to start lightly resenting some of the cockeyed math.

My weekly salary was a generous—but capped—$2500. My

paycheck stayed locked in, regardless of the amount of shows played in any given week. Meanwhile, the more *vital* members of the band were paid on a "per show" basis. And if a concert was filmed or televised, they received double pay for that performance. (For those of you keeping score at home, our second night at the Tokyo Dome was filmed for broadcast on HBO.)

Crunching the Tokyo numbers, me and my fellow rookies were pulling down a little over $600 a night to perform in front of a crowd equal to the size of a large town. With all due respect, I've made that much playing at wedding receptions in New York City (to considerably smaller audiences). Needless to say, these calculations were not lost on us second-stringers. One night, as Tracy and I rollicked across the stage, she leaned in, nodded toward the gigantic crowd and chuckled, "Nice club-date, huh?"

On the other (and more talented) hand, the power players in the band cleaned up in Tokyo. I'll be a gentleman and avoid specifics, but if you add an extra zero to my weekly check, you'll get the basic picture. As Country and Western great Charley Pride said, "I ain't complaining, just explaining." Again, I assure you I understood, and accepted, the sideman hierarchy. I knew damn well I was no Marsalis or Kirkland. But even our road manager took issue with the lopsided numbers. Always the straight shooter, Billy said he'd never seen such a wide disparity between band member salaries. He branded the income inequality as "bad for morale."

* * *

Japan's Emperor Hirohito lay near death during our Tokyo stand—and the public seemed to already be in a state of mourning. (Hirohito died a couple of months later.) It was kind of spooky to peer out into the venue before our show and see 50,000 people sitting quietly. The hushed Dome felt more like the world's largest library than a rock concert.

Meanwhile, our mix engineer's penchant for mellow music only served to magnify the gloom. Paul Simon's *Graceland* and Steely Dan's *Aja* were hi-fi catnip for audio professionals at the time. (Matter of fact, they still are today.) Consequently, those two laid-back albums dominated our pre-show, walk-in music. Each night, the audience was held hostage by our soundman's snoozy soundtrack as they waited for us to take the stage. The band hated the sophisticated playlist. Instead of warming the crowd up, we felt the smooth sounds cooled them down. Screw the egghead music; we wanted our soundman to get the party started. How about some high-energy stuff like Prince, James Brown, or Sly and the Family Stone? You know, the kind of music people could enjoy from the neck down.

The Tokyo Dome also played host to Nippon Professional Baseball. (The stadium was home to the Yomiuri Giants, "The New York Yankees of Japan.") Our stage was erected in what would've normally been center field, so the area behind the bandstand was perfect for our traditional pre-show game of catch. Like tennis, playing catch had become one of my favorite pastimes. With so much free time on our hands, I'd learned to appreciate the therapeutic, almost meditative value of simply tossing a baseball back and forth. And since a game of catch could break out anywhere, anytime (indoors, outdoors, no court required), the pseudo-jocks among us always kept our gloves handy.

Our first night at the Dome, Branford and I wolfed down dinner, grabbed our mitts, and raced to the AstroTurf. We romped around like little kids in the backyard, creating fantasy scenarios as we lobbed the ball high against the padded outfield wall. *Bottom of the ninth... Crack!... The ball is deep... Marsalis climbs the fence to make a game-saving circus catch... The Mets win!* Unfortunately, security guards approached after only a few minutes of play and asked us to cease and desist. Citing the Emperor's poor health, the officials deemed our frolics inappropriate, especially in full view of the somber fans. The request seemed a bit odd considering the circumstances: NO fun allowed, this is a rock concert dammit! Nevertheless, we deferred to their wishes... sort of. We didn't exactly "cease," but we did move to a deserted hallway near the dressing rooms.

Branford saw our new, more restrictive environment as the perfect setting to work on his pitching repertoire. (Pitching?!? My kingdom for a mask and a chest-protector.) I reluctantly agreed to catch the erratic right-hander and copped a squat. Branford started out with a few lazy curveballs, which were easy enough to handle. But amid all the noise backstage, I missed Branford's warning of an incoming fastball. He went into his windup and BOOM! He nailed me right in the chest with a blazing pitch. Scaring the shit out of both of us, we decided to put our mitts away before I landed on the 15-day disabled list.

* * *

Sting pulled me aside after our final show in Tokyo and whispered, "Follow me, I want you to meet somebody." I fell in behind my boss, trailing him down a long hallway without giving the cryptic invite a second thought. We wound up in a secluded, empty room, where I was introduced to Sting's "somebody"—Mr. Eric Clapton. Holy shit, I could not believe what was happening. I shook hands with the rock guitar legend, fully expecting to wake up in my teenage bedroom at any moment. This HAD to be a dream. The low-key Clapton was cordial and complimentary, definitely falling into the "bigger they are/nicer they are" category.

I was in guitar-geek heaven as Clapton and I chatted about OUR craft. "Slowhand" even asked what type of strings I used. And as if that wasn't enough, Eric and I ended up going out on the town together. (Branford and Clapton's world-class bassist, Nathan East tagged along.) Surreal doesn't begin to describe that evening. Rocking a sold-out baseball stadium in Tokyo with Sting...and then barhopping with Eric Clapton? Like I said, big cities can yield BIG things. Of all my amazing experiences on Sting's tour, my hang with Clapton might rank as number one. Or as Koko would want me to say: *ichiban*.

I crossed paths with Eric Clapton many years later in NYC and just like my emotionally lopsided reunion with Chet Atkins, the exchange proved to be humbling. I excitedly reintroduced myself to Eric, gushing about our evening together in Tokyo. He mustered a weak smile before responding with the bare minimum of interest. Clapton clearly didn't give a damn about my moldy Sting credit, nor that we'd ever even met. Imagine that! Hanging out with Jeffrey Lee Campbell didn't rate as a memorable moment in the life and times of Eric ("Clapton is God") Clapton.

Osaka | Koshien Stadium | October 29, 30

Trading the runway for the railway, we traveled to Osaka via Japan's high-speed Bullet Train. Boredom and hunger eventually converged, so a few of us made our way to the dining car for a change of scenery and a bite to eat. During our meal, we couldn't help but notice a nearby table of giggly Japanese girls sneaking glances in our direction. I'd only been in Japan for a little over a week, but I was already accustomed to being ogled by curious citizens. (Americans—and especially American musicians—don't exactly blend in with the homogeneous Asian population.) We made several attempts to engage the young ladies, but we were left hanging as they retreated into classic Japanese modesty. A couple of the girls even hid their blushing faces behind window curtains to avoid making eye contact with us. I loved it. After a lifetime of battling aggressive Westerners, I found the shy Eastern demeanor quite charming.

I encountered another shining example of Japanese virtue as we checked into our hotel. In my tour-program profile, I'd jokingly cited my favorite junk food to be "chocolate anything." Some devoted fans in Osaka obviously took this throwaway line to heart and sent a smorgasbord of chocolate treats to my hotel. Hotel staffers aided and abetted the kind gesture, delivering the goodies to my room in advance of our arrival. When I unlocked my door, I was surprised (and touched) to discover a mother lode of chocolate waiting for me. The candy was artfully arranged around my room, making it look like the Easter bunny had tracked me down…in Japan…in October.

Hollywood royalty was on hand at our concert in Osaka. Oscar-winner Michael Douglas was in town shooting the cop movie *Black Rain*, and dropped by for a taste of home-cooked rock 'n' roll. Douglas came backstage before the show to say hello and shoot the breeze with his fellow Yankees. Looking to enhance his evening, the actor asked if we had any *party favors* on us, specifically of the herbal variety. Unfortunately, Mr. Douglas was out of luck. (A rock band with no pot? What's the world coming to?) Hey, we were no dummies. Japan isn't like laid-back Italy, where a stack of complimentary concert tickets can get authorities to look the other way. On the contrary, Japan's anti-drug laws are notoriously strict. Just ask Paul McCartney. He spent nine days in a Tokyo jail for trying to smuggle marijuana into the country—and faced a prison sentence of up to seven YEARS. Accordingly, we were clean as a whistle.

Always the pragmatist, I viewed harsh possession penalties as the perfect argument for making booze my official drug of choice. (Along with the simple fact that I loved to drink.) Unpacking my beer-and-pretzel logic, the widespread—and LEGAL—availability of alcohol makes it the *ideal* substance to abuse on the road. If the monkey on your back in merely thirsty, you'll seldom have to worry about international borders triggering an involuntary detox. Our hotels always had a well-stocked bar—or at least they did when we checked in.

My eyes were immediately drawn to Michael Douglas each time I looked out into the Osaka audience. The movie star sat dead center, making it impossible to miss his chiseled American jawline floating among the sea of Asian faces. And if his Anglo features didn't give him away, his dark sunglasses at night certainly did. Typical celebrity behavior: desperate to blend OUT.

We headed back to Tokyo after Osaka for a little R&R. (Sounds like something from an episode of *M*A*S*H*.) With a rare three-day break on the itinerary, our Japanese promoter wanted to make sure the troops were entertained, and since I still lacked anything approaching good judgment, I accepted another one of those pre-paid "dates." But this time around, instead of visiting a homey brothel nestled in a quiet neighborhood, the *magic* happened in some nondescript office building. Department of Ill Repute? Fifth floor.

My local wingman ushered me off the elevator and down a drab hallway. We entered a small waiting room where I took my seat among the other beacons of Tokyo society. Adding just the right touch of *class*, an out-of-focus TV sat in the corner looping Japanese porn. The joint was seriously bluesy, but news flash: so was I. A hostess eventually appeared from the back and motioned for me to follow.

I was led to a cramped, dimly lit room furnished with a hot tub, a small bed, mirrored walls...and, of course, a total stranger (kneeling at my feet, no less). Dispensing with any formalities, we got right down to business—literally. Chop-chop, time is money. My mind wandered as my petite companion doled out various carnal pleasures with a paint-by-number efficiency. Not that I expected anything different, but it was clearly just another day at the office for my Tokyo rose. How depressing: two naked adults, alone together.

After the *transaction* was complete, the young lady reached into her mini-fridge and grabbed a bottle of water, while handing me a much-welcomed beer. We sat on the edge of her bunk, sipping, smiling, nodding...but not saying a word. There was no point: she spoke no English, I spoke no Japanese. (Where's that Koko when you really need her?) Considering the intimate context, it was by far the most awkward silence of my life. The inelegant evening scored the trifecta: sleazy, comical, and sad. Lust in translation.

Fukuoka | Uminonakamichi Seaside Park | November 3

Fukuoka was only a short flight from Tokyo but, following standard operating procedure, we traveled the day before our concert. Unless it's unavoidable, flying on the "day of show" is just asking for trouble. Shit happens, especially when commercial airlines are involved. Unfortunately, allowing for this margin of error occasionally results in downtime in some less-than-exciting locales. Hello Fukuoka.

Mino and I set out in search of dinner, but unlike Tokyo, our options were somewhat limited. We eventually stumbled upon a place that looked promising, so we ducked in and grabbed a booth. After getting settled, we opened the menus and our eyes widened: a jumble of Japanese calligraphy was staring back at us. Uh oh. In my admittedly limited experience with Japan, I'd been able to count on English subtitles to bail me out, but those courtesy translations were nowhere to be found at *Café Fukuoka*. Compounding our dilemma, nobody on the staff spoke any English. Just like with my rental girlfriend in Tokyo, we were at a clumsy impasse. (At least we were all clothed.) After a few failed attempts at communication, our waitress shrugged and signaled for us to follow her. She led us back outside and directed our attention to the front window. Aha! So *that's* why there's a display of plastic food at many Japanese restaurants. Relieved, we pointed out our selections and then headed back inside to our table. A plate of fake sushi is worth a thousand words.

The Fukuoka show was the only gig of the entire tour where our commute included a boat. After the concert, we drove to a nearby marina and boarded a private yacht back to our hotel. I'm not much of a sailor, so I was relieved the trip didn't involve any open waters. Faced with only a short cruise across Hakata Bay, there was never a threat of being lost at sea. But thanks to my fertile imagination (pollenated by 60's sitcoms), I had everything figured out just in case. If we'd somehow ended up marooned on *Gilligan's Island*, we had our bases covered. Sting was intelligent, wealthy, and good-looking. He could serve as our Professor, Thurston Howell III, AND Ginger…all rolled into one.

Fukuoka fulfilled our Japanese commitments. Next up: The Land Down Under. And from the looks of my flight itinerary, Australia was seriously "down" and seriously "under." Our hemisphere-hopping journey featured a twelve-hour flight from Tokyo to Sydney, followed by a five-hour, cross-country flight to Perth. But the marathon day of travel yielded a substantial upside. Welcome to the beginning of the end: OZ.

Australia

November 7 — 21 (8 shows in 5 cities)

In sharp contrast to the wonder of Japan, my first visit to Australia felt more like a nagging case of déjà vu. Yes, I was technically in a new, distant land, but you could have fooled me. Australians spoke English, employed a dollar-based currency, and even liked their beer served cold. In essence, Down Under was a lot like Down Home...maybe to a fault. Instead of comforting me, the familiar trappings only seemed to magnify my weariness. By that late hour, if I wasn't expanding my horizons, I'd just as soon have been on my couch in NYC. Numb and exhausted, I'd seen enough of the big, bad world for one year.

Perth | Entertainment Centre | November 7

After averaging three or four shows a week for almost a year, I'd developed an understandable aversion to wasting any of my precious downtime sitting in a loud, dark arena. But I took leave of my senses in Perth and actually went to a concert—voluntarily.

At the time, Sting's publicist Kathy Schenker was also repping the red-hot Australian rockers, INXS. The group was performing at Perth's Entertainment Centre the night before us, so I jumped when Kathy offered up a VIP pass. It was an evening well spent. INXS put on a killer show and temporarily cured what ailed me. The band's raw funk-rock—coupled with their fresh, understated stagecraft—soothed my savage blahs.

We piled into our van the next day and set out for work. I couldn't stop gushing about the mighty INXS as we motored down the highway. An exasperated Kathy eventually turned around, shot me a dirty look and pressed her index finger to her lips. (The international sign for "Please shut the fuck up.") Oops. I guess Kathy didn't appreciate me rubbing Sting's nose in her other client's awesomeness. Luckily my big mouth didn't cause any lasting damage. Kathy ultimately scaled the corporate ladder to become Sting's manager.

Adelaide | Memorial Drive Park | November 10

Despite my moratorium on concerts (except of the salaried variety), I did check out another band while we were in Adelaide—but that's only because the Musician's Union of Australia (MUA) made me. As per union bylaws, all touring artists were required to add a local supporting act.

We hadn't used any warm-up acts since our initial string of shows at the beginning of the tour. Why should we? The ticket buyers were coming to see Sting, so that's what he delivered.

Each night, when the lights went down, the audience got their money's worth—and then some. Two full sets, plus two multi-song encores; two-and-a-half hours of uncut Sting. James Brown may have been the "hardest working man in show business," but Sting was no slouch. Nevertheless, with no desire to tangle with the MUA, Sting acquiesced and brought "plus special guest" on board for our show…but on his terms.

Sting went with every rock fan's *favorite* and added a classical string quartet to the bill. Advantage Sting. If he was going to be forced to include an opener, then it would be an act HE liked. (I assume tweaking the "powers that be" also figured into Sting's calculations.)

The highbrow sounds of Mozart and Beethoven echoed through the backstage area as we readied for work. Sting was all smiles—until the chamber group launched into a Beatles medley. His ears perked up, but his face dropped. Sting immediately instructed Billy to ask the group to please stick with a purely classical repertoire. "NO pop tunes." Sting seemed determined to enlighten the Aussie audience, whether they liked it or not. He may have lost the union battle, but he won the culture war.

Melbourne | National Tennis Centre | November 12, 13

We played two nights in Melbourne, but one probably would've been plenty. Although the crowds were enthusiastic, our shows were far from sell-outs. In fact, I heard the concert promoters resorted to "papering the house" (giving away free tickets) to keep up appearances. Sadly, our Down Under buzz factor seemed to be facing a slight headwind. For one thing, the *Nothing Like the Sun* album was over a year old by that point—a little long in the tooth by showbiz standards. But maybe more significantly, management had conceded Australia wasn't really considered rabid Sting territory in the first place. Oh well, you can't win 'em all. Despite my partisan bias, I could understand how Sting's jazzy pop might be something of an acquired taste for the rugged, free-wheeling Aussies. Truth is, when I think of Australian music, my mind goes straight to the kick-ass, cock rock of AC/DC. (I love those guys!)

The muted response in Melbourne underscored the anti-climatic feel of our final frontier. Instead of going out on a high note, it felt like we were limping to the finish line. Everybody—and I mean *everybody*—was ready to wrap things up and go the hell home. In spite of chalking up the most incredible year of my life, I was a broke-down, shell of a man. On the bright side, my burnout had provided a liberating sense of detachment. After spending most of the year worrying about my job security, the fear had lifted. With only a handful of shows left on the schedule, I could exhale. My fifteen-month audition was finally over.

Emboldened by the scent of the finish line, I vowed to loosen up and at least *try* to act like one of the big boys. Sting's tenured sidemen (Branford, Kenny, and Mino) possessed an easy-going, carefree manner, and had no problem treating the boss like one of the guys. They constantly joked around with Sting, busting his chops at will…and dammit, I wanted in on the fun. Ask and ye shall receive, courtesy of Sting's lush ballad, "Sister Moon."

Kenny Kirkland's piano solo on "Sister Moon" was consistently one of the highlights of our show. Each night, when it came time for Kenny to strut his stuff, I'd sling my guitar behind my back, cop a seat on the edge of the drum riser, and watch/listen in awe. (I have a recording from one concert where Kenny organically incorporates disparate quotes from Debussy's "Clair De Lune," jazz standard "Willow Weep for Me," AND funkster Sheila E's "A Love Bizarre" all into the same brilliant solo.) The dude was a monster.

I sat snapping my fingers to Kenny's masterpiece in Melbourne, when Sting strolled over and plopped down beside me. Sting leaned in after a couple of backbeats and snarled, "Don't snap your fingers in *my* face." Without hesitation, I placed my hand two inches in front of his world-famous nose and—with full defiance—snapped. Sting knew I was joking, but he seemed momentarily taken aback nonetheless. Meanwhile, I'm thinking to myself (halfway seriously by that point), "Go ahead, make my day, FIRE ME. I am SO ready to go home."

Unfortunately, the University of Miami's curriculum didn't offer a course in "How to Treat a Rock Star." It would have been much more beneficial than those hours I spent studying Schenkerian analysis. (If you don't know what that is, count yourself among the lucky.) As it turns out, navigating a leader's artistic temperament is one of the most important—if not underrated—aspects of any gig. I eventually became pretty adept at straddling the line between subordinate and peer, but it was a balancing act at times. Obviously, stars want confident, self-assured players in their band, but that being said, there are still occasions where a little bit of genuflecting goes a long way. The trick is knowing when to zig—and when to zag. Luckily, Sting was secure enough in his own skin to withstand some pushback now and then. In fact, I think he actually relished it.

* * *

Searching for any diversion to help run out the clock, the band/crew athletic rivalry bubbled up once again. But this time around, instead of a soccer ball, our weapon of choice was a cricket bat. Cool! One quick question: "How the hell do you play cricket?" Class was back in session as the sophisticated Brits gave me a remedial course in "the gentleman's game." Meanwhile, since rock tours tend to view everything through the prism of "merch," management printed up another batch of custom-made jerseys to commemorate the big contest. (But unlike our inspired "skull and crossbones" soccer outfits of yore, our cricket uniform consisted of a generic white pullover with a small, modest logo. Even our swag was limping to the finish line.)

We suited up in our polo—ahem—cricket shirts, commandeered an out-of-the-way city park, marked off a *pitch,* and spent the afternoon *bowling* at the *wickets.* (Say what?) The slow-moving sport resembles baseball to an extent—just lazier—so it was the perfect vehicle for our top priority: talking trash. Confounding the experts, Team Band prevailed yet again. And believe it or not, the game-winning hit came from a Southern boy who grew up thinking cricket was a noisy bug in the backyard.

Brisbane | Entertainment Centre | November 16

Airline personnel stopped me as I attempted to board our flight to Brisbane. Gate officials deemed my carry-on was too large for the cabin and insisted I check the offending item. I begged for leniency, pointing out my pliable bag was only slightly over the size limit, but my pleas were in vain. Accepting defeat, I stepped aside and began extracting my in-flight essentials before surrendering my belongings to the belly of the plane. Meanwhile, just behind me, Sting and his enormous pieces of luggage were being waved right on through. Forgetting my station in life, I shouted, "Hey, no fair! His bag is a LOT bigger than mine—plus he's got TWO of 'em." My argument fell on deaf ears; the agents were much too busy being mesmerized by an international rock star. In the end, I had nothing to show for my protest, except a vigorous "Shut up, Jeff" from my irritated boss. High mileage had obviously taken its toll on the filter between my brain and my mouth. Am I fired yet?

We touched down in Brisbane and were whisked away to the secluded resort of Sanctuary Cove. Our hotels were usually located in the middle of our host city, so the non-urban setting provided a therapeutic change of pace. Actually, by that point, any "change of pace" was, by definition, "therapeutic." I embraced the hideaway's pampered lifestyle—and the Southern hemisphere's counterintuitive November warmth. I spent my mornings carving divots in the resort's manicured golf course, and my afternoons swimming in the man-made, sandy lagoon, while hotel staff threw shrimp after shrimp on the "barbie."

Occupancy was curiously light during our stay at the remote lodge, conjuring the eerie vibe of a Hitchcock film noir. I kept myself company in the deserted hotel bar one evening, nursing my cocktail in solitude as a distracted Sting plinked on a piano tucked in the corner. It's not every day you see one of the world's biggest rock stars sitting undisturbed in a hotel lounge—especially behind a baby grand, performing the works of Chopin. I leaned back and smiled, savoring my private recital from the unheralded concert pianist.

Sydney | *Entertainment Centre* | *November 18, 19, 21*

And the distinction of being the FINAL stop on our tour goes to…(drumroll please) Sydney, Australia. There was talk of possibly stopping off in Hawaii for a couple more shows, but that idea was humanely put down. As a wise man once sang, "Bring on the night."

I joined Sting and Kim for breakfast one morning in Sydney. Choosing the path of least resistance, we defaulted to the hotel's utilitarian restaurant. We'd placed our orders and were mid-conversation when Sting paused and gazed upwards. I was confused by the abrupt silence until my ears locked in on the soft background music wafting through the air. A cheesy, *elevator* version of "Every Breath You Take" dripped from the ceiling. Sting and Kim sat quietly, smiling their multi-platinum smiles. Nothing lifts the spirits like racking up residuals as you sip your morning coffee. Voted Billboard's number one song of 1983, "Every Breath You Take" was the gift that kept on giving…

…and giving. In 1997, fourteen years after its initial release,

"Every Breath You Take" struck pay dirt again. But this time around, instead of syrupy Muzak, it was hip-hop bringing the smile to Sting's face. Rapper Puff Daddy used the iconic "Every Breath" guitar hook as the cornerstone for his hit, "I'll Be Missing You," and dragged Sting back to the top of the charts in the process. Thanks to copyright law, the moment Puffy appropriated the Police sample, Sting became an official co-writer...without lifting a finger. But the plot thickens. Puff Daddy reportedly neglected to secure Sting's permission before borrowing the "Breath" snippet. This slip-up gave Sting the leverage to demand—and receive—100% of the song's royalties. Boom! Time to get a bigger mailbox. A single composition spawned TWO #1 international hits. Ka-ching, Ka-ching.

* * *

Even with the end in sight, sentimentality would have to take a number. Pragmatism ruled the day as one very important piece of business loomed on the horizon: the time-honored (and beloved) "End of Tour" bonus. With Christmas-like anticipation, everybody—the naughty and the nice—wondered just how generous *Santa* would be. We tried to keep it classy, but some of us couldn't resist speculating on the size of our presumed windfall. Unfortunately, Kenny Kirkland had been in my ear for a couple of weeks, maintaining I'd been woefully underpaid from the get-go. Kenny was no fan of the tour's salary discrepancies, and contended my paycheck had been light by a thousand dollars a week—at least.

According to Kenny's math, after a full year of service, I was deserving of a bonus in the neighborhood of FIFTY-THOUSAND DOLLARS! I didn't necessarily buy into Kenny's inflated estimate, but his socialist leanings did help nudge my hopes upward.

The night of our final show, Sting summoned each band member to his dressing room, one by one. When my turn came, I anxiously entered the boss's lair, having no idea what to expect. Sting's tone was sober and sincere as he thanked me for my hard work and excellent musicianship. He wished me continued good luck, gave me a hug and then handed me a sealed envelope. Despite the distracting visions of dollar signs dancing in my head, I was present enough to appreciate the gravity of the moment. I was humbled and moved by Sting's grace. But as soon as I exited Sting's dressing room, I rushed to the nearest private corner and ripped open the envelope. Inside, I found a check for…fifteen thousand dollars. And I have to confess, I was a little disappointed. *Only* fifteen thousand dollars?

The formerly sweet and innocent boy from Carrboro had clearly lost all perspective. But in fairness, perspective was in short supply after my whirlwind year of excess and extravagance. Early in the tour, an industry fat cat had lectured me over late-night cocktails, "Look kid, in showbiz, money is like water in the ocean. Take as many buckets of it as you can, no one will ever miss it." Thanks to mercenary advice like that, I'd become profoundly jaded. But now that I'm a bit wiser—and nobody's lining up to hand me any five-figure gratuities—I realize my reaction in Sydney was shameful. Sting's gift was generous and appropriate. Greed ain't good; gratitude is good.

* * *

SHOWTIME! Once more, with feeling—and I mean "once." Our final concert was one big party, but that pretty much describes all our concerts. (Ignore my intermittent bellyaching; being a musician beats the hell out of working for a living.) As the show got underway, I quickly realized we were in for a bruising night of practical jokes. The crew had obviously been granted full immunity, and they weren't going to take any prisoners. They pranked anybody—and everybody—throughout the evening. The shenanigans were flying fast and furious, but a few highlights stand out:

1. The band got a good laugh during the "Englishman in New York" hip-hop breakbeat. The sound crew had covertly replaced JT's bombastic kick and snare samples with the sounds of pigs and cows. When JT started beating on his electronic drum pad, the arena was transformed into a high-decibel barnyard, featuring a funky breakdown of "oinks" and "moos."

2. The crew erected a curtained booth adjacent to Kenny's keyboard rig. The shrouded cubicle was strategically tucked behind (and below) our multi-level stage, making its contents visible only from Kenny's vantage point. When I asked my guitar tech about the mysterious nook, he just smiled. My curiosity grew exponentially when I saw Tracy—Kenny's girlfriend at the time—glide over during a song, take a peek inside, and recoil in disgust.

As soon as the setlist allowed, I bounced to Kenny's side of the stage (courtesy of my wireless guitar) to investigate. I peered down into the stall without breaking strum. Whoa! I was stunned to see a topless stripper smiling up at me as she *fiddled* with one of the sex toys from her vast arsenal. Kudos to our resourceful (and raunchy) roadies. They outdid themselves, building—and concealing—an X-rated, Times Square peepshow right beneath the noses of fifteen thousand none-the-wiser Australians.

3. Don't think for a minute the boss was off-limits. It took until the first encore, but Sting finally fell victim to the crew's wicked sense of humor. As Sting launched into his patented "Don't Stand So Close" striptease, a pair of speedo-clad bodybuilders rushed from the wings to flank our topless leader. Always the pro, Sting kept singing…but nobody was listening. The well-oiled brutes ran through their repertoire of freakish flexes and successfully hijacked Sting's spotlight in the process. The band (and crowd) howled with laughter as the pumped-up bookends dwarfed our exhibitionist leader—and his *formerly* impressive chest.

At the conclusion of the Mr. Olympia competition, we tackled "Every Breath You Take" for the last time. Sting's trademark number was always one of my favorite moments of the show. Even after a year of repetition, I still got goose bumps when Sting would look over at me and nod, cueing the iconic intro. For eight blissful bars, it was just me and THE man, dueting on one of the best-known arpeggios in rock music. Back when I was playing

"Every Breath" in cover bands, I never dreamed I'd have the honor of performing it with the actual composer; let alone in twenty-five different countries around the globe.

Sting returned for the final encore with his solo renditions of "Roxanne" and "Message in a Bottle." As always, the band rejoined Sting on stage toward the end of "Message" for our customary call-and-response hoedown. And after one hundred and eighty-one concerts, we shouted out our very last "Sending out an SOS!"

* * *

The next day—with #181 still ringing in our hung-over ears—the American contingent boarded our flight back to the States. Meanwhile, Sting and his British counterparts were already airborne, London-bound. In a flash, the tour was over and, like proverbial "army buddies," we were all going our separate ways. It was only fitting my last day on the job involved a brutal seventeen-hour flight to LA, followed by another six-hour leg to New York.

We deplaned at JFK and staggered zombie-like toward baggage claim. It'd been over twenty-four hours (and counting) since we'd departed Australia, and everybody was off in his or her private coma. The luggage carousel eventually wheezed to life and started spitting out suitcases. I lowered my head and elbowed through the scrum to gather my belongings. Loaded down for my final limo ride back to reality, it was time for the official goodbye. I knew better than to get sentimental over the magnitude of the moment, so I observed standard tour etiquette and low-keyed my farewell. "OK guys, see you soon." A weary Tracy just stared at me and grunted, "Yeah, right."

To Hell's Kitchen and Back

Now what? The tour was over, but in some respects my education was just beginning. And the lessons that lay ahead were tough ones.

Tracy was right. After an intense year of thick and thin, the band's close-knit relationships dissipated quickly. Everyone turned the page and moved on with their Sting-free lives. Paths crossed from time to time, but none of us made any real efforts to maintain contact—except for my old pal, Branford.

Branford and I saw each other quite a bit for the first couple of years after the tour ended. Our mutual love of sports—along with *his* Mets and Knicks season tickets—gave us a perfect excuse to hang out. We summered at Shea Stadium and wintered at Madison Square Garden. But unlike yours truly, Branford was still a hot commodity post-Sting. Consequently, there were times where last-minute work forced him to bail on boy's night out. When duty inconveniently called, Branford would apologize for standing me up, and then atone by dumping the tickets in my lap. The games weren't nearly as much fun without Branford's pithy color commentary, but I loved playing Mr. Big Shot as I doled out the windfall comps to my cash-strapped cronies.

One such night, Branford gave me all three of his Knicks tickets, but I could only rustle up one partner in crime. No big deal. When an out-of-work musician and a struggling actor end up with an extra NBA ticket, there's one logical move: scalp it for beer money. Flush with funds after our black-market transaction, me and my buddy, Sam, enjoyed an all-expense-paid evening of b-ball and brews—courtesy of our missing musketeer. Fast-forwarding to present day, I'm happy to report my "struggling actor" pal struggles no more. But you probably know Sam better by his full name: Samuel L. Jackson. Jeez, now THERE'S a New York success story.

* * *

Loose on the streets of Manhattan with an oversized bank account, and an ego to match, I was destined for cautionary-tale infamy. I was convinced my one-year stint with Sting had granted me lifetime membership in *Club Rock Star*, so I knew it was only a matter of time until I landed my next plum gig. Therefore, I didn't see any point in pursuing smaller, local jobs. Instead, my *brilliant* game plan was to just sit back and wait for the imminent high-profile offers worthy of my elite status. Regrettably, I'd become "that guy"—a cocky bachelor with a stockpile of cash, a distorted sense of self-importance, and a bottomless thirst for booze. The perfect storm was brewing.

I moved into a studio apartment in Hell's Kitchen and proceeded to party around the clock. Unmarried and unemployed,

I lacked any compelling reason to go home at night—and there were plenty of times I didn't.

One night (actually, more like five o'clock in the morning), I wound up at an illegal after-hours joint on the Lower East Side. The makeshift club was located in the basement of a run-down building and—just like in the movies—you needed to know the password to gain entrance. A folding table served as the bar; bootleg booze was sold in plastic cups; and "house rules" required all drugs be consumed out in the open: NO hiding in the bathroom. (That last one's still a puzzler.) Topping it all off, some lanky, Super Fly dude sat behind an electric piano in the corner, providing a bluesy soundtrack for us high-as-a-kite low-lifes. The wanton depravity didn't faze me in the least, but I was stunned by the presence of live entertainment. I struck up a conversation with the pianist during one of his breaks. "Damn man, what time does your gig end?" He replied nonchalantly, "7:30...AM."

Daylight was in full swing when I finally crawled out of that hellhole. I yearned for a pair of sunglasses to shield my eyes from the harsh glare...and to hide my shame from the respectable members of society on their way to work. I somehow made it back uptown, but before crashing, I foolishly decided to stop by the ATM outside my bank to replenish my once-again empty wallet. What an idiot—GO HOME! In my stupor, I repeatedly tried to enter an invalid PIN. Needless to say, account access was denied. I was certain it was the stupid machine's fault, so I stormed inside the bank and drunkenly demanded to speak with a manager. I was quickly escorted to a secluded customer service area where I received humanitarian assistance in filling out a withdrawal slip. Money in hand, I stumbled home and collapsed.

I regained consciousness late in the afternoon. My nausea intensified as I slowly recalled my humiliating spectacle at Chemical Bank. (Perfect name huh?) Thoroughly disgusted with myself, I knew something HAD to change. *God, grant me the serenity to* …do my banking at a different location for a little while. Classic denial in all its glory. My lame strategy exploded in my face less than a week later when, attempting to lay low, I hiked up to my former Chem Bank on the Upper West Side. A familiar representative flagged me down as I walked in the door and cackled, "Hey Jeff, I heard you were over at Branch Eight the other morning." I'm still embarrassed.

On the domestic front, although I was still technically involved with my long-suffering girlfriend, Denise, that murky situation was deteriorating rapidly. It was official: my life had crumbled into an unqualified mess. Without realizing it, I'd embarked on my own extended "Lost Weekend."

I continued to spend freely—with no real income to speak of—and inevitably crossed the Rubicon where my debts exceeded my assets. (Thank you, Mr. Credit Card.) Painted into a financial corner, I had no choice but to put my tail between my legs and join a wedding band. But it wasn't just ANY wedding band; it was the exact same band I was working with when I landed the Sting gig. (And believe it or not, they actually made me re-audition!) It's a damn good thing I'd decided against burning that bridge when I was *temporarily* called up to the Majors. I needed the work.

Turns out I wasn't the only one trolling the job market. Sting also found himself among the ranks of the unemployed after a brutally short stint on Broadway in *3 Penny Opera*. But instead of going the wedding band route, Sting retreated to a Parisian studio and began work on his next album, *The Soul Cages*. When the record was finished, it was time once again to mount a world tour. I knew it was a long shot, but I held out a sliver of hope that Sting might invite me back into the fold.

I thought my prayers had been answered one afternoon when Kim Turner called out of the blue. My heart pounded as Sting's manager unwittingly tortured me with his rolling disclosure. "Hey Jeff, Sting is putting a band together for the upcoming tour and wants to know ... *thump thump, thump thump* ... if you have any drummer recommendations." Not exactly what I was waiting to hear, but I was flattered Sting still valued my opinion. I obliged with a few names before working up the courage to ask Kim about the guitar situation. He coughed and sputtered, saying he wasn't totally sure what was happening on that front. I seized my opening and mentioned I'd love to be considered for the gig. Kim quietly conceded my name "had not come up."

Fade to black. The rejection was painful, my destruction complete. There was only one saving grace for my battered ego: Sting ended up using all new musicians on his next tour. When friends asked why I was no longer working with Sting, "whole new band" made for a handy alibi.

I'm still haunted by my failure to parlay my Sting year into a Sting career. Fair or not, I'll always feel like I let a golden opportunity slip through my fingers. Did my drinking hurt my status with Sting? It sure as hell didn't help. There's no way I was at the top of my game with my incessant partying. I've seen truly gifted musicians flourish in spite of their substance abuse—but my earthbound talents weren't near strong enough to offset my addiction issues.

On a positive note, the guitarist who followed me, Dominic Miller, is still working with Sting today. I doubt even a sober version of Jeffrey Lee Campbell could have achieved such impressive longevity. A philosophical friend of mine used to say, "If *you* didn't get the gig, then it wasn't *your* gig." Hats off to Dominic. He didn't take my gig, he took his.

* * *

Only a couple of years removed from my crowning glory, I was basically right back where I'd started. Sting had a brand-new band; I had a brand-old one. My life was miserable. I was broke, newly single (dumped), and desperately trying to manage an unmanageable drinking habit. Technically speaking, I was fucked. Then, for my next trick, I got mugged.

Getting mugged was practically a rite of passage back in the bad old days of NYC. It seemed like everybody I knew had some kind of war story. My number came up one night in the West Village neighborhood known as the Meatpacking District. NOT the upscale Meatpacking District of today (synonymous with *Sex and the City*, trendy nightclubs, and haute couture), but the scary Meatpacking District of yesteryear—a desolate area that actually featured smelly meatpacking plants and a nightly parade of transvestite hookers.

My deflowering, so to speak, took place on a darkened West 14th Street. I was waiting to be buzzed in to a friend's recording studio when an opportunistic thug snuck up behind me, poked an unidentified weapon in my ribs and growled, "Give me your shit." The dude obviously meant business, so I handed over my wallet without argument. But we weren't done. The greedy bandit nodded at my guitar and pedalboard and hissed, "I mean ALL your shit!" The thought of resisting never entered my mind; mugging victims were getting killed for a whole lot less during those hellish days of the crack epidemic. As soon as the thief (and my gear) disappeared into the night, I raced to the corner and flagged down a cop car. I filed a police report and then made a beeline to the nearest tavern to calm my nerves.

I paid a visit to the NYPD's 10th precinct the following morning and spent a couple of hours browsing through ream after ream of terrifying mug shots. But it was a lost cause; I had no idea what my assailant looked like. Survival instincts had clearly prompted me to avoid direct eye contact with the Grim Reaper. I wasn't able to ID the perp, the crime remained unsolved, and I never saw that guitar again. My world was bleak—and getting bleaker with each passing day.

Then I caught a break. A Kentucky angel appeared in my life: the lovely and loving Patty Murray. Casual acquaintances from the neighborhood, Patty and I bumped into each other one afternoon on Ninth Avenue. As we chatted, Patty, a talented singer, mentioned she was learning to play the guitar . . . and well, that was that. I showed up at Patty's place a few days later for a friendly little guitar lesson, and basically never left. It was love at first strum. We lived together for a couple of years before exchanging "I do's" in a small ceremony at the United Nations Chapel.

Married life agreed with me, settling down was exactly what I needed. Unfortunately, it still took another year for me to admit my drinking was totally out of control. I finally got the message after having not one but TWO life-threatening seizures. My first seizure happened right after a wedding gig in New Rochelle. (Our lead singer found me thrashing about on the men's room floor. When I came to, he was cradling me in his arms. Thanks, Paul.) The attack occurred moments before I was going to climb behind the wheel of my rusted-out Honda. The angels were definitely watching over me that night. I'm literally lucky to be alive.

Heeding my near-lethal wake-up call, I stopped drinking. I didn't touch a drop of booze for a couple of months, and I felt great. So great, in fact, I decided to climb back into the gorilla's cage. Convinced I'd learned my lesson, I vowed to drink responsibly. That wishful thinking lasted three or four weeks, tops. Moderation quickly unraveled into excess and before I knew it, I was back on the floor convulsing…but this time with an audience.

My second seizure happened at a midtown rock club—ON-STAGE. The crowd got its money's worth that night. I guess when God saw my initial brush with death didn't scare me straight, he decided to up the ante and try to "humiliate" me straight. Ironically, my seizures resulted from trying to do the right thing: quit drinking. But due to my deep chemical dependency, cold turkey almost killed me. (Three years later, my dear friend Richie Douglas wasn't as lucky. RIP Richie, I'll never forget you.) Public Service Announcement: alcohol withdrawal can be deadly, seek professional help.

I finally saw myself for the pathetic drunk I'd become, and committed wholly to cleaning up. Through the grace of God—and my dear Patty—it somehow stuck. I got sober for myself, but I'm not sure I could have pulled it off without my loving wife's patience and support. Patty was there for me, every sweaty, trembly step of the way. My gratitude is beyond eternal.

Sure enough, my life improved when I stopped drinking. As my boozy fog slowly lifted, I began to see many truths. One of my biggest revelations was the good news/bad news aspect of my meteoric NYC rise. Needless to say, winning the Sting lottery right out of the gate was incredible. But as a result, I skipped over the crucial step of establishing roots on the New York music scene. I went straight from being "the new kid in town" to "the new kid out-of-town," bypassing a lot of freshman (and sophomore) dues in the process. Consequently, I was in for a rude awakening when I returned from my triumphant year on the road. (There's only one direction to go when you start at the top.) I may have thought Jeffrey Lee Campbell was famous, but the city of New York collectively yawned. As I was waiting around for my phone to ring, it never dawned on me nobody knew my number. I was living in a bubble of Sting-induced arrogance, adrift on a sea of vodka.

But let me be VERY clear: I don't want—or deserve—an ounce of sympathy. I'm one of the luckiest guys I know. Few musicians ever get to be part of a major world tour, especially with an artist of Sting's stature. That said, I can't help but wonder if my dream gig may have come too soon (and too easily) in the grand scheme of things. Maybe I would've handled my success a little better if I'd had a couple of humbling NYC years under my belt first. But that's not how fate works. Opportunity knocks when it damn well pleases—and with that being the case, I'd always choose "too soon" over "never."

Clean and sober, I set out to tackle New York—again. Fortunately, I wasn't completely back at square one. This go-round, I was armed with a highly valuable Sting credit. I began a second wave of networking with renewed purpose, determined to meet and play with as many musicians as possible. Thanks to clear-headed dedication—and the tri-state area's flourishing wedding band industry—my workload quickly increased.

In addition to my "meat and potato" tuxedo gigs, I fleshed out my schedule with the usual hodgepodge of sideman fare. I backed singer/songwriters in bars and nightclubs, played on low-budget indie records, and on rare occasions, even bagged a few of those elusive, verge-of-extinction jingle sessions. I was also lucky enough to land some A-list gigs along the way, playing with artists including Aretha Franklin, Michael Bublé, and Jon Bon Jovi. (A fellow musician used to joke these types of high-profile jobs scored invaluable "mother points." Translation: Your mom could brag about your latest gig to HER friends...and they'd actually know who the hell she was talking about.)

My phone was ringing, but I was nowhere near Easy Street. Life as a self-employed musician is tough sledding, so I was constantly searching for new sources of income. (I once dated a girl who summed up the professional musician's plight concisely: "You guys can make a killing...but you can't make a living." Harsh, but all too often true.) Fortunately, I had the foresight—or dumb luck—to fall in love with a musician. My wife Patty gets it. As a fellow performer, she understands the feast/famine struggle of the music biz all too well.

Things finally looked up when I looked down—into the orchestra pits of Broadway. Broadway is one of the few places where a musician can make a decent income...without being famous.

Consequently, working on a Broadway musical is one of New York's most coveted gigs. And as technology continues to shrink the demand for actual humans in the music biz, Broadway is becoming more and more desirable—and competitive.

In the world of musical theater, full-time orchestra members maintain a stable of handpicked substitutes; skilled players who stay at the ready for any stray crumbs of fill-in work. But subbing on Broadway is not for the faint of heart. First, you have to find someone in need of a sub—and convince them you're a worthy candidate. If you can swing that, roll up your sleeves. You'll spend weeks (or months, if necessary) learning the music, inside and out, backwards and forwards...for FREE. Once you feel sufficiently prepared, you're expected to come in, withstand the game-time pressure, and nail the show. If the conductor is pleased with your performance: congratulations, you're added to the list of approved subs. If the conductor is not pleased: buh-bye. And all those unbillable hours of homework? Up in smoke. Subbing is incredibly stressful, but it's how you crack the scene.

In a typical NYC twist, my Broadway break came from yet another one of my six-string heroes: legendary session guitarist, David Spinozza. (His impressive discography includes Paul McCartney, John Lennon, Paul Simon, and tons more.) At the time, David was playing guitar on the hooker-themed, R&B musical, *The Life*. The show's colorful conductor was quite a stickler, so David was burning through subs at an alarming rate. A mutual friend recommended me, and Spinozza agreed to give me a shot. I spent two full months preparing for my big debut, dissecting every nuance of David's guitar part. (The orchestra's piano player quipped, "Damn man, you even learned David's mistakes!") Fortunately, my painstaking work paid off. I survived my trial by fire, and ended up subbing regularly for Spinozza on *The Life,* as well as his next show, *Fosse.*

After a few years of *sub*-servience in various pits, I snagged my first full-time Broadway chair in the screen-to-stage adaptation of *Saturday Night Fever.* I'd come of age during the disco era so the Bee Gees tuner was tailor-made for my skill set. (I spoke fluent wah-wah.) I was thrilled to finally have a steady gig, but as they say, work begets work. A mere four months into my *Fever* tenure, I found myself being wooed away by the highly-anticipated musical, *Seussical.*

Decision time: should I stay or should I go? Leaving one show for another almost always involves an element of risk. There's no guarantee your new job will outlive your old one. Patty and I weighed the pros and cons, and ultimately concluded I should take the Cat-in-the-Hat plunge. Tipping the scales in *Seussical's* favor, the show's veteran music contractor had pitched the family-friendly production to me as a sure-fire hit, predicting it would run "ten years…minimum!" A no-brainer, right?

Wrong. *Seussical* barely lasted six months. Horton Hears a Flop. But before I could even dread looking for a new job, a new job came looking for me. *Seussical's* musical director, David Holcenberg, pulled me aside as our show was bleeding out, and asked if I'd be interested in joining him on an upcoming show built around the music of ABBA. (Swedish popsters ABBA? On Broadway???) I was skeptical, but in no position to be choosy, so I shrugged, "Yeah, sure" and fell ass-backwards into the unforeseen global phenomenon known as *Mamma Mia!*

A Broadway musical is generally considered a success if it

runs for two or three years. But the feel-good *Mamma Mia!* ended up running an astounding FOURTEEN years. Not bad for a show widely panned by critics and theater snobs. (The New York Times review called the musical "bland, hokey, corny.") Apparently, nobody liked *Mamma Mia!* but the public. The ABBA-inspired blockbuster chalked up 5,773 performances, and currently ranks #9 among the longest running shows in Broadway history.

But please hold your applause. My extraordinary stint with *Mamma Mia!* wasn't the result of some savvy career move on my part. I was simply in the right place at the right time. Landing a Broadway gig requires high-level skills, but landing a Broadway HIT requires high-level LUCK. As the saying goes, "Timing is everything."

Of course, I wasn't feeling very lucky as I watched my "can't miss" *Seussical* circle the drain, but my premature pink slip wound up being my golden ticket. *Seussical's* untimely demise cleared the decks for an amazing (and quite prosperous) 14-year ride with *Mamma Mia!* Pessimists take note. My reversal of *misfortune* underscores one of life's true enigmas: "bad" news can actually be good news. Stay positive. You're always exactly where you're supposed to be.

Miraculously, my hot streak continues. Shortly after *Mamma Mia!* announced its closing notice, my phone rang with an offer to join Andrew Lloyd Webber's Broadway-bound, *School of Rock*. I pounced, and thanks to a serendipitous dovetail between the two shows, I was unemployed for only a matter of weeks. I was extremely grateful to have a seamless transition from one secure job to another, but I wrestled with twinges of survivor guilt. (Most of my *Mamma Mia!* bandmates were forced to return to the freelance jungle.) Steadfast friends pooh-poohed my qualms, contending I deserved my latest gig. And while that may be true to an extent, I'm always quick to point out the sobering math. There are a LOT more "deserving" Broadway musicians than there are Broadway chairs. Like I said, "lucky."

Although my original NYC fantasies didn't involve musical theater, Broadway has turned out to be a perfect fit for my meticulous (read: wacky) nature. People always ask how I can stand to play the exact same songs…night after night, week after week, month after month, year after year. Whew, that's a damn good question. Am I searching for order amid the chaos of the universe? It's possible. But my primary motivation is, without a doubt, my taste for the finer things in life: namely, food and shelter. Stating the obvious, relentless gigs come with relentless paychecks. And at eight shows a week, fifty-two weeks a year, there's nothing more relentless than Broadway.

Thanks to my steady Broadway income, I've been able to build a respectable nest egg, and still sleep in MY bed every night. Ask any musician, that's rare in this biz. Most of my peers spend an inordinate chunk of their lives in vans, airports, and hotels in order to maintain the cash flow. Meanwhile, I'm at the other end of the spectrum: I walk to work EVERY day. (Talk about blessings, I haven't owned a car in years.) The commute from my Hell's Kitchen apartment to the Theater District clocks in at a breezy ten minutes; I feel like I live in Mayberry. Life on Broadway has proven to be the exact opposite of touring for me. No planes, trains, or automobiles—just shoe leather. The physical wear and tear is negligible. In fact, I may be getting younger.

* * *

Things are great. I sobered up, and I grew up. Patty and I have been happily married for over twenty years and—somehow, someway—I've defied the odds to make a living as a musician in the city of my dreams. I'm happier, healthier, and more creative than I've ever been in my life.

On the day he hired me, Sting looked me straight in the eye and said, "I'm going to make you famous." OK, maybe he got a *little* carried away. Despite Sting's bold prediction, I never became a household name. But I have endured—and that in itself is no small feat. Nevertheless, if you glance at my resumé, one name still jumps off the page: STING. The man may not have made me famous, but his gold-plated seal of approval has generated DECADES of work for me.

Like it or not, credentialism is a reality in the music business; celebrity endorsements carry a lot of weight. Accordingly, having a big-name credit in your back pocket is like knowing the secret handshake. In our family, we lovingly refer to Sting as "the five-letter word." Whenever I've ended up in situations that begged for a little self-promotion, Patty always asks afterward if I had a chance to mention "the five-letter word." The answer is usually yes. Sting is a fun name to drop. A few years back, Jack Morer (my old college pal, and Manny's Music/Bushrock tipster) chuckled, "Dude, you might as well change your name to Jeff '*played with Sting*' Campbell. That credit is going to follow you around forever."

It's impossible to overstate the impact Sting had on my life—

both professionally and personally. He plucked me from obscurity and triggered a seismic shift that reverberates to this day. And while I hope to have many triumphs still ahead of me, a comparable leap is unimaginable. Going from selling candy bars to playing guitar with one of the biggest rock stars in the world will be hard to top. The way I see it, my life has been nothing but gravy ever since that glorious afternoon when Sting uttered matter-of-factly, "Jeff, you can have the gig...if you want it."

I haven't stayed in touch with Sting over the years, but we occasionally bump into each other around NYC. The last time our paths crossed, Sting gave me a big hug, looked me up and down and beamed, "Jeff—WE look great!"

I love that guy.

Acknowledgments

Until I tackled this project, my writing had been confined to four-minute pop tunes. Consequently, I had NO idea what I was getting myself into. It was like trying to swim across the ocean; by the time I realized my predicament, it was too late to turn back. So I kept my head down . . . and eventually made it to the distant shore. The experience was profound and eye-opening; I'll never read another book the same way again. Praise be to writers everywhere.

Bringing a book to fruition requires tenacity, immeasurable elbow grease, and extreme attention to detail. That said, due to the passage of time—and a little too much "fun" all those years ago—my storytelling may contain the stray *accounting* error. Any discrepancies are minor and inadvertent.

Thanks to:

Mom and Dad, Mike Campbell, Doug Travis, Bill Covington, Tony Bowman, Jeff Kazee, Rodney Howard, Charlotte Sabina, Michael Bugdanowitz, Karine Bugdanowitz, Andy Church, Kim Church, Dietmar Cloes, Nuno Leite, Anita Adsit, Harriet Whelchel, Sandy Aquila, Emanuel Chulo Gatewood, Ned Matura, David Allen, Warren Odze, Luther Rix, Larry Elliott, David Holcenberg, Michael Keller, Brian Dennis, Tom Merkel, Jon Bon Jovi, Robert Wilson, Maryann Karinch . . . and Sting.

Extra thanks to:

Bill Baucom—After indulging yet another of my Sting war stories, you strongly urged me to "write this stuff down." I heeded your advice, and blindly scampered down what turned out to be a multi-year rabbit hole. Thanks for that initial nudge, and your ongoing support throughout my lengthy learning process.

Mark Sloan—I told you over lunch I was writing a book. Your unconditional enthusiasm spurred me on. Thanks for believing in me, suffering through a clunky first draft, and putting your reputation on the line with YOUR agent.

Sue Olsen—Thanks for the decades of friendship, and traveling cross-country every summer for OUR Algonquin Round Table. Having a fellow writer's shoulder to cry on was invaluable. Onward and . . . onward!

Mark Belair—You talked me off the ledge numerous times as we walked up 8th Avenue after yet another round of "Dancing Queen." You warned, "Getting the words from your head onto the page is the easy part . . . getting the words from the page into your reader's head is the tricky part." I hope I achieved that goal in some small measure. Thanks for your support and guidance. Your mantra "hard writing equals easy reading" was my North Star.

Will Campbell—I don't know where to start. Thanks for ALWAYS being there for me.

Jim Henderson — Only a true friend would edit a single-spaced, first draft, hard copy by hand. Thanks for being a great mentor, always leading with generosity, compassion and laughter. The world needs more Jim Hendersons.

Jimmy Kissane — I still have your full-throated voice mail on my iPhone. It helped more than you'll ever know. Rest in peace you big lug.

David Bulitt — Life is so random. After years of chasing countless promising leads into dead ends, I flung a final Hail Mary — and you reeled it in. Spectacular catch! Thanks for taking the time to care.

To Bob, Jan, Mark, Matt, and the entire team at Deeds Publishing. Thanks for believing in this book — and all your great work.

To ALL my beta readers: thanks for your gentle patience while I learned how to write. Your input, feedback and cheerleading was invaluable. You helped me get from there to here.

In memory of: Delmar Brown, Kenny Kirkland, Kim Turner, Fiona Williams, Mike Strout, Ian Copeland, and Richie Douglas.

About the Author

Jeffrey Lee Campbell, originally from North Carolina, is a guitarist, composer, and producer. He has been a professional musician for over forty years—thirty and counting in New York City. In addition to touring the world with Sting, he's performed with artists including Sammy Davis Jr., Aretha Franklin, Michael Bublé, and Jon Bon Jovi. A grateful journeyman, Jeffrey has played guitar on countless recordings, jingles, and Broadway shows.